THE
SILENCE
OF THE
RATIONAL
CENTER

THE
SILENCE
OF THE
RATIONAL
CENTER

WHY AMERICAN FOREIGN POLICY IS FAILING

Stefan Halper and Jonathan Clarke

BASIC
BOOKS

A Member of the Perseus Books Group
New York

Books published by Basic Books are available at special discounts for
bulk purchases in the United States by corporations, institutions, and
other organizations. For more information, please contact the Special
Markets Department at the Perseus Books Group, 11 Cambridge Center,
Cambridge MA 02142, or call (617) 252-5298 or (800) 255-1514, or
e-mail special.markets@perseusbooks.com.

Designed by Trish Wilkinson
Set in 12-point Adobe Garamond

Library of Congress Cataloging-in-Publication Data

Halper, Stefan A.
  The silence of the rational center : why American foreign policy is failing /
Stefan Halper and Jonathan Clarke.
      p.   cm.
  Includes bibliographical references and index.
  ISBN-13: 978-0-465-01141-4 (alk. paper)
  ISBN-10: 0-465-01141-1 (alk. paper)
  1. United States—Foreign relations—2001– I. Clarke, Jonathan,
1947– II. Title.
JZ1480.H36 2007
327.73—dc22
                                                                 2006032291

10 9 8 7 6 5 4 3 2 1

Stefan dedicates this book to his wife, Lezlee, and
his children Elizabeth and Marin.

———————

Jonathan Clarke dedicates this book
with love and affection to his wife, Suzanne, and children,
Crispin, Robin, and Tiffany, truth-seekers all.

Contents

Introduction

At times, United States foreign policy has been extraordinarily successful. The current era, sadly, is not one of those times. With the American image tracking new lows in almost every part of the world and American policies meeting nearly unprecedented resistance, the state of US relations with the rest of the world is bleak.

People who are dissatisfied, as we are, with the nation's foreign policy have often written books to critique the offending elements or priorities and propose better ones. That is not our intention here. Instead, in this book based on a lecture series delivered by Stefan Halper at Cambridge in 2005 and 2006, we invite the reader to consider a broader question centered on foreign policy but also reaching into contemporary culture. The administration of American foreign policy, particularly if it involves significant human and financial costs, can proceed only with the support of the public. This means that in advance of major decisions a debate about the options takes place in the public space. In considering this critical juncture in the policy process, we suggest that embedded flaws within the structure of foreign policy deliberation produce irrational impulses rather than rational calculation and that these flaws are especially apparent in times of crisis.

The format of the foreign policy debate has been shaped by two mutually reinforcing elements. The first is the unusual American susceptibility to what we call Big Ideas. Some of these, phrases like Manifest Destiny, have achieved iconic status. Others, such as "Axis of Evil," are little more than transitory clichés. In both their grandiloquent manifestations, as in today's Freedom on the March and more modest renditions like Stay the Course, these phrases allude to a *deus ex machina* that tends to compress complex issues into simple nostrums and obfuscate rather than illuminate. At their worst, these phrases—like Domino Theory during the Vietnam era and "drain the swamp," the neoconservative rallying cry for ridding the Middle East of terrorists—are disastrously misleading to both policymakers and the public. The second element is the requirements of 24–7 media, which, with large blocks of time and space to fill, are hungry for a constant stream of catchy notions and fresh faces to attract eyes, ears, and advertising dollars. In combination these elements produce a distorted public discourse in which the nature and implications of important policy decisions are obscured. Superficial explanations are rewarded and expert analysis, which is usually complex, is penalized. Slogans dominate the discourse in place of the subtle balancing of interests and resources typically needed in executing a successful foreign policy.

The people responsible for this balancing of interests and resources are sometimes the career professionals, scholars, and analysts working in government offices and think tanks, and at other times they are political activists, editors, and those with experience on the ground. Their expertise is often narrow but very deep: They have read the long histories of arcane subjects and are familiar with the nuances of local cultures. In conversation, they are able to explain why some dramatic scheme will likely encounter difficulty, raise factual complications to glib and fashionable ideas, or refer to the lessons of some long-forgotten misadventure.

Experience and learning have turned most into pragmatists, distrustful of ideology and mindful of long-term interests and enduring issues. Their function in the nation's political life is to bring their knowledge and judgment to bear on the issues of the day and to find solutions that safeguard the nation's varied interests. This is the group we have termed the "rational center." Its role is not limited to foreign policy, but foreign policy is where its influence has traditionally been most crucial and to-day, most endangered.

During relatively calm periods, experts from the rational center face an uphill battle in making their voices heard over the hubbub of media-enhanced Big Ideas. In times of stress, their voices are barely audible. For example, Senator Joseph McCarthy's insistence that communism was a monolithic force marginalized prominent experts who could have told us that the Korean War was a peninsular affair inspired as much by Kim Il-Sung as by Moscow or Beijing, or that Moscow and Beijing had dis-tinct worldviews and often clashing interests. In the late 1950s, as the United States considered how to respond to the looming crisis in In-dochina, the experienced voices that might have offered sage perspective about Chinese intentions and historical conflicts in Southeast Asia had been driven from government. In the run-up to the Iraq war, those few prominent figures from the diplomatic and military communities who warned in prescient detail of the problems the occupation would en-counter were ignored or bundled off into premature retirement.

The problem becomes critical when, rather than resisting these forces, leading experts themselves start coining or adhering uncritically to Big Ideas. In such cases, academic luminaries strike a Faustian bargain in which they trade in their expert status for media-blessed celebrity or po-litical influence. The workings of the modern media amplify, package, and distort—often with political intention—the product of public intel-lectuals like Samuel Huntington and Bernard Lewis in a manner unheard of when George Kennan and Henry Kissinger were starting their careers.

WHAT IS A BIG IDEA?

In many ways America was born as a Big Idea that was rooted in the con-cept of American Exceptionalism. John Winthrop's "City on a Hill" speech of 1630 still resonates as the defining image of American Exceptionalism. Since that time, rhetorical renditions of Big Ideas have provided cohesion, identity, and a sense of national, often providential, "mission." Unlike its European counterparts, whose sense of nationhood is deeply grounded in a shared culture and history, America is a land of immigrants who have consciously forged a nation. In effect, they have forged the *idea of a nation.*

The Big Ideas running through the American discourse often have strong spiritual or religious roots: Redeemer Nation, New Jerusalem, Manifest Destiny, or Last Best Hope on Earth. These slogans provide rhetorical emphasis to the notion that America is both special and separate, with its own version of the rules.[1] They contrast it sharply, for example, with the European Union, which takes the form of a "project." While the European Union as an undertaking echoes the creation of the United States, there is a complete lack of spiritual content in its founding and successor treaties. America, by contrast, was animated by a series of Big Ideas that welded identity and direction to a quasireligious mission.

Because these ideas are now seen as hallowed statements of national purpose, it is easy to forget that they often originated in the newsroom or the pulpit as popularizing expressions. This underlying purpose forms a common thread that joins these earlier slogans with contemporary ones such as "Indispensable Nation" or "Unipolar Moment." Big Ideas are often moral assertions disguised as strategic doctrines or objective factual statements (e.g., Ronald Reagan's use of the phrase "Shining City on a Hill" to depict the American example in global affairs or the early twentieth-century phrase "Imperialism of Righteousness" to describe America's ambitions on the world stage); or else they wear their moralism more openly. For nearly four hundred years, these ideas have expressed a continuing belief that the complexity of America and its place in the world can be distilled into a simple phrase.

The Big Idea is a broad and idiosyncratic class. While it often includes the enduring headlines of American history, many political slogans en route to obscurity are also rooted in Big Ideas. The common element is that the Big Idea is a rhetorical device that rests on shared assumptions reflecting

American Exceptionalism and functions as a direction-setting form of shorthand, an easily grasped metaphor or signpost for an underlying notion that is difficult or tiresome to spell out or, indeed, may not be well understood. For a person or a nation in a hurry, Big Ideas save time. It is much easier to dream up a concept like Axis of Evil than to enunciate a common policy toward nations as different as Iraq, Iran, and North Korea. In political discourse the Big Idea may act in several ways: as a simplifier (Containment), an illuminator (Evil Empire), or a mobilizer (Freedom on the March). Notions like Axis of Evil, which was a speechwriter's phrase, can develop their own momentum and take over policy—and even become the policy.

Big Ideas themselves, are neither good or bad. In certain respects they are simply instruments used by politicians around the world to solidify opinion and to generate support for their causes.[2] They might be described as "macroslogans." But left unchecked, this more or less harmless norm contains a systemic danger: Big Ideas tend to foreshorten debate, unleash emotions, and create false realities. They often lead to truncated thinking—as when President George W. Bush, referring to the War on Terror, declared "You are either with us or against us"—and policy volatility. In fact, when it comes to foreign affairs, those who claim to have a simple solution are often trying to promote their version of a Big Idea . . . and we should be skeptical.

Consider two modern examples. The first is 9/11 Changed Everything. Here, the notion is that the events of 9/11 suspended what was previously known about regional politics, culture, and personalities in the Middle East and particularly in Iraq. This argument enabled the Bush Administration, through use of a framing concept, to impose strong conformist pressure on what became a one-way debate over "weapons of mass destruction" (WMDs). Slogans and apocalyptic images abounded. Condoleezza Rice, then the national security adviser, argued that "we don't want the smoking gun to be a mushroom cloud."[3] This assertion illustrates how unfounded assumptions can capture the space that should be occupied by careful analysis. Political leaders on both sides of the Atlantic, abetted by errors—or worse—on the part of top intelligence officials, were able to use the "everything has changed" concept to suppress dissent so successfully that prominent newspapers like the *New York Times* were subsequently moved to apologize to their readers for having been intimidated and having not, for nearly three crucial years, challenged the Administration's rationale for war in Iraq.[4]

As we know, some experts did dissent. For instance, former Secretaries of State James Baker and Lawrence Eagleberger and former National Security Advisors Brent Scowcroft and Zbigniew Brzezinski challenged the Administration's rationale privately and then in public before the war began. They were ignored. And UN weapons inspectors Hans Blix and Mohammed El-Baradei, in a report released on January 27, 2003, expressed doubt that a WMD program existed in Iraq. They were also ignored. Later, the Administration sought unsuccessfully to have El-Baradei removed. Recent research identifies a clear pattern of skepticism within the CIA and the Pentagon about the Administration's approach to the war.[5]

A second framing concept, Nation at War, provides political advantages to the Administration but distorts the political and legal environment. The political implications are obvious. Being on a war footing rallies the population around the executive, increasing presidential power. The Nation at War notion permitted President Bush to campaign for re-election as a war president, implying that times were too perilous for a change in leadership. Moreover, the legal status of being at war accords certain rights under the UN Charter and provides the executive with legal powers governing such areas as privacy, speech, search and seizure, and the use of the military justice system that otherwise would be unavailable.

The run-up to the war and the first years of the Iraq occupation saw a marked failure of the institutions Americans rely upon to analyze and, when necessary, challenge Administration policy governing major foreign engagements. Until the spring of 2004, though some influential analysts and writers spoke out, most remained silent. The Brookings Institution continued to publish tendentious statistics about progress in Iraq well into 2006.[6] And the Council on Foreign Relations (CFR), the quintessential establishment voice in foreign affairs, advanced little criticism of the effects of the Nation at War idea on political or legal discourse. It was not until the conventional wisdom shifted away from "all is well" that CFR officials went public with full-throated criticism.[7] Congress is notable for not having challenged the Administration's rationale for the war until questions were raised in the Democratic presidential primaries by Howard Dean—and then only after public dismay became palpable. The media were especially slow off the mark. Books by senior journalists acknowledging their profession's shortcomings after 9/11 are only now, as we write, beginning to appear.[8]

Taking a concept from trauma surgery, we argue that the "golden hour," when intervention can be most effective, was allowed to pass. In 2006 we saw the emergence of generals, State Department officials, and scholars decrying the mistakes that were made. We value our public policy institutions and the analysts and experts who inform them for their contributions under pressure. Yet the time for performance is during the crisis before irrevocable decisions are made, not after the storm has passed.

All too often the Administration's narrative acted to suppress difficult issues. For example, at a conference convened by Cambridge University in June 2005 on the legal issues surrounding the Coalition's use of force in Iraq, NATO officials raised the following questions:

- What is meant by the right of self-defense accorded under Article 51 of the UN Charter?
- Can states that claim they are "at war" launch preemptive or preventive actions if they believe their security is threatened?
- Do some states or groups, for example, threaten North Korean, Syrian, or Iranian security? If so, do the latter have the right to launch preventative strikes?
- Can a strike be justified based on intelligence information that indicates an attack is likely and where there could be little or no warning?

These are all legitimate questions that must be asked before, not after, hostilities have commenced.

Yet, the Nation at War idea has proven politically potent. Spooked by their successive electoral defeats, the Democrats—and many moderate Republicans—were pulled to the right after 9/11. They replaced their long-time reliance on diplomacy with the assumption that to be credible they had to express a willingness to project power, including both pre-emptive and preventive war.[9] Only with the 2006 mid-term elections, as the nation sought to regain its equlibrium, did these tendencies abate. In fact as late as 2005, the Washington, D.C.-based Center for American Progress provided an example of liberal acquiescence to the notion of force as an early option. Founded ostensibly to offer an alternative to the Republican version of the war on terror, it has taken pride in advocating, as a matter of broad policy, "vigorous military action." The many possible steps short of military action and the art of risk management get second-ary consideration even in a forum established to look critically at just such concepts. The Nation at War Big Idea thus goes unchallenged.

In his 2005 commencement address Yale President Richard Levin urged the university's graduating class to confront this phenomenon. He said: "In the last presidential election . . . every issue . . . was reduced to a formula. 'Staying on message' was the name of the game. There was no real debate, no progression in the argument. The tendency to over-simplification and polarization leads us to represent too many important public choices as false dichotomies."[10]

THE INFLUENCE OF FAITH

The lure of Big Ideas in American politics is as old as the republic itself. The young nation was animated by the notion that it was exceptional in its moral clarity, its foundation in divine providence, and its appointment to a higher purpose. These ideas mark the United States as fundamentally different from its European ancestor nations. It is rooted in this sense of higher, providential purpose. We can not easily imagine a modern European leader describing his country, as President Bush did in January 2005, as having "a calling from beyond the stars."[11]

Nearly all Big Ideas have strong spiritual roots. This dimension is important to the connections among different eras. By any measure of international comparison, the United States stands out as a deeply religious nation. It is unusual in the prevalence of religious belief and acceptance of revealed, nonrational truth. Americans are far more likely to attend weekly religious services and believe in a supreme creator than the citizens of other industrialized countries. They do not hide their faith. When Karen Hughes, then the Under Secretary of State for Public Diplomacy, toured four Middle Eastern Islamic countries in 2005, one of her specific goals was to convey to her audiences the importance of faith in American life. Since 9/11, especially, much of America's foreign policy has been justified in religious terms, such as this line in President Bush's 2003 State of the Union address, given on the eve of the Iraq war: "The liberty we prize is not America's gift to the world. It is God's gift to humanity."[12] We ask, therefore, whether the large role played by faith in the United States may render Americans more susceptible to the notion of American Exceptionalism.

BIG IDEAS AND THE MEDIA

If Big Ideas in various rhetorical guises are a persistent phenomenon throughout American history, the rise of the 24–7 media has placed them firmly at the center of public discourse. The primary agenda of cable television outlets, talk radio, and the networks is to build ratings, gain market share, and accumulate advertising dollars. Their interest in issues and policy runs a distant second. Hungry for sensation, they feed off of simplified ideas, expressed without nuance or qualification and often pitted against other simplifications in a "point-counterpoint" format. Like prizefighters, guests are urged to go "head-to-head" as if there were only two, mutually exclusive, options to each policy choice and no common ground existed.

Those whose education and experience would qualify them as experts quickly learn that sound bites and repartee, not analysis, are the keys to being invited back. This means playing the game according to the format. As Bruce Bartlett, formerly a senior fellow at the National Center for Policy Analysis, put it:

> I just got off the phone with a booker for one of the cable news channels who wanted me to play the role of the knee-jerk Bush supporter and I had to decline . . . The fact is—and everyone knows this—that few issues are black-and-white. There are always nuances that are impossible to discuss in a debate format. But the debate format creates the illusion that there is always a simple answer to every complex problem and encourages average television viewers to assume that those of us in the Washington policymaking community are all idiots totally beholden to our party, without a lick of common sense or integrity.[13]

This format is ideally suited to advancing Big Ideas, a skill in which the anchors of the popular shows excel. They are expert at attracting audiences with snappy phrases. Unfortunately, this entertainment skill has nothing to do with illuminating the complexity of foreign policy choices. Take a catchphrase like "shock and awe." Harlan Ullman, a former naval officer and co-inventor of the term, told us that he intended it to describe a policy of both carrots and sticks, with two components: short-term "shock" and long-term "awe." But it has been appropriated by the media to mean simply a dramatic bombing campaign.

America's fixation with framing concepts and the demands of commercial media thus feed off of each other. Together they turn the policy process back to front, so that mythology too often precedes rationality. This sets the stage for the third and decisive element in the decline of American foreign policy.

THE COLLAPSE OF
THE RATIONAL CENTER

Big Ideas and the news media are what they are. We may regret our culture's susceptibility to glib political merchandizing, but we cannot change it. There are whole library shelves full of works that deplore the shallowness of the mass media. Moreover, the new media—the Internet, blogs, e-mail lists, and podcasts—do not herald any dramatic improvement. So in this book, out of a concern for conciseness and the reader's blood pressure, we treat these elements as given.

What is not a given is the role of the foreign policy experts who inhabit the rational center. It is not that experts don't make mistakes; they do and there are many examples of egregious errors. Experts believed, for example, that General Douglas MacArthur's plan to introduce democracy to Japan would not work and counseled against it. But effective policy is rarely achievable without them, and impediments to their participation in the policy debate need to be minimized.

We devote a good part of this book to charting the rational center's occasional moments of ascendancy in foreign policy—for example, the remarkably successful diplomacy that accompanied the end of the Cold War and the adroit diplomacy that has managed the US-China relationship. Much of the rest of the book looks at the rational center's opportunism, which has contributed to recent diplomatic dysfunction and could result in catastrophic outcomes should the US-China relationship be driven by Big Ideas, not American interests, going forward.

Because all Americans have (often quite strong) views on national security it is easy to underestimate the value of experts. In so complex an area as foreign policy, where the choice between particular options is always subject to vigorous competition between values and means, we are obviously not suggesting that there is ever a single "right" answer available only to the expert; experts have been wrong on many occasions. But the delicate weighting of complex political, military, and economic variables that together determine the nation's strategy in specific arenas, and that strategy's execution, require the participation of people who have devoted time and effort to acquiring the necessary knowledge and experience. The probability of a terrorist nuclear attack, balancing the complex factors underpinning the transatlantic relationship, or plotting an integrated response to emergent giants in Asia are highly complex matters. We depend on experts to analyze these challenges objectively and to carry out the decisions reached through the democratic process. The expert role in foreign policy is thus to examine policy options with reference to the data—to historical developments and the record—and then recommend policy and guide its implementation. This role is inconsistent with the easy celebrity offered by talk-show programs.

Many esteemed academics are lured by media hungry for credentialed authorities. Those with TV-friendly skills, namely a forthright, telegenic presence and an ability to squeeze complex issues into forty-five-second sound bites, are in particular demand. All too often, however, they are persuaded to give producers what they want: either credentialed justification for national policy they know is questionable, or else reflexive opposition. The problem is that citizens who watch these Punch and Judy acts come to believe these are real policy discussions and then go out and vote.

We have nearly reached the point where experts devote more time to packaging their ideas in a media-friendly way than to the rigor or implications of their analysis. It is entirely counterproductive that distinguished former Secretaries of State such as Madeleine Albright and Lawrence Eagleburger should lend dignity and credibility to confrontational talk shows whose truncated, rapid-fire format effectively excludes expertise from the debate.

It would be bad enough if scholars merely misrepresented ideas that were fundamentally sound. But the infection cannot be quarantined; it comes back to distort the ideas themselves. For example, Harvard professor Samuel Huntington's influential concept, the Clash of Civilizations, started life in the journal *Foreign Affairs* as a phrase borrowed from another scholar and appearing with a modest question mark after it: "The Clash of Civilizations?"[14] By the time the idea went between hard covers, there was no sign of academic modesty. Clash of Civilizations had become an assertion with cosmic validity despite an outpouring of serious and pointed criticism across the academy.[15]

When experts of distinction reinforce the Big Idea/media nexus instead of resisting it, they become enablers of what is, often, misconceived policy. In effect, they cease to function as experts and become advocates for one or another set of ready-made policy positions. Henry Kissinger, for example, is perilously close to acting in this way with regard to preventative war.[16] In times of national stress the rational center's failure to perform its vital function threatens to return the United States to a pre-Enlightenment way of thought, where its conception of the world is defined by overbearing nationalism, scare scenarios, and religious rhetoric at the expense of reason, skepticism, and analysis.

To illustrate this state of affairs, we reintroduce readers to the ways in which information is offered to them. In some cases we discuss familiar fixtures of the national media: the hosts of popular shows, the stars of the opinion circuit on television and radio, trendsetting editorial writers. In others we will describe less well-known figures who, out of the public eye, play a critical issues as intelligence, the role of the military, and US policy towards China.

WHAT WE HAVE LOST

The silencing of the rational center by the culture of the Big Idea is not simply an academic problem. It imposes difficulties on American decision makers when developments in the real world—whether in China, the Middle East, Russia, or Latin America—fail to fit ideologically driven policy. To see what we have lost, let us look at an earlier crisis that was successfully managed, the reunification of Germany in 1989–1990.

Now that the fall of the Berlin Wall and the emergence of present-day Germany have been subsumed in triumphalist narrative about the inevitable demise of Soviet communism, it is difficult to remember that when popular demonstrations first erupted across Eastern Europe in 1989 and mass emigrations signaled the collapse of East German authority, there was a dangerous feeling of anarchy in the air. When the Berlin Wall was breached that November, there was no reason for confidence that the revolt would turn out well. In Washington events had taken the leadership by surprise. No master plan existed, and there were divided counsels about how to proceed.[17] In East Germany the government had collapsed; in West Germany the ruling coalition was divided on next steps; in Moscow the Soviet leadership was anxiously contemplating its own demise; in London and Paris old suspicions of German revanchism greatly subdued the leaders' enthusiasm for reunification. Furthermore, Germany represented the strategic cauldron of the Cold War. The Fulda Gap in northern Germany was the point where allied war planning had focused for fifty years. In 1989 over 300,000 Soviet troops were still stationed there and the Soviet presence in Berlin represented its salient into Western Europe.

A rational solution to these problems was far from inevitable. Bitter disagreement broke out at the beginning of the negotiations about whether this was a process of "unification" or "reunification." Yet some ten months later a treaty was signed in Moscow in which all parties agreed that the two parts of Germany would become one country through the simplest mechanism: a short amendment to one article of the West German Basic Law. It was further agreed that the new country would remain a member of NATO and the European Union, with Berlin as its prospective capital and all non-NATO forces withdrawn. The stability of Europe as a military and political entity was affirmed. The division of Europe that had been the source of global tension for half a century came to an end without a shot being fired.

This was a diplomatic triumph of the first order in which there were many heroes—notably the people of East Germany, whose street demonstrations left no doubt that the communist era was over, and the (West) German chancellor Helmut Kohl, who understood that delay was not an option. Yet the chief credit for handling the crisis and designing the new era in Europe undoubtedly lies with the United States and specifically with the team assembled and led by President George H. W. Bush, especially Secretary of State James A. Baker and National Security Advisor Brent Scowcroft. The present Secretary of State, Condoleezza Rice, played a supporting role in her capacity as a Soviet expert at the National Security Council.

The talks demanded, over nine months, an intensive commitment to multiparty diplomacy, support for the policy of an ally (West Germany), overcoming the objections of friends (the United Kingdom and France), and reassuring a potential adversary (the Soviet Union). All of this was set against a background of massive street demonstrations throughout Eastern Europe. A miscalculation—particularly one that lost the trust of the Soviet Union—could have sent Europe down a deadly spiral.

Instead, American diplomacy rose to the challenge, sometimes developing highly ingenious formulations to cut through divisions and retrieve momentum. At one point, for instance, the negotiations threatened to stall, with the United States and West Germany facing sustained delaying tactics from the United Kingdom, France, and the Soviet Union, as it became increasingly apparent that East Germany was a humanitarian disaster in the waiting. The time had long past for the three non-United States victors of World War II to be defending their prerogatives. The question was how to soothe their *amour propre* while addressing the needs on the ground. The State Department's "two plus four" formula fit the bill. The "two" were the parts of Germany, which would be allowed to negotiate their own form of reunification, while the "four"—the United States, France, the United Kingdom, and the Soviet Union—would handle the international aspects. This apt formulation carried the negotiations through the summer of 1990 and eventually allowed all the participants to accede enthusiastically to the Treaty of the Final Settlement of September 1990.

The reunification of Germany took place less than twenty years ago, but as a diplomatic accomplishment it seems to come from another age. The Bush team's quiet competence in securing American interests and advancing global good without causing resentment seems a distant memory now.

We can isolate four strands of what we have lost:

1. Balancing ideals and policy. The American approach to German unification found an ideal balance between ideology and realism. When British prime minister Margaret Thatcher raised realistic concerns about slowing down the process to avoid offending the Soviet Union, President Bush countered with the long-held American vision of a "Europe whole and free."[18] But this vision never became a substitute for a pragmatic policy for implementing the vision—as shown by the "two plus four" process.

By contrast today's vision of democratization as the solution to US foreign policy challenges (for instance in the Middle East) is treated as self-implementing, without the need for ongoing, detailed administrative engagement. We have seen American idealism harden into ideology, and then ideology become policy.

2. Knowledge. Look at any picture of those involved with German re-unification and you will see people with deep personal knowledge of the other parties' views grounded in extensive diplomatic stays in each other's countries. This applies not just to the NATO allies but to the intimate personal connections between the US and Soviet leaders, which were built on a long tradition of meetings, formal and informal, in both countries to work out differences.

Now look at the Camp David pictures of the top policy makers in the fateful days preceding the March 2003 attack on Iraq. Only one person,

Defense Secretary Donald Rumsfeld, had ever been to Baghdad. There was no United States Embassy there. The pattern repeats itself in other trouble spots: Iran, Syria, North Korea. American leaders have little or no contact with leaders in these places, and diplomatic representation is minimal or nonexistent. Language capabilities are deficient. There is no feel for what one American official has called the "pulse" of countries, even those where vital American interests are involved.[19] Too often American leaders are making grave decisions about countries and leaders they know largely through briefing books, which can contain, as we now know, inaccurate judgments. In testimony of the Senate Foreign Relations Committee on September 19, 2006, Under Secretary of State Nicholas Burns commented that he had never met an Iranian official.[20]

3. Listening. During the German negotiations there were few instances when the participants held the same views. Many differences were substantial and emotionally powerful, including the deep European fear of a resurgent Germany. These concerns were heard with respect in Washington. President Bush, for example, out of respect for the Soviet leader Mikhail Gorbachev, made a conscious decision not to assert claims of victory as the Berlin Wall fell.

4. The Political-Military Balance. Perhaps most significantly, in times of national crisis or challenge, we have seen a shift in authority from diplomatic to military power structures. During the German negotiations generals participated only to advise on technical matters relating to the troop levels between NATO and the Warsaw Pact. Their advice tended to be hard-line, but it was never allowed to dominate. Interestingly, this pattern was also evident during the Cuban missile crisis, when President Kennedy spoke dismissively of the advice he received from the military.

Since the mid-1990s, however, the rise of neoconservative influence, coupled with the breathtaking advances in targeting accuracy and strike capability brought about by the Revolution in Military Affairs (which we discuss in chapter 6), has provided increased scope to military operations previously circumscribed by political concerns.[21] Precision munitions, for example, that in theory minimize civilian casualties, have increased the range of possible objectives. This, together with the types of foreign problems we face, has contributed to a shift in the locus of political-military decision making to the Pentagon.

More recently, with the ebbing of neoconservative influence and greater push-back from the rational center, the definition, and thus perception, of major international challenges has changed, and the result is that diplomacy has begun again to play a greater role.

RESTORING THE RATIONAL CENTER

David Halberstam's classic book, *The Best and the Brightest,* published in 1973 as the Vietnam War was winding down, exposed the fatal combination of brilliance and arrogance that lay at the heart of that debacle. His objective was to show how such a brilliant assemblage of talent could get things so wrong.[22] Our book embarks on a similar quest, but with one important difference. America in the first decade of the twenty-first century is at a different stage of development. The terms of trade in technology and economics are not as favorable to the United States as they were in the mid-1970s. Outside of military technology, America's competitive lead is subject to increasing challenge.

China, a coolly rational society with an ancient culture, is rising rapidly, and it maintains a complex relationship with the United States that we discuss in some detail in order to illustrate the critical role of the rational center in the decades ahead. On its current trajectory Chinese investment in raw materials, infrastructure, and military modernization—and its critical role in the purchase of US debt, which provides it with unprecedented leverage on American consumers—presages a challenge that, if not properly handled, could within two decades change the quality of American life for the worse. Others, including the European Union and India, and the changing dynamics of the energy market, pose challenges in distinct arenas. Under these circumstances, a poor performance by America's elite will be much more damaging than it would have been during the Vietnam era. The world is simply more competitive.

As the Iraq war proceeded from the spring of 2003 through early 2005, we encountered mounting skepticism about whether the rational center could be reconstituted. We were told time and again that in a country as commercially attuned and fragmented as the United States, with a media format that tended to suppress substantive policy debate, and with the political parties so concentrated on short-term advantage, trying to find and restore a center of gravity was, at best, a difficult task. We were told that our strictures against celebrity-seeking academics were too harsh because, after all, no one (certainly, few other academics) really took them seriously any more. In a disheartening way, this makes our point that the compromises our intellectual leaders have so willingly made has taken away the gravitas and perspective they once provided.

Yet the rational center is regaining its traction as the sense of crisis abates. This means that the issue is more than simply the toxic political exchange or the media format. There is a recurring syndrome evident at times of crisis in which the rational center is submerged both because it is hesitant to challenge patriotic passions and because the format is not encouraging.

The implication that American society is not capable of self-reformation is dispiriting and incorrect. What is apparent is that in times of crisis or stress, America is particularly susceptible to Big Idea rhetoric, which causes passion to replace rationality in important parts of the national discourse, and the institutions that normally provide perspective—the editorial pages, research centers, the Congress—to become silent. That this condition is temporary is apparent from our experience following the Red Scare, the Vietnam War, and more recently the 2006 mid-term elections when the rational center reasserted itself. It remains, however, that a more competitive world will not afford the luxury of our enthrall to Big Ideas and their debilitating passions in the future. To avoid unwanted outcomes, the rational center must dominate the national discourse as crises arise and, indeed, impose its own definition as challenges arise, to ensure that the policy response is measured, logical, and effective. Should this prove beyond our ability, the outcome will be determined by external factors and the results, for the United States, will not be so congenial.

We do not believe this unhappy end is preordained. We firmly believe that the rational center has the capacity for both effectiveness and brilliance. It needs to show these qualities not only when the cycle of events creates a favorable moment but also at moments of stress when mistakes can be least afforded and when its expertise is most urgently needed to understand foreign policy risks in their true context.

ONE

The Big Idea in History

In March 2003 Americans went off to invade Iraq with the tune "Freedom on the March" swelling the national breast. The country proudly embarked upon a great enterprise inspired by a Big Idea and confident that the means would somehow arise to achieve its noble ends. It was a war of choice. Operation Iraqi Freedom took place not simply because a dark cabal of unelected officials foisted their views on an inexperienced president, or because the intelligence process failed or was corrupted, or because secretive industrial interests manipulated democratic accountability.

These things may have happened. And most Americans believed at the time that Saddam Hussein had weapons of mass destruction capable of bringing regional chaos. The decisive element, however, was that a large majority of Americans—elite and ordinary, conservatives and liberals—embraced the Big Idea that they were conferring freedom on the Iraqi people, that this was a noble and quintessentially American duty, and that by bearing the gift of liberty they would be welcomed with open arms. They found the notion of "Freedom on the March" so alluring that few challenged the Administration's rationale for the policy or demanded that the media or Congress ask the required questions on their behalf. Those who did make such demands were dismissed or barely heard.

Something very similar happened when the nation, enthralled with the notion of "monolithic communism," embraced the Domino Theory and became embroiled in Vietnam. There is a recurring quality to this phenomenon that is most pronounced in times of crisis: we have seen its ascendancy in our generation and the preceding one. And with the accelerated news cycle, it is able to gain traction more widely and rapidly than before.

America's foreign policy discourse is so fragile today because at a critical point two forces—Big Ideas and Big Media—come together to force the debate through a *format* that de-emphasizes fact-based analysis and replaces it with a glib and fashionable media-speak called infotainment. The combination of American susceptibility to the Big Idea and the infotainment requirements of today's ratings-driven 24–7 media strongly favor impulse over rational calculation and sound bites over expertise.

Precisely when it is most needed, the rational center is left to fight for a place at the foreign policy table. As the renowned American diplomat George Kennan observed, the truth is often a poor competitor in the marketplace of American ideas because it is "complicated, unsatisfying, full of dilemmas and always vulnerable to misinterpretation and abuse."[1]

In this chapter we look at the phenomenon of Big Ideas in American foreign policy history. We cannot hope to provide an exhaustive survey— there are far too many examples. But we can offer a sketch that shows the use of notions and catchphrases to convey policies rooted in American Exceptionalism. It is an old American habit.

American Exceptionalism is the mother of the nation's Big Ideas. The notion that its citizens are a special people born of exceptional circumstances with a unique role in humankind's salvation is the oldest, most enduring theme in the nation's public space. It informed the rhetorical premise on which Americans asserted their right to separate from their British ruler; it was vital in fashioning a homogeneous, sociopolitical whole out of so many heterogeneous parts throughout initial and subsequent waves of immigration; and it persists as a platform on which the modern United States interacts with the world. It is reflected on a recurring basis in the public square, especially at times when the nation is challenged. Orators and leaders often fashion their rhetorical prescriptions with reference to the nation's common belief in its unique and exceptional nature—a belief that is ever present just beneath the surface of the public discourse. At critical junctures, politicians and pundits dip into this pool of collectively held "truths" to validate their proposals for public consumption. The notion of Exceptionalism has functioned like a conceptual umbrella under which various expressions of this idea become powerful framing themes in their own right, such as "Detachment" from European toil and conflict, "New Beginnings" and "Providential Mission" in the progress of human society, and "Manifest Destiny" and an "Imperialism of Righteousness" in the territorial expansion of the nation's borders.

AMERICA AS AN IDEA

If all nations are to some extent imagined communities, and all aspiring republics face the challenge of defining the illusive matter of national identity, then America began life as the ultimate imagined community. The very idea of America was consciously forged by its founders when they extracted national and mythic meaning from an otherwise inchoate mass of beliefs, aspirations, and disharmonous settlements previously united largely in the act of rebellion. There was no definitive "people" to serve as a point of reference. Neither was there a definitive geographical entity, given that America's land mass remained only partly explored and still subject to competing historical, imperial, religious, and indigenous claims. Without racial or spatial definition, the new geopolitical identity had to be legitimized in both nonethnic and nonterritorial terms. This problem was solved by creating the idea of America.[2]

Big Ideas have always been central to the process of nation-building. Yet, more than other modern nations, America has employed Big Ideas to describe an age or an aspiration. From its colonial period through the present day the arts, literature, and the political and spiritual realms have all brought forth themes that emphasized the "exceptional" nature of the American experience to present America in various guises.[3]

In earlier times, the nation saw itself, as a moral exemplar, in harmony with nature, a land of moral renewal, God's chosen nation, the new order of the ages, the land of the Enlightenment, the first consciously wrought modern nation and the universal model for all societies. We were the "City upon a Hill," the "New Eden," and the "Redeemer Nation." Later on America was thought the land of equality, and the guarantor of world peace.[4]

Thus with the self-construction of America there began a recurring process—a perpetual industry of themes that fashioned and illuminated the substance of nationhood.[5] America was ever recasting itself, ready to reconceptualize its Exceptionalism to meet the next challenge. For each such challenge, a rhetoritician was there to coin the phrase that defined that era's Exceptionalism.[6]

Exceptionalism

A closer look at the concept of Exceptionalism reveals that during it's early period as a colonial settlement, America's intellectual discourse centered on the idea that Americans were a chosen people delivered from corruption and evil to a New World. The phrase *New World* dates from the first European exploration of the Americas and was widely adopted after the 1504 publication of the celebrated series of letters by Amerigo Vespucci under the title *Mundus Novus*. But by the time Jamestown was founded in 1607, followed by the Mayflower's landing at Plymouth Rock thirteen years later, the phrase *New World* enjoyed an entirely new significance.

Many of the intrepid colonists of the eastern seaboard saw themselves as agents of God, handed the gift of starting again and building a new way of life. Their sense of mission contrasted sharply with that of earlier ventures, which reflected various seventeenth-century European commercial rivalries. The Massachusetts and Virginia colonists were there to reinvigorate a corrupted and spoiled world. The most famous orator of the colonial period to give voice to this idea, Massachusetts Governor John Winthrop, delivered his classic sermon in 1630 under the title "A Model of Christian Charity." He told his parishioners, "Thus stands the cause between God and us . . . For we must consider ourselves a city upon a hill, the eyes of all people upon us."[7]

The idea of the "City Upon a Hill" found ready acceptance among the colonists and their descendents. Other Puritans, such as Jonathan Edwards, Cotton Mather, and John Cotton, were quick to echo Winthrop's vision with similar proclamations, like "the glorious work of God . . . shall *renew* the world of mankind . . . and shall begin in America."[8] The message was clear: Americans were a special people and an example to the world. It was a dynamic concept; for Americans, the universal applicability of their values emerged as a constant refrain over the three centuries that followed. It can be traced, for instance, to Walt Rostow's 1960 *The Stages of Economic Growth: Non-Communist Manifesto*, in which his economic model, which asserted the universal applicability of American values, was used by the Kennedy Administration in Southeast Asia.[9] In a similar vein is Secretary of State Condoleezza Rice's statement in October 2005: "But when impatient patriots in this country finally demanded their freedom and their rights, what once seemed impossible suddenly became inevitable. So it was in America. So it was in much the world. And so it will be in the Middle East."[10]

The late eighteenth century colonials held much the same idea. Their nation was destined to be different and better than all others on earth. The man who most successfully articulated this sensibility was Thomas Paine, who published *Common Sense* in January 1776. This small but influential pamphlet argued for independence as the only course that would secure the rights to which the peoples of the New World were entitled. "This new world has been the asylum for the persecuted lovers of civil and religious liberty from every part of Europe," Paine argued. "We have every opportunity and every encouragement before us, to form the noblest, purest constitution on the face of the earth. We have it in our power to begin the world over again."[11] This theme reverberates today in America's determination to deliver democratic pluralism to Iraq.

Prominent revolutionaries such as Benjamin Franklin, John Adams, and Thomas Jefferson were very much in the business of fashioning a fresh national identity. In their writings and speeches they likened the new America to Republican Rome before Octavian's proclamation of an empire and claimed Cato the Younger and Cicero as forbearers. George Washington was described as a modern-day Cincinnatus. Just as the heroes of Roman republicanism had strived to defend liberty from tyrants like Julius Caesar, so John Jay, James Madison, Alexander Hamilton, and others were engaged in a struggle to defy the corrupt powers of the old world.

Jefferson urged the extension of this analogy to the design of state buildings. It was crucial, he emphasized, to abandon the colonial Georgian architecture of plantation houses and public buildings associated with British rule. In their stead, the new nation should create the "pure architecture of Republican Rome." Jefferson's drawings for the Virginia State Capitol mark the beginnings of a classical revival in the United States. This was truly a Big Idea in motion: the American creation was a return to classical ideals and ancient virtues that had been lost in the vortex of European civilization.[12]

And so the nation embraced one concept after another , each reflecting the idea of America's exceptional nature in an effort to identify and promote a coherent notion of national character and purpose. The core message was that America had turned away from the vices of the Old World and had made a new beginning for human history: notions like "First

New Nation," "New Israel," and "New Eden" became popular across the arts, literature, and academia. Noah Webster declared America an "Empire of Reason," and Ezra Stiles asserted that "the Lord shall have made his American Israel high above all nations which he hath made."

Alexis de Tocqueville, Louis Hartz, and Frederick Jackson Turner all sought to emphasize that America liked to think of itself as, and to some extent was, an escape from the bondage of the past, that the conditions of American life had prevented feudal institutions from emerging, and that this new republic was thus a living manifestation of "pure modernity." As the *Democratic Review* asserted in 1839, "our national birth was the beginning of a new history." Ralph Waldo Emerson agreed, arguing that Americans had established an "original relation to the universe."[13]

This idea also occupied the primary place in the earliest philosophies of official government. The Founding Fathers embedded within the Great Seal the Latin phrase *Novus Ordo Seclorum*, meaning "New Order of the Ages," which, beginning in 1935, appeared on the back of the American dollar bill. America's first diplomats, from Washington to Franklin, Jefferson, and Madison, all strenuously expounded the grand dream of a new republican diplomacy informed by reason and contrasting with the Machiavellian ways of Europe. When French Foreign Minister Count de Vergennes told John Adams to be less pompous with such ideals in the chambers of international diplomacy, Adams replied, "the dignity of North America does not consist in diplomatic ceremonials or any of the subtlety of etiquette; it consists in reason, justice, truth, the rights of mankind."[14]

From Winthrop to the dollar bill, Americans were seldom allowed to forget Exceptionalism, the original Big Idea on which their nation was founded. This theme reverberates throughout the nation's political rhetoric, perhaps nowhere more vividly than in President John F. Kennedy's 1961 inaugural address. After reminding his audience that they were the "heirs of the first revolution," Kennedy assured the world that America would "pay any price, bear any burden . . . to assure the survival and the success of liberty."[15]

Exceptionalism may have been America's original Big Idea, but it was by no means the only one. Rather, it served as the wellspring for countless others.

Detachment

The original notion of "Detachment" from the toil of European balance of powers provides an example of both the tumultuous political realities facing the earliest practitioners of American foreign policy and the function provided by narratives of Exceptionalism. It holds that America should conduct its foreign relations independent of the iniquities and cynical power politics of Europe in order to protect the exceptional conditions of American liberty at home. If the nation became involved in warfare and imperialism with the Old World, taxes and conscription would compromise Americans' unique level of individual freedom, European powers might compete for favor among different states and break up the Union, alliances with greater powers might compel America into a subordinate role that could force a compromise of national interests, and warfare might become a part of the American way of life. In his farewell address Washington asserted, "it is our policy to steer clear of permanent alliances with any portion of the foreign world."[16] Quite obviously, the U.S has since seen the benefit of alliances, bilateral and multilateral agreements and organizations, the UN foremost among them. Still, hesitation is apparent in certain circumstances. The roots of the American rejection of the League of Nations after World War I might be seen in Washington's farewell address, and, in our time, impatience with, if not a skeptical attitude toward, international agreements such as the International Criminal Court and the Kyoto Protocol is clear.

Interpreting what was seen as a divine mandate, we find another dimension of detachment. John Quincy Adams believed America should provide an example to the rest of the world.[17] He said that America should not venture overseas "in search of monsters to destroy" but should act as "the well-wisher to the freedom and independence of all" while remaining "champion and vindicator only of her own."[18] In a similar vein, Jefferson went so far as to argue that America would need no diplomats, only commercial councils in the liberal interaction of free trade. Subsequent challenges from Spanish, French, British, and Indian quarters soon pierced early illusions regarding the feasibility of the Big Idea of American detachment. But it served the infant republic well as a guide to the otherwise bewildering and complex world of foreign relations.[19]

Both Detachment and interventionist policies that project American values on global affairs are expressions of American Exceptionalism. American Exceptionalism provides a context for both. Just as isolationism and more recently, Libertarianism have reflected the theme of detachment, so activist intervention, as expressed by the neoconservatives, reflects a separate strain of Exceptionalism. Both are expressions of American Exceptionalism, though detachment and activism each express different policy prescriptions.

Detachment may be seen as a strategy to address specific challenges. But, used in rhetorical terms, as in the case of the Monroe Doctrine, it advanced a national discourse in its time that defined what it was to be an American. Thus leaders, depending upon the circumstances or challenges, utilize different rhetoric for each; they can use one or the other to play to this soft spot in the American psyche. This underscores why the American public space is so unique.

The Monroe Doctrine

The first practical manifestation of the twin ideas of Exceptionalism and Detachment may be seen in the Monroe Declaration, or "doctrine" as it soon came to be called.

To protect their idea of America from the convulsions then occupying Europe, Americans would have to ensure that these convulsions never reached the New World. With considerable input from his Secretary of

FIGURE 1   No less than the oratories of New England diplomats and Puritan governors, the artists of the new republic sought to leave little doubt as to its exceptionality and distance from European perfidy. The plate at right, from 1796, depicts American liberty as Hebe, the goddess of youth, who treads on chains, a key, and a scepter—symbolic objects of the old world. She offers her cup to an eagle, and the outline of Boston can been seen in the background behind an altar and under a sky of lightning. (*Liberty. In the Form of the Goddess of Youth; Giving Support to the Bald Eagle*, American Political Prints, 1776–1876, Library of Congress.)

State, John Quincy Adams, President James Monroe announced in December 1823 that "we owe it . . . to candor and the amicable relations existing between the United States and those powers to declare that we should consider any attempt on their part to extend their system to any portion of this hemisphere as dangerous to our peace and safety."[20]

The Monroe Doctrine, in its rhetorical presentation, is a classic example of a Big Idea. A declaration of a vague and sweeping vision of nonintervention, it had little practical effect for many decades. In its dealings with Britain over the future of Oregon, its annexation of the Falkland Islands, and the expansion of British Honduras, or with Russia over the southern boundary of Alaska, the United States never invoked the Monroe Doctrine. Even as an abstraction, however, it marked an effort to assert America's position in an inhospitable world by recasting the boundaries of national identity with big concepts. European rivalries would be kept out of the new American hemisphere.[21]

If the early practical impact was minimal, the diplomatic impact in European courts was more immediate. Austro-Hungarian count Klemens von Metternich remarked that "these United States whom we have seen grow . . . have suddenly left a sphere too narrow for their ambition and have astonished Europe by a new act of revolt, more unprovoked, fully as audacious, and no less dangerous than the former." Metternich's disapproval was echoed by Moscow, which announced that Monroe's declaration deserved "only the most profound contempt." German chancellor Otto von Bismarck described it as "insolent dogma . . . a species of arrogance peculiarly American and inexcusable."[22]

Among Americans, however, Monroe's Big Idea was an unbridled success. Its popularity helped define an American sense of self. As the chief of the British Diplomatic Mission reported to London, the Monroe Declaration "seem[ed] to have been received with acclamation throughout the United States," a response that "echoed from one end of the Union to the other. It would, indeed, be difficult, in a country composed of elements so various, to find a more perfect unanimity than has been displayed on every side." The Monroe Declaration engendered a sense of unity among disparate peoples now sharing the same sovereign boundaries. It drew on a common discourse that was increasingly familiar to Americans and reminiscent of the ideals enshrined in their struggle for independence forty years earlier. It also affirmed to European monarchs and chancellors a strong sense of national identity; their reactions were proof enough of that.[23]

Manifest Destiny

When John O'Sullivan, the editor of *Democratic Review*, wrote in 1839 that America's real claim to the Oregon territory rested in "the right of

FIGURE 2   The vague but determined sensibility underpinning the Monroe Doctrine developed to no small extent out of the new nationalism that followed the War of 1812 between the United States and Britain. This early-nineteenth-century cartoon reflected the perspective in American diplomacy that the time had come for Americans to assert their proper dominion on and around their home continent in spite of European machinations. Satirists would refer to the British in this period as "John Bull," while the British similarly referred to Americans as "Cousin Jonathan." In this satire of Anglo-American and Franco-American relations, an American maiden with a staff and liberty cap delivers a stiff lesson to "John Bull" and "Mounseer Beau Napperty" about respecting American rights while the two are forced to listen. ("Columbia Teaching John Bull His New Lesson," American Political Prints, 1776–1876, Library of Congress.)

our manifest destiny to overspread and to process the whole of the continent which Providence has given us for development of the great experiment of Liberty," the notion of "Manifest Destiny" became a way to explain what was already happening on the ground and rationalize it as an American right.[24]

As Big Ideas had became something of a fashion in America midcentury, Manifest Destiny emerged as a mobilizing and legitimizing

FIGURE 3   In John Gast's famous painting from the 1870s, westward expansion is portrayed as a goddesslike figure of divine providence, who watches over the settlers from above as they move into new territory. The female icon carries a book in one hand, symbolizing the Enlightenment and the reason of Anglo-Saxon civilization, and with the other she lays the telegraph wires that bind the nation together. Behind her, farmers, railways, plows, livestock, and settlers' caravans follow, while Indians and animals take flight, implying that nothing can stand in the way of American progress. This work became a marvelous piece of visual propaganda and was widely circulated. It was alluring to Americans seduced by the promises and purposes of Manifest Destiny. (John Gast, "American Progress," Library of Congress.)

concept that enabled Americans to understand the nation's westward expansion, subjugation of native peoples, and territorial acquisition in a way consistent with their founding ideals. This rhetorical function of Manifest Destiny as a Big Idea endures today. In 2005 it allowed Yale historian John Lewis Gaddis to transcend what he calls the "moral ambiguity" of the Iraq war by making the case for America's historical role as global "savior."[25]

The Westward migration proceeded simply because the land and opportunity were there, and little, with the sometime exception of rough country and hostile native tribes, stood in the way. It was facilitated by expanding commerce and the railroads, and driven, in essence, by the notion of the Frontier and hopes for a better life. As settlers migrated west, encouraged by government promises of "forty acres and a mule," through uncharted spaces, they eventually reached Mexico, California, and British Oregon. Questions of law, order, and security were left to the military and federal marshals, whose presence, not to mention administration, was uneven at best.

Magazines, posters, newspapers, religious leaders, and politicians all came to celebrate the westward spread of American civilization. As Colorado's Governor William Gilpin remarked in 1859, "The American realizes that 'Progress is God.' The destiny of the American people is to subdue the continent—to rush over this vast field to the Pacific Ocean, to change darkness into light and confirm the destiny of the human race. Divine task! Immortal mission!" Senator Daniel Dickinson (D-NY), reflecting the spirit of the times, said to Congress, "Our form of government is admirably adapted to extended empire. Founded in the virtue and intelligence of the people, and deriving its just powers from the consent of the governed, its influences are as powerful for good at the remotest limits as at the political center."[26] This sense—that, unlike the predatory nations of the past, American interventions are based on goodwill and sacrifice designed to share the gifts of good government enjoyed by Americans with those less fortunate than themselves, whether in the Philippines, the Dominican Republic, or Iraq—has time and again been an important dimension in American foreign policy.

In the mid-nineteenth century these sentiments were on full display in the arts and literature. The Western Frontier was a metaphor for opportunity and renewal. Eliza Farnham's eye-witness account, *Life in Prairie Land*, describes how the stage had been set for a "theatre of a life." The West was new and virgin ground—a theatre in which to craft

FIGURE 4   Andrew Melrose's "Westward the Star of Empire Makes its Way" is a perfect example of how Big Ideas captured people's imagination through mainstream art. Hugely popular, it depicted American expansion as the light of a higher civilization moving across the continent. ("Westward the Star of Empire Makes its Way" by Andrew Melrose. Museum of the American West, Autry National Center, Los Angeles.)

a perfect self.[27] William Cullen Bryant's famous poem "The Prairies" exemplified what one historian described as the Anglo-European will to write North American prehistory and thus define the antecedent of its own destiny. An undiscovered land, the frontier had not yet fallen *into* history. Its territories somehow belonged to a time before time that was now the preserve of Americans, as God's chosen race, to discover.[28]

In a missionary age, Manifest Destiny was the bumper sticker sentiment that asserted the civilizing impulse of Anglo-European culture and the innate supremacy of its practices. The treatment of indigenous populations and the practical necessity for expansion were explained by the notion that America stood in a pivotal position in human history. Manifest Destiny turned an unstoppable popular migration into an affirmation of American identity.

During the presidency of James Polk, Manifest Destiny informed many of the arguments for war with Mexico, leading to the acquisition of what are now Texas, Arizona, New Mexico, Utah, Nevada, and California. A Boston newspaperman commented: "The conquest which carries peace into a land where the sword has always been the sole arbiter . . . must necessarily be a great blessing to the conquered. It is a work worthy of the supremacy of humanity over the accidents of birth and fortune."[29] In Philadelphia, Admiral Robert F. Stockton made himself an overnight celebrity by announcing, "If I were now the sovereign authority . . . I would prosecute this war for the express purpose of redeeming Mexico from misrule and civil strife . . . I would with a magnanimous and kindly hand gather these wretched people within the fold of republicanism."[30]

The Imperialism of Righteousness

At the end of the nineteenth century Manifest Destiny faded from the political discourse, to be replaced by the Imperialism of Righteousness. First appearing in the 1890s in the speeches of prominent advocates for territorial expansion such as the Reverend Alexander Blackburn and Senator Albert Beveridge of Indiana, this phrase stood for the notion that Americans were a chosen people destined to transform and reform other civilizations and peoples. The Imperialism of Righteousness was thus descended from both Manifest Destiny and the Monroe Doctrine, and presented a strong dash of Victorian moralism.

When the American battleship *USS Maine* exploded in Havana Harbor in February 1898, having been sent to protect American property and citizens, politicians and clergy urged a renewed spirit of national greatness, actively encouraging newspaper publishers such as William Randolph Hearst and Joseph Pulitzer to whip the public into a war frenzy. These "Manifest Destinarians" envisioned a grand opportunity to embellish the national myth by inserting America into the competition among the "Great European Powers" while fighting a war that served the nation's economic and military interests. The Imperialism of Righteousness, however, required that the war be justified not only by "liberating" the Cuban people from Spain but by extending America's enlightened rule for their salvation and regeneration. In this sense America acceded to the European antecedents it had been trying so earnestly to escape, the British "white man's burden" and the French "*mission civilisatrice.*"

Hearst's *New York Journal* and Pulitzer's *New York World* led the way. Despite its implausibility, the *Journal* published diagrams that purported to show how Spanish saboteurs had attached underwater mines to the ship and exploded them from the beach. Both publishers showed few qualms about stretching and fabricating stories of Spanish atrocities to sway public opinion. The Spanish had allegedly confined some Cubans in brutal prison camps, which the newspapers used to full effect as justification for war. Headlines of Spanish cannibalism and disgusting forms of torture overwhelmed the newsstands.[31]

Hundreds of correspondents were dispatched to report on these atrocities. As the famous anecdote goes, when the journalist Frederick Remington arrived in Cuba and found little of substance to report, he sent a cable to his editor saying, "There is no war. Request to be recalled," to which Hearst replied, "Please remain. You furnish the pictures, I'll furnish the war."[32] Whether the tale is accurate or not, that is precisely what Hearst and Pulitzer did, devoting up to ten pages a day to stories about Cuba. Other newspapers soon followed. Dozens and then hundreds of headlines, articles, and editorials demanded that the loss of American lives be avenged. This growing support for military intervention and annexation became conflated with powerful notions about how the expansion of American power would benefit not only US citizens but, more importantly, the rest of the world.

The *New York Times* quickly joined the war fever, publishing unfounded and alarmist headlines such as "Madrid Press Feels Alarm: Talk of Destroying American Commerce and of Sending an Army to the

THE SPIRIT OF WAR PERVADES THE BREASTS OF ALL AMERICANS.

Patriotic Citizens Advocate Recourse to Arms to Wreak Vengeance Upon Spain for the Cruel and Cowardly Destruction of the Maine

FIGURE 5   This is an image of the front page of the *San Francisco Examiner* shortly after the *USS Maine* exploded. Over half of the page is occupied by George Washington and the national flag. This hyperpatriotic imagery typified the new spirit of national assertiveness driven by the sensationalist press and the idea that America's contribution to world affairs was an Imperialism of Righteousness. (As reproduced from microfilm of the *San Francisco Examiner* in John Baker, "Effects of the Press on Spanish-American Relations in 1898," Library of Congress.)

United States." The *World* ran a story titled "American Women Ready to Give Up Husbands, Sons, and Sweethearts to Defend Nation's Honor." Regional newspapers succumbed to the same formula. As the *Humboldt Times* observed on April 12 following the Maine's explosion, it was the thirty-seventh anniversary of the Battle of Fort Sumter: "how patriotic

FIGURE 6   In this 1898 cartoon the heroic Uncle Sam places himself defiantly between the young, vulnerable maiden of Cuba and the evil rogue of Spain. (Published in *Puck,* 3 June 1896. Library of Congress.)

Americans would like to hear the cannon's reverberation on this 12th of April to avenge the slaughter of the boys in blue on board the *Maine* in Havana's harbor two months ago."[33]

Pulitzer's *New York World* had been the first newspaper to introduce colored comic strips, followed almost immediately by the *Journal.* Among the first of these strips was the "Yellow Kid," a young boy who was always dressed in yellow. But because printing techniques were imperfect the colors often smudged and ran over the rest of the paper, dyeing parts of it yellow.[34] By the end of the nineteenth century, the term "Yellow Press" had come to symbolize the jingoistic and sensationalist reporting that turned the Maine event into a popular *casus belli.*

WHAT SENATOR PRCOTOR SAW IN CUBA

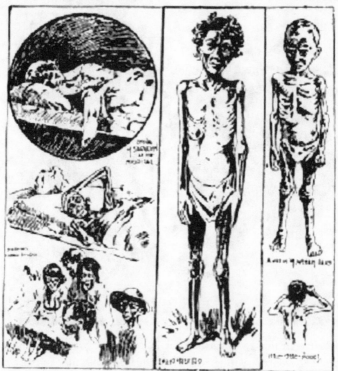

FIGURE 7   This illustration, published on January 25, 1898, was based on what one senator claimed to have seen the previous year. That this sort of information was unconfirmed was not as important to the newspaper publishers as the fact that it added to the hysteria. ("Cuban Babes Prey to Famine. Thousands of Children of the Reconcentrados Perishing in Island Towns." As reproduced from microfilm of the *San Francisco Examiner* in Baker, "Effects of the Press on Spanish-American Relations in 1898." Library of Congress.)

The press was closely followed by prominent figures from the churches. Powerful Christian organizations such as the Methodist Episcopal Church described war with Spain as a divine mission involving "the manifest favor and help of Almighty God." Protestant missionaries and evangelical organizations rallied behind the new slogan, the "Imperialism of Righteousness."[35] The religious press provided enormous support for figures such as Senator Albert Beveridge, who argued that God "has not been preparing the English-speaking and Teutonic peoples for a thousand years for nothing but vain and idle self-admiration. No! He has made us the master organizers of the world to establish system where chaos reigns . . . He has made us adept in government that we may administer government among savages and senile peoples."[36]

Within months of its sinking, the phrase "Remember the Maine! To Hell with Spain!" could be heard from newsstand to church gathering. Even street venders and manufacturers seized the opportunity to link their products to the increasingly popular slogans. The Chicago Dry Goods Reporter published a column in March 1898 explaining how to make an effective window display based on the disaster: "The window dresser who is ever alert for novelty will not allow the disaster to the battleship Maine to pass without getting an idea out of it for a window display." Similarly, an advertisement for Connick and Cousins Wholesalers in Eureka proclaimed, "Don't wait till the war is over or until prices advance on eatables before you lay in a supply of the necessaries in that line."[37]

The slogans worked. By the time the McKinley Administration declared war on Spain, on April 25, popular support was almost unanimous. By the time the Spanish surrendered, with US forces in possession of Guam, Puerto Rico, Hawaii, and the Philippine Islands, annexation had already been rationalized with the idea that what was good for America was good for others. McKinley observed that the United States had a duty to help "oppressed peoples." Control of Spain's former empire was a "great trust," which Americans carried "under the providence of God and in the name of human progress and civilization."[38]

It is possible to see in the Imperialism of Righteousness the early inspiration for self-authorized military intervention set forth in the "National Security Strategy of the United States" of 2002. In this modern form, its variants are much celebrated by neoimperial enthusiasts, such as Harvard professor Niall Ferguson, who advocate a modern American empire.[39]

FIGURE 8   A classic example of a Big Idea in motion, this cartoon, published in the aftermath of the Spanish-American War, depicts both Cuba and America as beautiful women, reflecting the pure and noble undertaking of the war to defeat Spain. Cuba is young, upright, and angelic, while America is superior and wise. The end of Spanish influence is represented by a broken ball and chain at Cuba's feet, as she is invited to join the Union. (As reproduced in "The Birth of the American Empire as Seen through Political Cartoons [1896–1905]," *Organization of American Historians Magazine of History* 12, no. 3 [Spring 1998]: 52. Library of Congress.)

Wilsonianism

For a brief moment at the end of World War I, writes historian Michael Mandelbaum, Woodrow Wilson bestrode the world like a colossus.[40] The American President arrived at the Paris peace conference in 1919 with a set of ideas for remaking the whole international system and ensuring that another Great War would be impossible. In his well-known fourteen-point blueprint for a better world, he looked forward to a new world order free from restricted trade, arms races, empires, and tyranny. The peoples of the world would receive the gift of self-determination, while the new League of Nations would prevent the repetition of war among the Great Powers. Wilson's new world order was not to be, but this did not mean that his ideas failed to gain traction at home. In stirring oratories to the American people, he successfully styled America's involvement in European conflict and his subsequent proposals for American leadership in the League of Nations as a crusade to make the world safe for democracy. It was the law of nature and God, he argued, that the world become a self-regulating realm of free individuals.[41]

Of course Wilson had detractors—then and now. Some scholars of the period believe that Wilson combined his ideas with compelling delivery to manipulate the Congress and defeat progressives at home—an irony lost on his admirers. Yet, the effect was to overcome the profound opposition in the country at large to involvement in World War I.[42]

As a phenomenon Wilsonianism combined the rationality of a Princeton University President with the presumption of an Episcopal minister's son, thus giving form to an evangelical commitment to reconstruction and equality that characterized American thought early in the century. Wilson dreamed of a world devoid of enduring rivalries, conflicts of interest, compromises of principle, spheres of influence, and compulsory alliances. He did not recognize America as a nation with rivals, allies, or partners. His was a world in which the only legitimate wars were those required to protect a universal order; war itself constituted a criminal interference with the very law of nature.

FIGURE 9   Following the declaration of war by Congress in 1917, the US Treasury sold "Liberty Bonds" to the American people to finance the Allied war effort. This poster, released soon afterward, combined a pertinent scare-scenario with appeal to deep sentiments of national identity. The very heart of American Exceptionalism and way of life—the Statue of Liberty—is shown under attack. This exemplified the Wilson Administration's effort to mobilize public opinion through themes and sentiments that recalled the nation's mythic beginnings. (Joseph Pennell, "That Liberty Shall Not Perish from the Earth," as reproduced in *The History Project,* University of California, http://historyproject.ucdavis.edu/imageapp.php. United States Library of Congress, Prints and Photographs Division, Washington, DC 20540, LC-USZC4-1347.)

FIGURE 10   The brief atmosphere of enthusiasm surrounding Wilson's vision for a better world at the end of World War I was summed up by this cartoon from the *Literary Digest*, in which Wilson's League had managed to muzzle the dog of war. The enthusiasm did not survive Wilson's political battle with the Senate, which ended America's postwar involvement in multilateral initiatives. ("Muzzled," *Literary Digest*, 13 September 1919; reproduced in "Harvard University World Model United Nations," 5 February 2000, www.hcs.harvard.edu/worldmun. Library of Congress.)

At another level, however, Wilson advanced a foreign policy predicated on the same rhetorical substance that had served Manifest Destiny and the Imperialism of Righteousness. In describing the peoples of the Philippines and Puerto Rico, Wilson proclaimed, "they are children and we are men in these deep matters of government and justice." When British representative Sir Edward Tyrell asked Wilson what he should report to London about America's Mexico policy Wilson replied, "I am going to teach the South American republics to elect good men." It was America's responsibility as the Exceptional Nation to show the way in lifting up these lesser civilizations. "When properly directed," Wilson argued, "there is no people not fitted for self-government." "The stage is set," he told the Senate in 1919, "the destiny disclosed. It has come about by no plan of our conceiving, but by the hand of God, who led us into the way." [43]

The end of the Wilson presidency marks an appropriate point to pause in this whirlwind tour of American history. The First World War saw the end of European primacy in world affairs and the emergence of the United States as a principal in an international system taking its first steps toward modern globalization. This is when American ideas first became linked to American power.

THE SENSE OF MISSION

The footprint of the first three hundred years of American history is visible everywhere in today's foreign policy decisions. The legacy comes in three parts:

- The nation's attachment to Big Ideas
- The unique character of America's Big Ideas
- The capacity of Big Ideas to mobilize opinion and participation

The first aspect establishes the context. Because of the special circumstances of its birth, America owes its identity to ideas. That was the basis on which it asserted the right to separate itself from Britain, and it remains the basis on which the nation interacts with the world, including interventions to bring about what is now called "Regime Change." Listen to President George W. Bush in his second inaugural address: "From the day of our Founding, we have proclaimed that every man and woman on this earth has rights . . . Advancing these ideals is the mission that created our Nation . . . America speaks anew to the peoples of the world."[44] Such declarations are so routine in American public life that they have lost their sharp edge. Yet while the American vision has been vital in democracy's global venture, there are few, if any, other world leaders who talk, let alone think, in such terms.

The second aspect is the ideas themselves: Providential Foundation, Exceptionalism, Detachment, Unilateralism, Manifest Destiny, Righteousness, and so on. All these are a part of the everyday thinking and behavior of modern American foreign policy figures. When Defense Secretary Donald Rumsfeld made his first visit to China in October 2005, he cautioned his hosts against building "another Great Wall" of limits on speech, information, and choices . . . substantive points with which we agree.[45] So normal is this behavior that it attracts no comment. Yet it is uniquely American. No other defense minister would offer such political advice to his hosts on an official visit. For an American to do so is unexceptional. It is in fact a feature of Exceptionalism.

We will discuss the third aspect in greater detail in the next chapter when we take up McCarthyism, Vietnam, and Iraq—all code words for moments in history when Big Ideas overwhelmed rational restraint to dominate public discourse and send American foreign policy in woefully unwise directions. Later we will examine whether such circumstances might arise again to bedevil a forthcoming major decision, for example regarding China. But the historical examples point in a clear direction. The rhetorical strength of Big Ideas place awesome power in the hands of certain elements of the body politic, enabling them to prevail over more focused and self-limiting conceptions of the national interest.

In the 1840s the Big Idea was that Americans were mastering a wilderness otherwise inhabited by savages who would benefit from America's civilizing mission. The land was being opened to all legal men who hoped to escape from class, bigotry, and persecution. In the 1890s, the

Big Idea was that Americans were offering a form of combined secular-religious salvation to the peoples of Spain's former empire.

Today, following 9/11, the idea is that the continued success of the American way of life—in all of its social, political, spiritual, and economic spheres—depends upon exporting that way of life to others, including the Middle East.

TWO

Three Institutional Failures

Three times since World War II, Big Ideas have seized the political discourse and driven policy experts to the sidelines: during the Red Scare of the early Cold War; during the entry to the Vietnam War, with its talk of democracy and dominos; and at the onset of the Iraq war. Each time, framing concepts rooted in Big Ideas turned complex foreign policy challenges into undifferentiated, apocalyptic threats to the nation's very existence. Professionals and area experts were excluded from the debate if they diverged from the patriotic consensus, and the mainstream institutions and publications that could have opposed the rush to simplification were either silent or instead provided an echo chamber for the dominant narrative. And in each case the suppression of debate and the exclusion of qualified experts led to a comprehensive foreign policy disaster.

A RECURRING SYNDROME

Each of the three generations since World War II has had to grapple with a ubiquitous, global threat, and each has suffered the consequences of a misconceived policy response by the nation's leaders. What is intriguing is not just that these episodes occur with regularity, but that they feature similar actors exploiting similar emotions. This was evident when syndicated columnist and television pundit Ann Coulter published a polemic after 9/11 arguing that, far from animating one of America's more disturbing episodes, Joseph McCarthy was in fact a neglected American hero. McCarthy, of course, was the senator who mounted a campaign in the early 1950s to convince Americans that their government had been infiltrated by hundreds of Communists intent on subversion. He first made national headlines on February 9, 1950, at the Republican Women's Club of Wheeling, West Virginia, when, at the climax of a speech, he announced, "I have here in my hand a list of 57 cases of individuals who appear to be either card-carrying members or certainly loyal to the Communist Party."[1] The list, if it existed, was never made public, but McCarthy's crusade caught fire across the nation.

Our look at this phenomenon is not intended to extend the bibliography on that period but to explore how slogans can overwhelm the political system. We will also examine how it is that ideas thought safely buried can rise up from the dead. Before the attacks of 9/11, anyone who seriously described the McCarthy era as exemplifying the aspects of the American democratic process would have been shown the door.

The mechanics of patriotism today, however, have turned that perception around. After 9/11 McCarthy's notion that Dissent Aids the Enemy is again found at the very heart of America's political discourse. This created an environment in which full discussion of the invasion of Iraq, which might at least in theory have produced a workable plan to anticipate the postinvasion difficulties, proved impossible. Thus, Coulter's defense of the man has an unconscious irony. The tapestry extending from McCarthy's heyday to the present is of a piece. When Big Ideas gain momentum, the rational center fades or is co-opted, policy deliberation is suppressed, core values are subverted, and national credibility, lives, and money are lost.

McCarthy and the Red Scare

Timing is everything in politics. When McCarthy made his first public accusations about Communist subversion in the heart of government, the American public was in a state of advanced anxiety. In Europe, the Soviet Union, now nuclear armed, was busy reneging on its undertakings at the Yalta Conference. In Asia, the People's Republic of China had been proclaimed and the stability of the Korean peninsula was far from certain. At home, a series of spy scandals, some involving the transmission of nuclear-related intelligence to the Soviet Union, were roiling the political scene.

It was in this atmosphere that McCarthy stepped forward with a simple explanation for Americans of the many crises around them. America was under attack from a Communist conspiracy, undetected in its extent and committed to the triumph of Soviet-style Communism. Alleging that the Truman Administration was "soft on communism," McCarthy promised to "clean house" (he wore a lapel-pin depicting a broom). Few were immune from his sloganeering. The State Department was filled with Communist sympathizers, who he called "commie symps." Democrats were "Comicrats" and other opponents were routinely smeared as "fellow travelers." McCarthy gave voice and form to the notion that America was being destroyed from within.

Though they disapproved of his message and his tactics, senior Republicans like Ohio senator Robert Taft and General Dwight Eisenhower chose not to engage McCarthy while his popularity was soaring. President Truman and senior members of his Administration also had no stomach for a fight. The rational center had collapsed. Institutions such as the press, the academy, and Congress that should have challenged McCarthy's charges were either mute or ineffective. In an interesting parallel to the 2003–2005 debate about Iraq, the little push-back that occurred came from cartoons.

Those who confronted McCarthy or his supporters paid the political price. Senator William Benton, a Democrat from Connecticut, was

FIGURE 11 Herb Block and the cartoonists were among the first to take on McCarthy, not unlike Jon Stewart and *The Daily Show* today. (Herb Block, *Washington Post*, 1950.)

accused of protecting "known Communists" when serving as Assistant Secretary of State, as well as purchasing explicitly sexual artwork. Benton lost his seat in the 1952 elections, along with numerous other Democrats, as the Republicans captured both the Senate and the White House. McCarthy was rewarded with the chairmanship of the Senate's Permanent Subcommitee on Investigations in the Committee on Government Operations, where he used the power of the subpoena to compel hundreds of government officials to appear at public hearings that served little purpose other than the public humiliation of the witnesses. Drawing on the successful tactics of the House Un-American Activities Committee (HUAC) hearings, McCarthy made it clear to his witnesses that the only sure way to show they had abandoned their left-wing views was by naming other "subversives."

The magic of McCarthyism was that it simplified. It provided an easy-to-grasp explanation of a confusing world in flux. But it also forged a link between prevailing anti-Communism and deeper notions of American Exceptionalism. Amid McCarthy's flamboyant rhetoric was a powerful connection between, on the one hand, a sense that the triumph of American values had produced a new age of affluence and national greatness, and on the other hand the fear that "Godless Communism," committed to America's destruction, threatened the nation's unique freedoms and its economic miracle.[2] Lacing his charges with outrage, he said, "the reason why we find ourselves in a position of impotency, is not because the enemy has sent men to invade our shores, but rather because of the traitorous actions of those who have had all the benefits that the wealthiest nation on earth has had to offer—the finest homes, the finest college educations, and the finest jobs in Government we can give."[3] This charge is echoed in today's denunciations of elitist liberals by the likes of Campus Watch. It is the most privileged—urbanites and academics, people in the media—who are betraying America's ideals. Significantly, this group includes elements of the rational center.

Fear and paranoia rise in times of threat and, once launched, join their handmaiden patriotism to travel quickly. At such times the voices of experts, members of the rational center, are quieted or mute. This atmosphere of suppressed debate often means that challenges are misunderstood, analysis is distorted, and policy does not effectively address problems on the ground.

From Thesis to Slogan

McCarthy's crusade against alleged traitors inside the most sensitive agencies, including the State Department, the White House, and the FBI (in 1995 the National Security Agency declassified the Venona files of intercepted Soviet communications identifying some 200 spies, but very few were on McCarthy's list) is the best-known aspect of his story.[4] A less familiar but ultimately more important aspect of his legacy is how his views influenced US policy toward the Soviet Union and the communist world in general. Through demagoguery and the intimidation of his subpoena power, he turned a well-crafted policy into a slogan. "Containment" the geo-political strategy became "Containment" the crusade against "Godless communism," which was a very different thing.

At the end of World War II, US policy toward the Soviet Union was based upon Stalin's promises, made at the 1945 Yalta Conference, that he had no territorial ambitions in Eastern Europe. President Franklin Roosevelt hoped to bind him into the postwar international system by making him a member of the club. With victory, however, Stalin quickly demonstrated that his commitments were worthless; Communist puppet governments were installed throughout Eastern Europe. The question was how to respond.

George F. Kennan, then serving in the US Embassy in Moscow, produced two documents, one a secret "Long Telegram" sent to the State Department in February 1946 and the other a public (albeit anonymous) article in the July 1947 issue of *Foreign Affairs* titled "Sources of Soviet Conduct." The latter contained the sentence: "In these circumstances it is clear that the main element of any United States policy toward the Soviet Union must be that of a long-term, patient but firm and vigilant containment of Russian expansive tendencies."[5] This was the only use of the word *containment* in an article of over seven thousand words.

Kennan and his State Department contemporaries tried to emphasize that, while the spread of international communism was a challenge for

American policy makers, it was not a cause for panic. Splits would inevitably develop between local Communists and the Kremlin, Kennan argued, provided the US did not intimidate the locals into seeking Moscow's protective care. While communists were still only revolutionaries striving for power, they would have little option but to rely on Moscow's support. Once in power, however, national and personal interests would likely bring local regimes into conflict with the self-aggrandizing policies of the Soviet Union.

The record of international communism, Kennan argued, was replete with examples of "the difficulty non-Russian individuals and groups have encountered in trying to follow Moscow's doctrine." The Kremlin's leaders were so inconsiderate and overbearing that few could stand their authority for very long. Washington should therefore make every attempt to exploit tensions between Moscow's leadership and the international communist movement. Kennan had welcomed Joseph Tito's break with Stalin and had foretold that Moscow would eventually struggle, and probably fail, to control the Chinese Communist movement. The Soviet leadership would "suddenly discover that this fluid and subtle oriental movement which they thought they had in the palm of their hand had quietly oozed away between their fingers and that there was nothing left there but a ceremonious bow and a polite and inscrutable Chinese giggle."[6]

A State Department Policy Planning Staff paper of 1949 suggested that the United States encourage "a heretical drifting-away process on the part of the satellite states," which might portend the emergence of "two opposing blocs in the communist world." This would provide Washington "an opportunity to operate on the basis of balance in the communist world, and to foster the tendencies towards accommodation with the West implicit in such a state of affairs."[7]

Kennan thus opposed direct US military action to prevent Communist takeovers. Such interventions, he argued, would only ensnare the nation in costly civil wars from which it could be difficult to disentangle. As he told an audience in Milwaukee in 1950, "I can conceive of no more ghastly and fateful mistake, and nothing more calculated to confuse the issues of this world, than for us to go into another great country and try to uphold by force of our own blood and treasures a regime which had clearly lost the confidence of its own people."[8]

At the core of Kennan's thesis, as he repeatedly sought to explain in lectures and speeches, was the notion that communism was not a monolith, and not all Communist movements posed a threat to American national security. "We are not necessarily always against the expansion of communism," Kennan told the Board of Governors of the Federal Reserve System in 1947, "and certainly not always against it to the same degree in every area." The strategy of containment thus did not require a universal level of engagement, as some advocated. Communist expansion could be contained "by the adroit and vigilant application of counterforce at a series of constantly shifting geographical and political points, corresponding to the shifts and maneuvers of Soviet policy." Certain core political-industrial centers were more important, such as Japan and Europe, while others, such as Indochina, were less so.[9]

Had this calm and nuanced approach been allowed to take root, American engagement with global Communism in the twentieth century might have taken a very different course, and the scourge might have died out earlier. But it was not so. Several forces, of which McCarthy was emblematic, would turn a rational policy into an irrational and moralizing catchphrase.

McCarthy's early momentum could not be sustained; his many accusations, investigations, and indictments produced few convictions. It was the rise of the China Lobby—whose Big Idea "Who Lost China?" played into McCarthy's charges that Truman was soft on Communism—that revitalized him. The China Lobby's rhetoric supported McCarthy's monolithic assumptions about Communism, reducing Kennan's delicate strategy, which counseled selective engagement, to a simple-minded policy of across-the-board confrontation. "Containment" was reduced to a slogan.

The China Lobby was born in the months after Mao Tse-tung's 1949 mainland victory over the Nationalist General Chiang Kai-Shek, when a powerful collection of pro-Nationalist Chinese businessmen, publishers, and military leaders joined forces with Republican members of Congress to attack Truman's White House for the disaster that had befallen US interests and for being "soft on China." Eminent figures like *Time-Life* publisher Henry Luce, Air Force general Claire Chennault, and Roosevelt intimate Tommy Corcoran vigorously supported Chiang Kai-Shek and criticized the Truman Administration's ineffectual attempt to resolve the Chinese Civil War by coaxing the Communists and Nationalists to the peace table. By the early 1950s, several more members of Congress had joined the cause. William Knowland became such a determined backer of the Nationalists that he was nicknamed the "Senator from Formosa." Other supporters included Senate floor leaders Kenneth Wherry, Styles Bridges, presidential candidate Robert Taft, Congressman Walter Judd, and the powerful silk importer Alfred Kohlberg.

The interests of McCarthy and the China Lobby converged. To keep his name in the headlines, McCarthy needed fresh grist for the mill to sustain his claim that Communism was on the march and America was being subverted from within. The well-connected members of the China Lobby and the FBI were happy to provide the Senator with fresh lists of people inside and outside government who they believed had minimized the dangers posed by Chinese Communism.

Like a hurricane feeding on warm tropical waters, McCarthy absorbed the Who Lost China? Big Idea and was re-energized by this new alliance. Communism was everywhere, its sympathizers had made America stand idle while communists took over the world's most populous country, and the battle now had to be joined at home and abroad. In this environment, the caveats and qualifications of Kennan's thesis were leached from the debate, along with the experts who formulated them.

These experts included many of America's foremost authorities on China. Owen Lattimore, for example, was Director of Johns Hopkins

University's Page School of International Relations in the early 1950s. He had grown up in China, spoke fluent Mandarin, enjoyed intimate familiarity with the country and some of its leaders, and had published five major works on the politics of China and Asia. But he antagonized prominent China Lobbyists with his criticism of Chiang Kai-Shek, his claim that "Mao was an agrarian reformer," and his ideas about how to confront what he saw as different forms of Asian communism.

He was highly controversial and remains so today. Moreover, in light of what we now know, his rose-tinted assessment of Mao could not have been more wrong. But his ideas never received a hearing. Lattimore was accused by McCarthy of being the Soviet Union's most senior spy in America. Two years later, after the FBI compiled a five-thousand-page file on him, he was indicted on seven counts of perjury. Although the charges against him were dismissed in 1955, he remained under suspicion of being a Communist agent for years. Other China specialists who had similar experiences included John Paton Davies Jr., who was personally attacked by McCarthy and dismissed from the State Department in 1954 by Secretary of State John Foster Dulles after a series of loyalty investigations, and John Service, another State Department China expert who was dismissed after the Loyalty Review Board decided he was a Communist sympathizer. The bitter experience of these men was a warning to others.

Those government experts who avoided being singled out did so by not challenging the prevailing political orthodoxy as defined by McCarthy and his supporters. This left only broad and simplified conceptions of international Communism to dominate the debate. By the mid-1950s, the Eisenhower Administration had officially endorsed the "Domino Theory," proclaiming that if a single country fell to Communism, its neighbors would collapse in a line after it (even though Eisenhower and other top officials, with the exception of Dulles, were deeply skeptical of McCarthy's views). Containment, which by that time meant the defense of every domino, had come to embody the very opposite of what Kennan argued. A victory for Communism anywhere now meant a defeat for America every-where. In Southeast Asia, this implied that the fall of South Vietnam would bring down Cambodia, Laos, Thailand, Malaysia, Burma, and Indonesia. Unadulterated anti-Communism became uncontested policy. McCarthy meanwhile enjoyed a substantial period of appeasement at all levels of gov-ernment until 1954 saw him defeated by a congressional and media back-lash as he made allegations against the military.

By 1957, McCarthy was dead from liver disease. What would survive him was the public conception of US policy in the Far East. William Fulbright, the chairman of the Senate Foreign Relations Committee, wrote in a 1961 letter to a friend about the "stubborn resistance in every instance" he still encountered in "trying to persuade my committee and the administration to reevaluate our policy in [China and Russia]."[10] The influence of McCarthyism was still sufficiently far-reaching to sup-press debate before it began, and underlying this phenomenon was a public opinion defined by ideological rigidity toward the Cold War.

Just as it is difficult today to have a nuanced discussion of international terrorism, there was no room in America's policy debate of the 1950s for in-depth policy analysis. McCarthy's assumptions about the nature of Communism and Soviet and Chinese ambitions triumphed in the public space and prevailed for two decades. This brought a profound and cata-strophic misunderstanding of the policy options surrounding the Korean and the Vietnam Wars.

Kennan later wrote that his initial proposals were twisted away from the political into the military sphere.[11] Looking back, it is clear that his policy recommendations were eclipsed by McCarthyism. His was a deli-cate and flexible concept embraced by a policy community that could not compete with McCarthy's simple certainty.

Cross out "Communism" and write in "terrorism" and McCarthy would have known very well how to work the levers of today's politics. The lesson for our time is the seemingly obvious point that the national interest is ill served when Big Ideas become populist slogans masquerading as policy.

INSTITUTIONAL FAILURE: VIETNAM

In American folk memory, the Vietnam era marks one of the most divisive periods in American politics. The images are those of massive, sometimes violent, protest. That is the mythology. In fact, the fateful decisions were made in an atmosphere of remarkable unity. From 1961, when President Kennedy gave his inaugural address, to 1964, when the Senate passed the Gulf of Tonkin Resolution, politics, the academy, and the media were all on the same track, all caught up by the concept of "monolithic communism" bequeathed by Joe McCarthy. At that time Noam Chomsky was still a professor of linguistics; Gore Vidal was still writing historical novels; Daniel Ellsberg was working on nuclear war plans for the RAND Corporation; Bob Dylan had yet to write his first song; and the killings at Kent State University still lay in the future.

At this golden hour, when options were still open, the zeitgeist flowed in one direction only. Robert McNamara, at the time Kennedy's Secretary of Defense, puts his capture by the Big Idea candidly and succinctly: "Like most Americans, I saw communism as monolithic."[12]

Let us turn now to three vital institutions: the media, Congress, and the academy. Each is entrusted with our hopes and guided by its responsibility to provide the nation with balance, leadership, and substantive analysis. How did they guide a nation then drifting into an Asian land war?

The Media

The situation in Vietnam was already deteriorating by 1955. Following the defeat of French forces at Dien Bien Phu by Ho Chi Minh Communist forces, the Geneva Conference of 1954 produced a treaty settlement that involved French withdrawal, a provisional division of the country between north and south at the seventeenth parallel, and the stipulation that free national elections would be held to decide Vietnam's future. But before these could take place, President Ngo Dinh Diem discerned signs of coordination between Moscow, Beijing, and Hanoi. He proclaimed a pro-Western government in the South and requested US assistance in resisting the growing pro-Communist insurgency supported by North Vietnam. The countdown to America's open military engagement in Vietnam had begun.

In a typical example of the reporting on Vietnam in this period, a *New York Times* story in early 1954 described a demonstration being held in Hanoi against American support for Diem. The story described in minute detail the Chinese and Soviet influence at the parade, which was evident in the uniforms, the marching style, and the surrounding crowds. Weeks later, another *New York Times* piece focused on Diem's growing popularity and depicted South Vietnam as a Western safe haven standing defiantly in the way of the encroaching communist monolith.[13] So went most of America's coverage of this region until well into the 1960s. Vietnam was not a Vietnam story. It was a Moscow-Beijing-Washington story in which the dynamics of Cold War confrontation provided the interpretive framework. Most of what America's news media published between 1955 and 1960 reflected and reinforced the popular fixation with Communism and the Cold War. Diem's despotic tendencies were downplayed, his anti-Communism was emphasized, and his Administration was portrayed as a beleaguered government attempting to transition from authoritarianism to pluralism. When Diem visited Washington in May 1957, the *New York Times Magazine* praised him as having "that high degree of courage that Ernest Hemingway once defined as grace under pressure."[14]

Diem's powerful supporters among the China Lobby had by then created a separate group known as "American Friends of Vietnam." By testifying before Congress, raising financial support, and providing commentary for high-profile publications like *U.S. News & World Report* and *Newsweek,* the Vietnam Lobby provided the South Vietnamese leadership with a substantial presence in Washington. And when the American Friends of Vietnam sought to portray Diem's government as a crucial element in America's effort to contain Communism, the nation's leading newspapers, magazines, and journals evinced little critical analysis.[15] What skepticism there was came from progressive publications with limited circulation such as I. F. Stone's weekly, *The Nation*, and *The Village Voice*.

The public had few alternatives to coverage that at best failed to present the whole story and at worst distorted what was happening in Vietnam.[16] Diem's regime, with its notably Catholic leadership, was, in fact, struggling desperately to establish itself within a Buddhist population that was progressively resistant to its corrupt and nepotistic leadership and increasingly receptive to blandishments from the North. Expanding guerilla actions against the South Vietnamese were led not only by Vietminh agents and indigenous Communists but also by non-Communist opponents of Diem's regime, including Buddhist monks such as Thich Tam Chou, Thich Tri Quang, and the Buddhist Institute. But in the American media the varied and growing opponents to the South Vietnamese government were too often lumped into a catch-all description that fit the entrenched anti-Communist discourse at home.[17]

Though Walter Lippmann, then considered the "Dean of American journalism" and writing for *Newsweek* magazine, rejected the Domino theory, eventually breaking with President Lyndon Johnson over Vietnam, he was the exception. The vast majority of reporters, editors, and columnists remained sympathetic to the Administration's view throughout the 1950s. When correspondents such as David Halberstam attempted to file stories on Vietnam that challenged the consensus view, they found it difficult or impossible to obtain space, especially on the front page. Forty years later the *Washington Post* ombudsman faulted his newspaper on exactly the same point in the run-up to the Iraq war.[18]

Popular columnists like Joseph Alsop who appeared in the *Washington Post* and James "Scotty" Reston writing in the *New York Times* remained committed, well into the mid-1960s, to reporting local developments through the lens of the Big Idea. If South Vietnam fell, Alsop warned, Laos and Cambodia would be the next dominoes seized by the communist monolith. This region was the key to Thailand; Thailand was the key to India and Japan; the loss of South Asia would then produce "grim repercussions further afield" in the "Middle East, North Africa and even Europe." As *New York Times* publisher Arthur Sulzberger told the American public, "a political battle more significant than Dien Bien Phu is now being fought in Vietnam," with the United States having committed "all its prestige."[19] And so the media debate on US Far East policy in the late 1950s and early 1960s was broadly framed by an undifferentiated anti-Communism.[20]

The US Congress

Although Fulbright would break with consensus in 1966 and begin to orchestrate congressional resistance to the Vietnam War, at that decade's beginning he, like most of the Senate, remained publicly uncritical of America's escalating involvement in Asia. Fulbright belonged to a group in the Senate, along with Hubert Humphrey, John Kennedy, Majority Leader Mike Mansfield, and others, that urged greater emphasis on economic aid and less military assistance to South Vietnam in order to promote stability. But until mid-decade they would not publicly challenge the Administration's policy rationale.

Mansfield was the Senate's expert on the Vietnam issue, but in the 1955–1965 period the questions he raised about America's expanding commitment to South Vietnam were only aired in private. When American journalist Albert Colegrove published an article in 1959 describing the corruption surrounding Diem's leadership, Mansfield attacked it for causing "a great deal of damage" to American efforts in Vietnam.[21]

This reflected the restrictive context in which Vietnam evolved as a policy issue in Congress. Dissent from the Cold War consensus was easily cast as unpatriotic. A small group of senators, starting around 1963, did attempt to persuade the Kennedy and Johnson Administrations that the entire basis of American South East Asia policy was flawed; they included

Frank Church, Wayne Morse, Gaylord Nelson, Ernest Gruening, and George McGovern. But as Church later described the more outspoken efforts of Morse and Gruening at that time, they operated in "the never-never-land of radically ineffectual dissent."[22]

These were the only members of Congress with grave reservations. A growing number were privately disturbed about America's slide into wider engagement. But at the critical juncture, the "go along, get along" political culture of the Senate prevailed. By 1965, a number of senators said privately that America was being drawn into a situation that had escalated out of control and from which it must extricate itself. But none found the courage until later to make this point in public.

The Tonkin Gulf incident in 1964 altered the character of US military and economic assistance. After the *USS Maddox* and the *USS Turner Joy* were "attacked" in international waters in the Gulf of Tonkin by North Vietnamese patrol boats on August 4 (following a similar incident two days earlier), economic development considerations gave way to a new strategic calculus. Despite Johnson's doubts (the facts surrounding US special operations inside North Vietnamese waters were withheld by the Pentagon), he had little difficulty in gaining broad public and congressional support for an immediate military response. Writing forty years later, Melvin Laird, who served as Secretary of Defense from 1969 to 1973, commented that the incident was "Johnson's ticket to escalate our role in Vietnam."[23]

The rational center lacked the grounds on which to challenge the Administration's account of the Tonkin Gulf incident and, in any case, could not compete with President Johnson's capacity to dominate the news. They could only note the inadvisability of an extended commitment to a land war in Vietnam. But these cautions were swept away by the exigencies of the moment. The claim that aggression was being directed from Beijing easily displaced the objections of policy critics, precisely when their views were most needed.

Johnson went on national television while his Secretary of Defense testified before Congress to advance the same arguments that had dominated US policy toward Southeast Asia for nearly fifteen years. "This is not just a jungle war," argued Johnson, "but a struggle for freedom on every front of human activity." A threat to any nation in that region, he proclaimed, was "a threat to all, and a threat to us." Congress was asked to authorize the use of force "in support of freedom and in defense of peace."[24] A majority of the Senate was swayed by the argument presented privately by the Administration and publicly by Fulbright, that Soviet and Chinese Cold War ambitions required congressional unity behind the President. With freedom and the American way of life under attack, nothing less than full congressional cooperation was expected by the public. And so the bill that Johnson sent to Congress requesting that America "take all necessary measures to repel any armed attack against US forces and to prevent further aggression" was unanimously passed in the House and passed by the Senate with a vote of 88 to 2, with only Senators Morse and Gruening voting against it.[25]

A $700 million supplemental appropriations bill passed the Senate in May 1965 by a vote of 88 to 3, with Nelson joining Morse and Gruening to cast the few "no" votes. This bill marked the point of no return. Although Johnson had promised the Senate that he had no intention of sending "American boys to do the job that Asian boys should do," deployment of ground troops officially began that July. Escalation took on a life of its own.[26]

Fulbright had accurately described how the long arm of ideological rigidity and McCarthyism reached into every area of debate. When Gruening attempted in March 1963 to broaden the discourse on foreign aid policies, Secretary of State Dean Rusk retorted, "those who would quit the struggle by letting down our own defenses, by gutting our foreign aid programs" are leaving "the field open to our adversaries." Rusk added that "insofar as anybody here or abroad pays attention to the quitters, they are lending aid and comfort to our enemies."[27]

To many observers of American debate after 9/11, this will sound depressingly familiar. Attorney General John Ashcroft, addressing critics of Administration policy in the months after the attacks, for example, said,

"My message is this: Your tactics only aid terrorists."[28] Similarly, Vice President Dick Cheney asserted that criticism from the Democrats was "thoroughly irresponsible and totally unworthy of national leaders in a time of war."[29] This theme was repeated, and amplified, by the media. During these crises, forty years apart, the national debate was successfully suppressed by the same framing concept: Dissent Aids the Enemy.

The Senate, as the nation's premier deliberative body, had thus failed in its institutional role to consider an alternative framework for understanding and addressing the Communist threat in Southeast Asia. Dissent, when it came, rose in the streets and on campuses as the reality of the war impressed itself upon those who would have to fight it and its flawed civil and economic development rationale became apparent. Some, like Daniel Ellsberg, who published *Secrets: A Memoir of Vietnam and the Pentagon Papers*,[30] challenged the Administration from the periphery—not unlike Howard Dean three decades later. And though his views were seen in the oratory of Senators Fulbright, Gruening, Morse, and others who were skeptical, the rational center, the expert policy community, had been marginalized by the Big Idea of Monolithic Communism.

The Academy

Soon after John F. Kennedy was elected President in 1960, it became clear that he had absorbed McCarthy's notions of Communism. His inaugural address connected the Domino Theory, as Eisenhower had applied it to Southeast Asia, with broader notions of American Exceptionalism and powerful historical refrains about a covenanted people with a mission to fulfill in the progress of human history. Kennedy declared, "Let every nation know, whether it wishes us well or ill, that we shall pay any price, bear any burden, meet any hardship, support any friend, oppose any foe, in order to assure the survival and the success of liberty."[31]

The academy embraced Kennedy's soaring rhetoric and gladly supplied the analysis to distill these aspirations to programs. Southeast Asia had become the test case for a new idea about the universal application of the American model.[32] Originating with a group of economists based at Harvard University and the Massachusetts Institute of Technology under the tutelage of Walt Rostow, the theory applied a model of economic "take-off" to the Third World—and especially South Vietnam. Rostow's idea, which he called "the Stages of Growth," was that one could identify all societies in their economic dimensions as lying within one of five economic-developmental categories: the traditional society, the preconditions for take-off, the take-off itself, the drive to maturity, and the age of high mass consumption. The United States, of course, represented the pinnacle of economic development toward which all other societies were evolving. Without dwelling on the details of this theory, we should note that the flawed ethnocentric notion that all countries are predestined to evolve toward convergence with the American model has remained influential, for instance in the Washington consensus of the 1990s and in books such as Thomas Friedman's *The World Is Flat.*[33]

Rostow's theory, which required almost no adulteration to make it into a Big Idea, became the operating template for various Administrations addressing development and geopolitical questions in the Third World. Beginning in the Eisenhower Administration and extending to the Kennedy and Johnson Administrations, his ideas of economic interdependency, nation-building, and macroeconomics became crucial elements of American Cold War discourse. Washington became increasingly convinced that the North Vietnamese were simply instruments of Moscow and Beijing, that Rostow's processes of economic modernization in Vietnam could succeed but merely required some time and insulation from insurgent Communist elements, and that the control of Asia itself relied largely on the fate of Vietnam.

The key objective was to prevent South Vietnam, in its preindustrial state, from being thrown off this path of economic virtue by Communist expansion. With Rostow's theory in hand, Washington championed the corrupt and unpopular South Vietnamese regimes of the Diem brothers and their successors as free-enterprise democracies in the making. The discourse, laced with images of an incipient democracy struggling to extend pluralism through local elections and buffeted by Communist guerillas, was framed for the American public through a steady supply of gripping, values-laden news and human interest stories.[34] There are, of course, parallels to the Iraq war here. Who can forget the faces of blue fingered, smiling Iraqis departing the polling places after voting for the first time in the long process to select a legislature and then a constitution?[35]

With Vietnam, the United States sent military forces overseas for the purpose of creating conditions in which civilian social programs could fashion a new democratic polity. It was not, of course, the first time; the United States had done much the same on a lesser scale in the Spanish-American War, Cuba, the Philippines, and Haiti. Each of these, however, was a clear departure from the perspectives of Alexander Hamilton and John Quincy Adams, who contended that America provided an example, but only an example, for the rest of the world to see.

Yet President Kennedy, mixing idealism and pragmatism, captured the Exceptionalist sensibilities of his time and perhaps of ours when he said, "To those people in the huts and villages of half the globe struggling to break the bonds of mass misery . . . we pledge our best efforts . . . If a free society cannot help the many who are poor, it cannot save the few who are rich."[36] In these words we can hear Containment, the World Made Safe for Democracy, the Imperialism of Righteousness, and the City on a Hill, an unbroken chain of Big Ideas stretching all the way back to Plymouth Rock.

THE IRAQ WAR

In the controversy over the Bush Administration's decision to invade Iraq in 2003, there was no figure immediately comparable to George Kennan, nor was there an equivalent McCarthy who seized the dis-

FIGURE 12   The political fallout from the Vietnam War proved to be more than enough to fell the Johnson administration by 1968, as the vast cost undermined the president's Great Society programs at home and the reversals abroad dominated the foreign policy discussion. Published in the *Peoria Journal Star* under the title "Columbus Days," this cartoon from the late 1960s underscored the contrast between the zeal of Johnson's Big Ideas about US Vietnam policy and how its effects were being perceived at home. (McCain Library and Archives, University of Southern Mississippi.)

course with accusations of subversion and conspiracy. Yet we witnessed a similar institutional failure, as an entire generation of Middle East experts from the State Department, the CIA, the uniformed military, the thank tanks, and the academy were left in the shadow of rising neoconservatives who seized and defined the debate.

Nearly four decades after Reston wrote in the *New York Times* that "we are in a war that is not only undeclared and unexplained, but that has not even been widely debated in Congress or the country," those institutions that could have challenged the scare scenarios governing the nation's perception of the terror challenge and Saddam Hussein failed to do so. The image of an amorphous, satanically evil enemy fostered a public willingness to accept simple patriotic ideas, while critics in Congress and opponents elsewhere were branded as un-American.

Just as Fulbright and the antiwar movement combined with events on the ground in Vietnam and at home to open the way for elected officials and others to bring their misgivings into the open, so it was left to former Vermont Governor and Democratic presidential aspirant Howard Dean to fracture Congress's reticence to challenge a "war" president.[37]

The Big Idea of the day, Freedom on the March was rooted in a strident linguistic code that emanated directly from the White House pressroom. Right after the 9/11 attacks, then White House Press Secretary Ari Fleischer scolded Bill Maher, then of ABC's *Politically Incorrect*, for asking if the word "cowardly" accurately described suicide bombers, saying, "It's a terrible thing to say . . . [Maher's comments are] reminders to all Americans that they need to watch what they say, watch what they do. This is not a time for remarks like that; there never is."[38] These were no longer "normal times," the American public was repeatedly told. With freedom under attack, dissent gave aid to the enemy, just as it had during the McCarthy years.

Writing in 1961, Kennan offered a chilling description of the unforgiving syndrome that seized America after 9/11: "There is nothing more egocentric than the embattled democracy." Under such circumstances, he argued, a democracy will attach to its cause "an absolute value that distorts its own vision of all else." Important questions are left unasked, unchecked assumptions harden into common knowledge, and the contest in which that society believes itself engaged assumes a "final apocalyptic quality." The public and its leaders alike come to think that "if we lose, all is lost and life will no longer be worth living; there will be nothing to be salvaged, but if we win, then everything will be possible; all our problems will be soluble; the one great source of evil, our enemy, will have been crushed; the forces of good will then sweep forward unimpeded, all worthy aspirations will be satisfied."[39]

Saddam Hussein duly became that one great source of evil. Take him down, neoconservatives argued, and democracy will blossom not only in Iraq but throughout the Middle East, where the forces of good would sweep forward unimpeded. But Kennan, of course, wasn't talking about Iraq. He was writing as a man disillusioned with how his own thesis of the 1940s—a sophisticated understanding of the variant forms of international Communism—had been transformed into a one-word slogan to justify the very policies he opposed.

Dean Acheson, Truman's Secretary of State, thought that sophisticated analyses like Kennan's were unsuitable for the political climate of the 1950s. It was better not to risk presenting arguments that were "unpalatable to believers in American omnipotence." The challenge, said Acheson, was to "so bludgeon the mass mind . . . that not only could the President make a decision, but that the decision could be carried out." Kennan reminded Acheson of his father's horse, which used to startle itself with the noise of its own hooves when it crossed wooden bridges. "The task of a public officer who is seeking to explain and gain support for a major policy is not that of the writer of a doctoral thesis. Qualification must give way to simplicity of statement, nicety and nuance to bluntness."[40] What Acheson was suggesting, which we discuss at length in chapter 5, is the co-optation of an expert, someone who knows better being dragged into a format that requires simplicity.

Just as McCarthy was a primary force in the assault on establishment expertise in the 1950s, the modern mass media was the twenty-first-century equivalent, which we address in chapter 3. The 24–7 media have been a vital element in structuring and formatting the information received by the public and thus shaping the public discourse. Administration-manufactured crisis narratives fed the media's endless search for sensation and drama while measured criticisms of these scenarios were far less exciting to watch or hear. Ratings-driven media competition exploited an insecure public's compulsion to learn as much about unfolding or worsening crises as quickly as possible. In this context themes advanced by Administration officials were echoed and repeated relentlessly by media outlets hungry for eyeballs and eardrums.

Given this confluence of powerful media and political interests, one asks how the cycle can be broken, how the informed public can regain its rightful place in the public debate. One might think the expert community would distill the cacophony of competing images and agendas to provide accurate assessments of policy. In subsequent chapters, we show why it did not.

THREE

Cable News:
Accelerating the Big Idea

If an unusual susceptibility to Big Ideas and their derivative concepts has led the nation to the brink of disaster in the past, what grounds are there for thinking the situation is worse today? We turn to a further impediment to the rational center, the modern cable news industry. So much criticism has been thrown at the modern media that one cannot believe (or even read) all of it. But we will make the case that, as a force multiplier of Big Ideas and the concepts that frame them, cable news creates a new and genuine foreign policy problem.

On the whole, the cable news industry is politically more or less neutral. Some shows and networks have one editorial policy, others a different one. The industry as a whole is a commercial enterprise aimed at carving out as large a market share as possible. To do this it adheres to an established formula that in most cases involves keeping things simple. Segments are short, advertising breaks are never more than seven minutes apart, the story mix is varied, discussion is staccato. As Joe Scarborough, host of *Scarborough Country*, notes: "It's hard to read Jefferson's 'Notes on Democracy' in the format we're given. You do your best to strip it down."[1]

73

This formula thrives on drama: wars, natural disasters, and grisly crime. At certain moments, such as in the aftermath of Hurricane Katrina, cable news has provided compelling viewing. But it is clearly not a natural home for the complexities of foreign policy unhappily sandwiched between scandals, abductions, and advertising breaks. And yet foreign policy experts, including some of the most distinguished, make regular appearances.

Unfortunately, these often brief appearances leave viewers with a largely distorted sense of the nature and dimensions of the foreign policy problems facing the nation. Because these programs are drawn to "breaking news," preferably with a human interest angle, they play more to viewer's ethics and emotions than their possible interest in analysis. Stories on the complexities of trade agreements, nonproliferation treaties, and UN procedures are normally put aside by the network anchors and may appear on niche programs such as *The News Hour with Jim Lehrer*. This has certainly been the case on most of the cable news channels. In the world presented by the rapidly growing cable industry foreign policy attention has been largely directed toward the Middle East, with the war in Iraq—due to loss of lives, financial costs, and because the nation's credibility is at stake—the predominant story. There correspondents, initially embedded with the military, reported the war's progress and the subsequent effort to install democracy. Financial limitations and limited personnel meant that, until the Iraq story became an all-encompassing national obsession, there was a paucity of correspondents on the ground able to absorb and assign meaning to the complex cultural, religious, tribal, and political elements that resisted the imposition of democratic government and that have now devolved into civil war. Thus, much of the reporting proceeded in accord with the Administration's narrative of "steady progress." The result was a "rip and read" culture in the cable newsrooms in which editors and producers drew their storylines from wire reports provided by the Associated Press and Reuters, which do have local bureaus. The effect has been that millions of viewers received what they believed to be full and accurate accounts of the coalition's political progress, which was written, until late 2004, by only a few correspondents. This inverted pyramid had the effect of flushing out nuance and simplifying complexity so that viewers, through no fault of their own, were left with a Manichaen world of blacks and whites. The policy decisions at hand were presented as choices between mutually exclusive catchphrases—"stay the course" or "cut and run"—with the implied message that every complexity can be understood in simple terms. It was left to the writing press, the Internet, and blogs to fill in the rest—and eventually challenge the Administration's rationale for the enterprise.

The effect of the inverted pyramid was again present in the case of Mahmoud Ahmadinejad's election in 2005 to be the new President of Iran. Because his victory was a surprise, not much was known about him. But the American cable news industry, drawing on this narrow base, was ready. Within forty-eight hours, show after show—*Special Report* with Brit Hume, *Hardball* with Chris Mathews, *Scarborough Country, Fox News Sunday, The Situation* with Tucker Carlson, Doyle McManus (a seasoned journalist with the *Los Angeles Times*) on *Washington Week* and so on—had labeled him with one of two words: *hardline* or *ultraconservative*. On top of this, they added unverified (and later refuted) speculation that he was among the original 1979 hostage takers at the American Embassy. These are all accomplished hosts who are aware that foreign policy is rarely binary. But they know their medium. Audiences "demand" that they characterize the event—in this case assess the meaning of an Ahmadinejad government—whether or not the information is available at that time, or they will switch channels.

Of course, they were correct, as far as they went. Ahmadinejad was all of those things. He has since proved to have radical, unsubstantiated ideas about the Holocaust, called for Israel to be "wiped from the map," and asserted Iran's right to have a nuclear program widely believed to include nuclear weapons. What was not reported in those early days—and what was vitally important—is that Iran's new President had broad support in the country and was an adroit, highly intelligent politician whose views were widely celebrated in the region. Most importantly for American viewers, the implied message—that he could and should be removed from power by the US military or through a coup supported by

Washington, in keeping with US policy to spread democracy in the region—was left on the table. Yet, as was apparent then, and is today, this solution would require a military capacity beyond current US capabilities and the political repercussions of such an action would be disastrous for American geopolitical interests in the region. All of this should have been a part of the early news coverage. But it was not.

This points to an underlying danger. By conditioning viewers to imagine that foreign policy involves simple choices and snap judgments, cable news accords a decided edge to those able to define events, often in the context of the Big Idea—in this case, Freedom on the March. The Administration of the day is advantaged by its superior reserve of information, its on-demand access to prime-time television, and its ability to stage events to create a message.[2] Experts outside the Administration lack these assets and are thus disadvantaged. At the entry point to a crisis—which we have stressed is by far the most important time for the injection of rational expertise—this places enormous leverage in the hands of the Administration.

Let us turn to some actual examples of how foreign policy experts have interacted with cable news hosts. Far more than in domestic affairs, where the hosts sometimes possess detailed knowledge, the cable format reinforces the Administration's ability to frame the issues in foreign policy and squeezes out expertise.

PROBLEM 1:
EXPERTS BECOME SOUNDING BOARDS

Simply because someone with established expertise appears on the air it doesn't mean that meaningful information is imparted to viewers. Even experts of great eminence must struggle against forceful hosts who, though vastly ignorant about foreign policy, control the format. All too often, the guest's perspectives and policy ideas are never actually heard: the expert becomes a mere foil for the host's prejudices.

Holbrooke vs. O'Reilly

On January 4, 2005, Bill O'Reilly had former Ambassador to the UN Richard Holbrooke as a guest on his Fox News show, *The O'Reilly Factor*, ostensibly to discuss the leadership of the United Nations. Holbrooke, despite being an extremely accomplished debater, quickly found himself maneuvered into discussing O'Reilly's ideas rather than talking about his own. Here are the highlights.

O'REILLY: With us now is Ambassador Holbrooke. Last December 5, there was a secret meeting at the home of Ambassador Richard Holbrooke here in New York City that the *New York Times* reports was held to help Kofi Annan save his job. Now since I don't trust the *New York Times,* is their report accurate? Did you guys get together? It was you and a few professors, a couple other pinheads trying to give him advice to save his job. Is that true?"

HOLBROOKE: Well, the pinhead thing is . . .

O'REILLY: All right, but you seem to be sympathetic to Annan, and that's what I'm not getting.

HOLBROOKE: Of course, I'm sympathetic to Annan. First . . .

O'REILLY: Look . . .

HOLBROOKE: So—well, let me finish, let me finish. The—in the tsunami [disaster relief efforts], in Iraq, the U.N. is doing essential things. The administration is utterly dependent on the outcome of that election in Baghdad at the end of this month.

O'REILLY: Right. I agree.

O'REILLY: Yes, have me in there, and I'll—but here's what I don't understand. I read your book, and everybody knows that you were involved in Bosnia, and you probably know Bosnia better than anybody, OK. Annan blew it in Bosnia.

HOLBROOKE: I wrote—I wrote a very critical account of the U.N. and . . .

O'REILLY: But it's . . . one after another.

HOLBROOKE: Look, our whole policy in Bosnia in '95, '96 was to throw the U.N. out, clean it up, send in NATO, negotiate.

O'REILLY: Because they couldn't do anything. Look, one after another, Annan is . . .

HOLBROOKE: I agree with—hey, you're . . .

O'REILLY: Then why do you want to keep him? He blows it . . .

HOLBROOKE: Why do I want . . .

O'REILLY: He blows it in Rwanda.

HOLBROOKE: Why do I want to keep Kofi . . .

O'REILLY: He blows it in Bosnia. He blows it in Iraq. He blows it in the oil-for-food scandal . . . I just don't think he's a strong leader, and that's my primary objection.

HOLBROOKE: And, quite honestly, Bill, knowing Kofi Annan well, I think you're being unfair to him.

O'REILLY: OK. And we'll be happy to talk to him any time. Mr. Ambassador, always good to see you. Thanks for coming in.

HOLBROOKE: Great to see you, Bill.[3]

In the combative, testosterone-charged exchange, O'Reilly skillfully avoided any challenge to his reflexively anti-UN position His line emerged triumphant, he demonstrated political diversity, and he enhanced the prestige of his show by presenting a distinguished Democratic Party foreign policy figure. Viewers learned nothing about the problems facing the United Nations, the optimal United States relationship to it, or Annan's stewardship. In a final humiliation, the guest thanks the host for mauling him.

Kissinger vs. Hannity

Henry Kissinger appeared on Fox News's *Hannity & Colmes* on July 29, 2003.

COLMES: Should an attempt be made to get Saddam alive, rather than dead?

KISSINGER: I think it's the nature of the way America does business that they don't kill people needlessly. If he is alive, he'll present many problems. If he's dead, he presents many problems. So I think it will be left to the local situation.

COLMES: If he's alive, should he be tried in an international court?

KISSINGER: Probably.

HANNITY: Yes, but one of the things I think we're seeing here is this day after day, night after night, criticism of President Bush. If you listen to the Democrats, he's done nothing right here, even in getting Saddam's sons, even in the quick military victory that none of these guys predicted. He can't even land on an aircraft carrier. He can't even leave the White House without being criticized.

KISSINGER: President Bush pulled the country together after September 11.

HANNITY: Yes, he did.

KISSINGER: He defeated the Taliban, he defeated Saddam Hussein. He is the dominant figure in the Middle East peace negotiations. And he has done, in my view, an outstanding job.

HANNITY: I agree with you.[4]

The distinguished former Secretary of State is used here to affirm the Administration's line, supported by the host, that all is well in the Iraq war—a dangerously blunt position. At Hannity's invitation, Kissinger moves to solidify support for President Bush rather than provide analysis of the substantive issues at hand. Kissinger is omnipresent on such shows, turning up for three minutes on *Fox & Friends* for a rapid-fire round about "What kind of man is Russian President Putin," on Greta Van Susteren's *On the Record* to discuss "South Korea's foreign policy," or on *The O'Reilly Factor* to debate "Iraq and Transatlantic Relations." One can only conclude that Kissinger wishes to keep his name and his views before the public, even if it is seen as partisan under the circumstances.

Clark vs. Hannity

The following comes from an interview with General Wesley Clark, a former NATO supreme commander, with Fox's Sean Hannity on June 15, 2005.

CLARK: We have a real policy issue for our country. We've got to get buy-in from other nations around the world on how to deal with these terrorists and other people that we've captured.

HANNITY: General, first of all, enemy combatants are afforded no protection under the Geneva Conventions. These are the combatants in the field that want to kill our soldiers. These are the people that want to destroy our country. There's 550 of them. But we're not murdering them. We're not torturing them. There is no comparison to Nazi Germany or the Soviet gulags or Pol Pot and the killing fields. It's an outrageous propaganda campaign. It gives aid and comfort to people that already hate this country. And I just cannot believe the Democrats, just like they stood by and listened to the comments of Howard Dean, that you guys are going to defend this? Rally around him? Circle the wagons? I—frankly, I guess, politically speaking, I should be glad, because I think it's—the American people are not going to like this.

CLARK: Well, Sean, I think we've got to focus on what's really at issue here. This shouldn't be a political issue. What it is, is a policy issue. And this is where the people in the United States, our government, we have to pull together. We've got to get a solution . . . [interrupted]

HANNITY: Tell that to Durbin . . . [5]

Clark's knowledge has been made to count for nothing. The show is nothing more than a vehicle for Hannity's simplistic views, given an aura of respectability by the appearance of a high-status expert like Clark. The viewing public has been promised a serious foreign policy discussion, but is given none. The format of the medium has seen to that. It makes smart people unsmart.

PROBLEM 2: FALSE EXPERTISE

That true foreign policy experts have a hard time getting their expertise across on cable news is bad enough. In another format, the roundtable discussion, we see a different problem: people who have genuine expertise in Washington politics speaking about a multitude of subjects, including foreign policy, about which they are often uninformed.

On August 14, 2004, for example, Bill O'Reilly of *The O'Reilly Factor* was invited on *The Tim Russert Show* to debate *New York Times* columnist and Princeton University economics professor Paul Krugman on such issues as tax cuts, Medicare, unemployment rates, Osama bin Laden, Pakistan, Iraq, Russian intelligence, North Korea, and weapons of mass destruction. O'Reilly and Krugman have an informed layperson's knowledge of most of these issues, but the fact that they are well known on the Washington political scene and recognized as media celebrities lends an air of authority to their personal opinions—an entirely unmerited authority.

The roundtable format provides little more than a recycling of conventional wisdom. Margaret Carlson, a distinguished columnist for *Time Magazine* with a side job as a commentator for CNN, where she was a long-running participant in CNN's *Capital Gang*, gave the secret away. She ascribed her success to the fact that TV producers are "looking for the person who can sound learned without confusing the matter with too much knowledge. I'm one of the people without too much knowledge. I'm perfect."[6]

The Capital Gang, The McLaughlin Group, Crossfire, The Newshour with Jim Lehrer, Washington Week with Gwen Ifill, The Dennis Miller Show, The Weekly Roundup on National Public Radio's *The Diane Rehm Show,* and others all hew to a common format. A handful of well-known "experts" are assembled for a roundtable discussion that, in thirty or sixty minutes can range from the appointment of the latest Supreme Court justice to intelligence reform, the use of medicinal marijuana to Iranian nuclear enrichment, the disappearance of a university co-ed in

Aruba to the Central American Free Trade Area, stem cell research to hurricane relief and human exploration to Mars. Jim Fallows of the *Atlantic Monthly* commented to us that proper preparation for the topics under discussion on any given "news roundup" would take all week. Obviously this kind of time is not available. So fifteen minutes must do. Experienced roundtable participants collect some interesting nuggets of Internet-based information and then bend the conversation around what they can talk about.

The Capital Gang *Invades Iraq*

This is taken from a December 25, 2004 *Capital Gang* discussion involving the columnists Marl Shields, Al Hunt, Robert Novak, Kate O'Beirne, and Margaret Carlson discussing the Iraq insurgency:

SHIELDS: To you Margaret.

CARLSON: The administration seems always to be surprised by the fact that there are all these insurgents and that Iraq is not secure, when it's the administration's failure to listen to the State Department and go with the Pentagon that meant we didn't have enough soldiers to immediately secure it. So these ordinary Iraqis, Kate, they're not sympathetic to the insurgents, necessarily, but they're too scared.

NOVAK: More soldiers . . .

CARLSON: They're too scared to turn them in.

NOVAK: More soldiers would not help. Come on! That's ridiculous!

SHIELDS: Well I disagree with that. I don't think there's any question that more soldiers would have helped . . . to stop the looting immediately afterwards. But the gang of five will be back with the president's priorities.

(*Commercial Break*)[7]

After the commercial break, the same team returned to discuss social security, tax matters, wages, immigration, Janet Jackson's "wardrobe malfunction," and the role of Hamas in Palestinian democratic reform. Later that month they started on intelligence reform, moved to the medicinal use of cannabis, and then finished with Canadian public opinion. This is typical of the roundtable format; it becomes a running seminar on everything and nothing. Not that the members of this group are unintelligent or uninformed: they are top Washington insiders with plenty of expertise on beltway politics. The problem is that the format forces them to discuss endless other topics on which they are certainly not experts and limits the time for discussion on issues where their authority counts.

In the case cited above, the viewing audience learns nothing about what the State Department's advice was or why the Pentagon has argued that there are enough soldiers in Iraq—both of which are important and contentious issues. Instead, we have point and counterpoint.

Such exchanges may make for good television, but they do little for foreign policy other than to recycle the various framing concepts currently in play. Moreover, foreign affairs by their very nature differ from domestic issues. To some extent, we all have something to say about education policy in American schools if we've gone to school in America, or on tax policy if we're American taxpayers. But many Americans have no meaningful experience whatsoever regarding China-Taiwan relations, Wahhabi influence in Syria, or re-emergent authoritarianism in Latin America. Foreign affairs require expert knowledge and first-hand experience; without those things one is often left to fill in the blanks with total conjecture.

The McLaughlin Group *Covers the World*

The first roundtable talk show was ABC's *The McLaughlin Group*, launched in 1982 and hosted by former journalist, Nixon White House staffer, and Jesuit priest John McLaughlin ever since. A typical discussion jumps from domestic issues to foreign policy and back again in a seamless blend of fact, conjecture, and imagination. The show of January 31, 2003, presented Eleanor Clift, Tony Blankley, and Gerard Baker, who moved from the cost of the Iraq occupation to funding for AIDS research, Medicare reform, North Korea, and taxation of dividends income, all in the space of just ten minutes.

MCLAUGHLIN: You see that new highballing figure on how much [the Iraq war] could cost, including occupation: $1.6 trillion, which means $1,600 billion. I presume that's a five—at least a five-year estimate, if not longer. But that's out there now as an outside figure. I ask you.

CLIFT: Yeah, those numbers are going to make it hard for the president to deliver on some of his other commitments. And if he doesn't make good on his promise to dramatically increase AIDS funding, he will have AIDS activists following him all over the campaign trail in 2004. His track record is not good. (*Laughter.*) He promised $500 million to prevent mother-to-child transmission.

MCLAUGHLIN: And?

CLIFT: —and not a penny of that has been distributed. First, the White House quietly got the money reduced from $500 million to $200 million, then it was killed in the end of the year crackdown on spending. Not one penny ever got out. But he had a press conference on it in the Rose Garden.

MCLAUGHLIN: Mm-hmm. Quickly. We're running out of time now.

BLANKLEY: The president's proposal to include prescription drug reform within a Medicare reform is going to fail, and he—

MCLAUGHLIN: Why?

BLANKLEY: Because there's not time to get the full Medicare reform passed, and the question is going to be whether he'll be willing to split it off. My guess is, he won't, and we won't get prescription drugs this year passed.

MCLAUGHLIN: What about incorporating the private sector into—in combination with Medicare?

BLANKLEY: Oh, it's all a wonderful idea. I just don't think—

MCLAUGHLIN: You don't think it'll work?

CLIFT: Terrible idea. (*Chuckles.*)

BLANKLEY: I don't think—

MCLAUGHLIN: I mean you don't think it'll pass. Okay. Then what do you have?

BAKER: North Korea will have a range of nuclear weapons within six months, and we'll be into a crisis with that country as soon as the Iraq situation is dealt with.

MCLAUGHLIN: Interesting, and fearful. I also think, by the way, the president was very sobering, if I had to pick one adjective, in that speech. I predict that the Bush proposal to end double taxation of dividends will be modified. Instead of ending it, the tax will be reduced, and the plan will survive in that form.

NEXT WEEK: The U.S. clergy condemn Bush policy on Iraq. Will they influence the president—or anyone? Bye-bye! [8]

In this cacophonous switching of subjects, foreign policy made two brief appearances from which the viewer would have gathered the stunning news that Iraq is expensive and North Korea is a problem.

Washington Week *Explains CAFTA*

One last aspect of the roundtable format is that the participants often mold a foreign topic around their real area of expertise, which is usually who's up and who's down in Washington. This exchange, on PBS's *Washington Week* about the Central American Free Trade Area between John Harwood of the *Wall Street Journal*, Karen Tumulty of *Newsweek*, and Anne Kornblut of the *New York Times*, took place on July 29, 2005.

HARWOOD: Speaking of "winning ugly," we've learned—I want to talk about the trade bill, CAFTA, Central American Free Trade Agreement.

We've learned a lot of the gory details over the last twenty-four hours of exactly how they got the votes to pass it. Why did President Bush want that deal, which isn't all that large, so badly?

TUMULTY: Well, you're right. It is—in the grand scheme of trade agreements this was a relatively minor one. But it had taken on—because of his difficulties of getting this thing passed—it had taken on enormous significance politically and symbolically. And if President Bush had been the first president in modern times to fail to get a trade bill through a Congress that is controlled by his own party, I think you would have had to stamp "lame duck" across his forehead.

KORNBLUT: How do you see these bills, the CAFTA bill or energy, affecting actual voters? Will it do anything to change their lives whether it's, you know, gas prices or air conditioning prices at this point?"[9]

Once the all-important matter of symbolic significance has been raised, real-life consequences seem anticlimactic: the last question went unanswered. Viewers might be excused for thinking CAFTA was simply a branch of Washington politics with the variables all under American control.

PROBLEM 3: WHAT FILLS THE VACUUM

Public policy analysis knows no softer target than American broadcast journalism. Any library or bookstore will reveal yards of shelves devoted to criticism: liberal bias, conservative bias, corporate ownership, an antibusiness slant, reporters who don't understand the people they're covering, reporters who identify with them too closely, sensationalism, anonymous sources, fabrication; there are few vices of which TV news has not been accused. Journalists are not held in high repute.

Our purpose here has been neither to refute these accusations nor add to them, but instead to point out how the inadequacies of television news affect what the public hears about foreign policy. When expertise is not respected—when those who actually know something are forced onto the same level as those who know much less, or are even made subordinate to them—then silly notions become equal to serious ones, and misconceptions become equal to facts. Weeds take over the garden: Big Ideas burst forth in all their shallow and destructive glory.

The American receptivity to Big Ideas and their rhetorical derivatives means that, early on, a debate may assume a compelling momentum that forces people to locate themselves within it; with this the 24–7 media reinforce audience predispositions rather than illuminating alternatives and exploring their implications. The community of experts, condemned to battle against these forces, then faces a stern challenge: how to introduce expertise, with some of the nuance, ambiguity, and emotionally unsatisfying answers this expertise brings with it, into a debate whose parameters have already been set.

In the next two chapters we look at the rational center's performance, both institutional and individual, in recent American foreign policy debates on such topics as nuclear proliferation, American identity, Islam, immigration, and the debate before the Iraq war. At issue is whether the rational center has been willing and able to act as a counterweight to the nation's natural tendency to inflame and oversimplify the debate. When it does, for example during the Cold War endgame, American interests prosper. When it does not, as during the McCarthy period and the Vietnam and Iraq wars, the damage to American interests and credibility is immense.

It can be readily understood, therefore, that the rational center has both an enormously difficult and enormously important role to play. This is almost impossible when experts fail to live up to their responsibility. The proper execution of foreign policy requires dispassionate, long-term expertise that is properly skeptical about the Big Ideas and media enthusiasms of the moment. Underinformed advocates of Big Ideas with big political and media bullhorns are a dime a dozen. Once experts allow themselves to become mixed up with this world, they become part of the problem. At times of foreign policy stress, this is a recipe for disaster.

FOUR

Think Tanks

T hough widely imitated throughout Europe and Asia, the think tank is an American invention and, in terms of scale and reach into government and media, a distinctly American phenomenon. The nation's major think tanks, with their dazzling array of scholars and practitioners, are, in theory, ideally placed to provide a forum for intellectual debate. They are more than capable of leading the assault against the primacy of entertainment over detailed exchange, and celebrity over substance.

This capability is, of course, precisely why the underperformance of the think tanks is so regrettable. In this chapter we focus on the cases where the think tanks have missed the mark, especially in times of crisis when the discourse of many has done more to reinforce Big Ideas than to challenge them. This was particularly the case as the nation moved toward war with Iraq, when those who were skeptical of the merits of the Administration's policy could not find a hearing in places like the Council on Foreign Relations, the Carnegie Endowment for International Peace, the American Enterprise Institute, and the Brookings Institution.[1] This was a true institutional failure. American taxpayers (who help support think tanks by granting them nonprofit status) and contributors alike are entitled to ask what they are getting for their money if the major institutions committed to open debate go silent precisely when they are most needed.

THE THINK-TANK WORLD

The RAND Corporation is generally thought to be the first modern think tank. Conceived during World War II, it issued its first report in 1946 and was first incorporated as a nonprofit organization in 1948. A 2004 article in *American Heritage, Technology and Invention* was modestly titled "How Rand Invented the Post-War World."[2] Since that time, some fifteen hundred think tanks have sprung into existence in the United States. This far eclipses the network available anywhere else in the world. Over two hundred of these sit in Washington, DC, alone, covering a full range of policy issues. We will focus on the fifteen or so that have the most influence on foreign policy.

One central feature of the think-tank system prevents it from functioning as an effective counterweight in the national policy discussion at crucial moments. Think-tank Washington is divided between two fundamentally different types of discourse: one designed to promote a coherent political message, and one designed to promote genuine debate. In times of crisis, the first enjoys far more influence in the public space than the second.

Among the most prominent think tanks is the Brookings Institution. One of the best-endowed think tanks in the world, it has an annual budget of over $25 million, a staff of nearly two hundred, and a collection of well-connected experts with experience from every branch of government. Watch national cable television for long enough, whether it's on Fox News, CNN, C-SPAN, or the BBC, and a Brookings expert will eventually appear. Other such organizations—the Center for Strategic & International Studies, the American Enterprise Institute, the Heritage Foundation, the Cato Institute, the Center for American Progress, and the Carnegie Endowment for International Peace—all command budgets approaching $20 million and staffs of one hundred or more. The Council on Foreign Relations (CFR) in New York runs at a cost of almost $30 million a year, and its flagship publication, *Foreign Affairs*, is the nation's leading journal on its subject.

The discussion panels and staff registers of these places feature some like Henry Kissinger, Jeanne Kirkpatrick, and George Shultz, who have supported the thrust of the Bush Administration's foreign policy, and others like Zbigniew Brzezinski, Brent Scowcroft, and James Baker, who advanced notable early criticism—though they proved to be the exceptions. This is a system with the highest levels of leadership, resources, talent, and outreach to the American public. Each major think tank has an impressive website and a publishing arm; each runs regular symposia and discussions; all dedicate extensive time, effort, and money to promoting their work in the public space. Each contains a depth of public policy experience.

Those who actually run these institutions will tell you that they play an invaluable role in the national discourse. CFR President Richard Haas, who has worked for four US presidents says, "of the many influences on US foreign policy, the role of the think tanks is among the most important." Think tanks, he says, generate new thinking, supply expertise, offer a venue in which to build shared understanding, provide third-party mediation between political sides, and educate US citizens about the world.[3] Strobe Talbot, a former Deputy Secretary of State and now the President of Brookings, similarly contends that "think tanks remain a principal source of information and expertise," providing studies and reports that are regularly relied upon to guide the public, Congress, and the media. Talbot cites a survey of congressional staff and journalists showing that 90 percent of them believe think tanks are a crucial element in the policy process.[4]

To get a sense of the space between the claims made by the think tanks and their actual performance, we embarked on a three-month odyssey in think-tank world in 2005.

The Heritage Foundation Regards Europe

Imagine being in a room with a group of people talking about America and the European Union. The first person remarks, "The EU is just a bad idea, like slavery, communism and high rise flats." All Europe wants to do, says a second, is "nothing about everything." Europeans and Americans are separated by "two different views of human nature," declares a third, while a fourth asserts that the EU is as wicked as "Communist Europe," and a fifth emphasizes that our job is "to expose it and fight it." You might think you had stumbled into the annual convention of the John Birch Society, but actually this discussion took place on June 28, 2005, in Washington, DC, at the Heritage Foundation, one of America's most prestigious research institutions; the speakers were a panel of experts at a conference on European integration and US foreign policy. They included Lord Pearson of Rannoch, a British businessman; former Director for the Congressional Task Force against Terrorism Yossef Bodansky; Member of the European Parliament David Hannan; Senator Gordon Smith (R-OR); Stephen Meyer, a senior fellow at the Discovery Institute; and Professor Marek Jan Chodakiewicz of the Institute of World Politics. Everything about this conference—from the complimentary breakfast to the cinema-sized auditorium to the Pentagon officials, journalists, congressional staff, and foreign diplomats in attendance—suggested wealth, influence, and professionalism.[5]

Yet, from the ten speakers, the audience heard just one monochromatic argument with little reference to substantive issues and no relevant data. The EU "is not in your interests," Lord Pearson intoned to his American listeners. "The EU project is invalid," proclaimed Hannan. Europe and America are locked in "a conflict of visions," said Meyer. Billed as a symposium on how an expanding Europe relates to US foreign policy, the debate avoided such specifics as transatlantic trade disputes, Balkan peacekeeping, Turkey's integration into Europe, the rise of Islamic fundamentalism, or any other subject where countervailing arguments had to be parsed and facts had to be weighed. It remained focused instead on vague maxims like "European politicians are corrupt," "the EU is like old fashioned totalitarianism," and "the Europeans never live up to their commitments." Pearson, Bodansky, Meyer, Hannan, Smith, and others simply lined up to repeat a single idea: *the EU is bad.*

The Big Idea that the EU is undesirable, which implicitly posits that America is superior—not only militarily and economically but morally— went unexamined and (with one exception noted below) unquestioned. The distinguished speakers were certainly within their areas of expertise but seemed, in this instance, unwilling to draw upon it. Those who attended left with their prejudices happily intact. The event was less a seminar than a pep rally with croissants.

Unipolarity at the New America Foundation

Someone who found the Heritage conference uninspired might look for a more open-minded discussion at, say, the New America Foundation, a smaller think tank that strives to "transcend the conventional political spectrum" as a "nonpartisan, nonprofit, public-policy institute." It does, in fact, bring together an unusually eclectic group of scholars and has recently established itself as the leader in this field. In place of a cinema auditorium, buffet tables, and large entrance foyers, it boasts an unpretentious office space with a single room that accommodates some forty people with room for a bowl of cookies and a table of canned drinks. But this modesty does not make it insignificant. The New America Foundation has a budget of over $3 million and a staff approaching fifty. It also supports a wide range of conferences and publications featuring notable public figures like former US Senate Majority Leader Tom Daschle, former Chief of Staff in the Clinton White House John Podesta, Michael Lind, E. J. Dionne, David Brooks, Daniel Schorr, and James Steinberg.

Yet, that same June the New America Foundation's panel "Why Foreign Policy Matters to the Democratic Party" offered a similar disappointment.[6]

It was billed as a discussion between Kurt Campbell, who occupies the Henry A. Kissinger Chair in National Security at the Center for Strategic & International Studies, and Clifford Kupchan, the director for Europe and Eurasia at the Eurasia Group. Both men were speaking as Democrats and qualified experts with established rèsumès from the Defense and State Departments on the subject of what the Democrats should be doing to re-establish themselves as "good stewards of the nation's security."

What followed, however, was another exposition about American power: Unipolarity. Campbell contended that "America has a preponder-ance of power and Democrats have to recognize that." Kupchan duly fol-lowed with the argument: "we must recognize and embrace unipolarity." Absent was any examination of the cracks in unipolarity such as the limi-tations on the US ability unilaterally to impose its will on Iraq or North Korea, to sustain democratic growth in Russia, to achieve consensus in the UN Security Council on vital matters like proliferation or to moder-ate China's scramble for critical world resources. Perhaps this omission was not the fault of the sponsoring think tank but an indication of how contrary thinking and complex arguments struggle to be heard.

Unipolarity is an old notion originally launched by Charles Kraut-hammer in an article for *Foreign Affairs* in 1990.[7] It describes America's unrivalled economic and military power following the fall of the Soviet Union, which is too often confused with omnipotence. The New Amer-ica Foundation, founded to bring "new voices and new ideas to the fore of our nation's public discourse," simply provided, in this instance, un-challenged confirmation of a misleading truism. The opportunity for fully fledged push-back was missed.

If a talk-show host resorts to Unipolarity as a one-word formula for American foreign relations writ large, that's one thing. His job requires him to use shorthand concepts to present abbreviated discussions of big issues. But the role of our experts at the nation's best think tanks is to counter the shorthand by restoring the substance and complexity the talk shows have taken out. Yet, here were two more experts embracing oversimplification instead of countering it. "We are in a period of unbridled American power," Kupchan stressed. "Democrats have to become comfortable again with hard power," Campbell affirmed. Clearly, the Democrats need to come to terms with unipolarity. But what emerged in the discussion was that this had more to do with winning elections (admittedly an urgent priority for the party) than with any realities on the international scene.

Terrorism at American Enterprise Institute

With our search for analysis free from slogans such as Bad Europe and Unipolar Power still unfulfilled, we next stopped at the corner of 17th and M Streets. Here stands the American Enterprise Institute (AEI), which is among the best known and best endowed of Washington's think tanks. Its offices, on the top three floors of this downtown high-rise, contain former intelligence analysts, UN ambassadors, White House speechwriters, State Department advisors, staff members for the US Senate Committee on Foreign Relations, and assistant secretaries of defense. There is no lack of expertise or resources here, a fact evident in AEI's complimentary lunches, which are unequalled on the think-tank circuit.

But let's say that in the wake of the London terrorist attacks of July 2005, for example, you were looking for intellectual refuge from the wall-to-wall cable-news diet of "could-it-happen-here?" stories, uninformed speculation, and idle commentary about bulky coats on the Washington Metro. If so, AEI's "Briefing on the London Attacks" would have offered little respite.[8]

The timing of this is important. Scheduled within days of the bombings, it unfolded while the British government had given out little information on the nature of the attacks and none on the culprits. At this early stage, the London attacks were an issue essentially without experts in the public space. Still, here was this panel discussion, advertised as "an AEI briefing," with a podium full of experts privy to no more information than the rest of us. The discussion that ensued is among the best examples of the think-tank system's habit of emphasizing format over substance and providing a venue for talking heads to present generalized chatter masquerading as informed expertise. AEI's executive-style twelfth-floor conference room was packed from wall to wall.

The event was full of unfounded assertions and offered little insight into the London attacks or the government's response. Peter Bergen, a man of considerable first-hand experience in international terrorism, came closest to informed analysis by listing the name of every European terrorist he could think of. In-house AEI scholar for the Middle East Michael Rubin quoted an Internet article by fellow Middle East expert Daniel Pipes suggesting that sixteen thousand British Muslim terrorists might be hiding in the United Kingdom. AEI military historian Frederick Kagan argued that these attacks are part of a broader struggle, akin to the Cold War, but that thankfully the positive ideology established by the Bush Administration has "proven to have a significant draw, even in places like Iraq." Last to speak, William Kristol, the editor of the *Weekly Standard,* suggested that "Islam in Western Europe is now more radical than Islam in the Middle East," a politically pregnant point, inviting simple conclusions to a complex and evolving situation.

This was not a briefing but a roundtable conversation of the sort that parallels cable news and might take place around the breakfast table: a great deal of idle speculation, misleading conjecture, and generalized opinion. One would hardly suspect that the purpose of the think tank is to provide an alternative to television discourse.

Democracy Building at the Hudson Institute

So far, having sampled three of Washington's elite research institutions and observed some fifteen hours of discussion involving over twenty experts, our search for a rational core of expertise among the think tanks had found little in the way of high-level, informative debate. Instead, we had found the same pseudocommentary, the same reductive speculation, the same sound-bite culture, and the same predominance of powerful framing ideas that afflict other elements of the mainstream political process. So where else could we look? For anyone concerned that the nation is increasingly being blown around by slogans and Big Ideas, an afternoon at the Hudson Institute offers little comfort.

Smaller than Heritage but larger than the New America Foundation, Hudson has a staff of almost one hundred and spends over $7 million a year on research, publications, and events. It has a powerful and distinguished board of trustees, including former Vice President Dan Quayle, Judge Robert Bork, former media giant Conrad Black, former Secretary of State Alexander Haig, and celebrated Yale historian Donald Kagan. Among its scholars are former White House advisors, government economists, retired generals, ambassadors, and foreign journalists. Its offices house people skeptical of recent shifts in US foreign policy as well as people who support them. But once again a wealth of expertise and finance failed to offer a counterweight to the culture of slogans.

A case in point is the Hudson's panel discussion "America's Mission: Debating Strategies for the Promotion of Democracy and Human Rights," held on June 20, 2005.[9] As US troops fought an elusive insurgency in Iraq, as Washington struggled to win hearts and minds in Arab-Islamic countries, as transatlantic relations grew strained over the question of trade relations with China, and as crowds of democratic reformers took to the streets in Lebanon, Kyrgyzstan, Palestine, and Ukraine, there was no debate more timely in 2005 than how to reconcile big principles with practical strategies to promote democracy and human rights.

Opening the symposium was Paula Dobriansky, the Under Secretary of State for Global Affairs. This could have been a moment of considerable import: here was a high-level member of the current administration with direct responsibility for the topic under discussion. It soon became apparent, however, that she was there mainly as a celebrity draw. After a ten-minute standard speech on America's commitment to human rights—filled with revelations such as "democracy is the cornerstone of the Bush administration's foreign policy"—she left for another appointment.

Following Dobriansky's departure, Tom Malinowski, Washington advocacy director for Human Rights Watch, praised the boldness of the Administration's "vision of spreading democracy." As a quick aside on the issue of Iraq, he added, "there's not much that can be done about Iraq except for getting the job done." No one in the audience stood up to ask what exactly this meant. After him came Jennifer Windsor, the executive director at Freedom House, whose comments centered on the high quality of the people serving the Administration. She was followed by Marc Platner, who gave a five-minute summary of America's dedication to promoting democracy since the beginning of the Reagan Administration, finishing with the suggestion that America had forever "changed the discourse" in places such as the Middle East. Last, resident Hudson fellow Michael Horowitz declared, "I am a great optimist about where we are," suggesting that Western Christendom could play a role in the Third World today "as it once did." He then asserted, "what we need is to pick a big fight and to focus on it as a counterpoint to Iraq . . . to pick a dictator and pull him down . . . We must pick a Syria, a North Korea, and an Iran. These are weak dictatorships. Once one falls, it will send a strong signal." Horowitz added that, "the president scores 'A' in my book," and concluded with the suggestion that we must "make China choose between North Korea and the US."

Again, we cite this example to illustrate the underperformance of the think-tank system. Among policy professionals, American think tanks are talked about and mythologized the world over. Names like Hudson, American Enterprise Institute, and New America Foundation appear on foreign affairs reading lists at Cambridge and Oxford. Yet, our quick tour leaves the distinct impression that most of the thinking goes in circles.

More Than an Off Day

If these instances seem extreme, it is not, alas, because we found a few think tanks having an off day. In the same period, we could have missed these examples and emerged with an identical narrative from countless others. For example, take a conference called "American Public Diplomacy: A Roadmap to Recovery," cosponsored by Heritage and another major Washington think tank, the Center for Strategic & International Studies (CSIS).[10] The latter has a budget of over $20 million and a platoon of former top policy makers that includes Henry Kissinger, Harold Brown, William Brock, and James Schlesinger.

The subject of this conference was how the US might improve its battered public image in the Arab world. Yet, despite being cosponsored by two of the nation's most powerful think tanks, the discussion consisted of mostly generalized and reductive inside-the-beltway speculation. The speakers focused on how "this great nation" is "distinguished from the rest of the world"; how we should teach better history in American schools about "great figures like Benjamin Franklin" so we can share a stronger sense of self with the rest of the world; how the greatest problem for American public relations today is that "we've handed too much influence over to the State Department"; and how we must never forget, when thinking about public relations, that "we are at war" and that "we do have enemies."

None of these examples is extraordinary. They are significant for precisely the opposite reason: they presented nothing out of the ordinary for their regular think-tank audience. No one stood up to challenge the discussants for pontificating on gigantic, reductive statements so general as to mean almost nothing. This brings us to another problem with think tank discourse: its audience.

THE AUDIENCE AS
IDEOLOGICAL BAROMETER

After the panelists have spoken, the custom at think-tank conferences calls for a question-and-answer session between panel and audience.

This element should offer a valuable opportunity for interface between experts and the public, or Administration officials and the academic community. Generally speaking, however, the audience is in ideological lockstep with the panel. If the discussion has been formatted around a single framing concept such as the Iraq War Is a Disaster, or Spreading Democracy Is Good, then the audience is usually as segregated as the substance matter. People apparently attend think-tank sessions not only because they are interested in the subjects under discussion but because they are on board with "the message."

That their minds are rarely open, let alone changed, may be seen in the question-and-answer sessions. Most questions simply reaffirm the speaker's message, for example, "When are we going to get tough on regime change in Iran?" or "How can we make the administration get real on climate change?" In journalism this kind of question is called a "softball." Sometimes, however, decorum is breached by questioners who deviate from the message. This tends to be done by people with little sense of how to make themselves heard effectively. During the European conference at Heritage the only dissenting question came from a woman who, while failing to ask a specific question, protested so loudly and for so long that the panelists and most of the audience stopped listening and left the room for their coffee break. Alternatively, an audience member deviates from the consensus because that is his purpose in attending. These people are sometimes loud, sometimes aggressive, and always defensive. They often frame their question within the context of the predominant idea, label it a falsehood, and on occasion have to be removed from the room, adding little to the discussion.

The result is a pseudodebate in which experts are like clergy preaching their gospel to the converted but hardly ever defending it before nonbelievers. The subtleties of rational discussion are trumped by a mixture of broad, vacuous messages and knee-jerk reactions. The audience, both a cause of substandard debate and a symptom of it, very often mirrors the panel discussion. Thus, if the panel has failed to inject tension into the dialogue, the question-and-answer session will be equally one-sided.

IT'S NOT ALL BAD

We would now like to give credit where it is due. What is frustrating for the observer of think-tank Washington is that there are parts of this system that function perfectly well. The same three-month period that featured the examples above saw numerous instances of think-tank discourse that were not slogan based, had no superimposed conceptual framework, attracted a diverse audience, provided substantive analysis, and showed a balance of perspectives from across the political spectrum. When think tanks concentrate on specific policies or issues, they often perform well.

For instance at the Woodrow Wilson International Center for Scholars—a federally supported institute designed to facilitate discourse between scholars and the public—we found insightful and focused debates such as "Hong Kong as China's Test Bed for Economic and Political Development" and "Bulgaria's Political Realignment." Both moved beyond the sound-bite debate to address specific issues. At the Cato Institute, a think tank known for its libertarian philosophies, we found substantive discussion on "Locking Down Loose Nukes" in which guests from the Carnegie Endowment for International Peace and the Foreign Policy Research Institute addressed specific challenges and options regarding nonproliferation, intelligence, and preemption dispassionately and at a granular level.

The United States Institute of Peace (USIP), a nonpartisan federal institution created by Congress in 1984 to promote the prevention, management, and peaceful resolution of international conflicts, provided numerous high-level debates in the same period on topics such as "Religious Education, Modernization, and Conflict in Indonesia, Pakistan, and the Philippines" and "The Hague Tribunal: Recent Developments and the Way Ahead." A cooperative venture coordinated by USIP and involving AEI, Heritage, CSIS, the Hoover Institution, and Brookings produced an interesting report on UN reform.[11]

Similarly, the Public Policy Institute (PPI), one of the smallest of the Washington think tanks, presented a debate focused on the first-hand experiences of guest speaker Larry Diamond, drawing on his time in Iraq as

senior advisor to the Coalition Provisional Authority in Baghdad. The
Brookings Institution presented a panel discussion titled "New Dynamics
in Syria," featuring veteran *Washington Post* reporter David Ignatius and former State Department official Flint Leverett. They were not there as "wise-
men" but as observers of the recent Ba'ath Party Congress in Damascus. At
Heritage and AEI, we found nuanced analysis and balanced panels: for example, the Heritage presentation "Finding Inspiration in Black History:
Radicals and the Thirst for Literacy,"[12] and AEI's debate "US Media Bias."

THINK-TANK OR POLITICAL LOBBY?

One senior fellow at Heritage told us that the organization does not
sponsor public events and voluminous literature in order to let the chips
of the argument fall where they may. The primary aim of the material is
to insert a coherent political position into the center of the national discourse. It is designed precisely to influence Congress, the media, the Administration, and the public with a specific agenda. Its panel discussions
and conferences are like controlled explosions, undertaken within a pre-
scribed environment and designed to serve an intended outcome.

Other organizations with this rationale include AEI, Hudson, the
Center for Security Policy, and the Washington Institute for Near East
Policy (WINEP). This does not mean that sensible, informative discussion is not to be found at these places. They are perfectly capable of orga-
nizing high-standard debate on issues like media bias, African-American
literacy, Medicare, and Mexican elections. But there is a sacred territory
in which core issues that are subject to intense political debate fall out
along a predictable left-right schism such as national security, US Middle
East policy, and relations with China and Europe. Here, the format does
not encourage questioning of the organization's central message. Think
tanks of this type, when addressing politically sensitive security issues, are
better thought of not as research institutions but as well-funded lobbies
with a support staff of scholars.

Organizations such as Brookings, on the other hand, lack an institutional political position on most things. Its fellows, in the summer of 2005, included supporters of the Iraq war and opponents of it, advocates of a realist engagement with Chinese economic expansion and advocates of a sustained trade embargo on grounds of human rights abuses. Discussion panels at Brookings are organized to communicate a mixture of perspectives rather than a powerful overall message. There are elaborate rules in its budget to ensure, as its President, Strobe Talbot, asserts, that financial providers have no influence over the design and outcome of Brookings research. In its own words, Brookings is financed largely by its endowment and by the support of philanthropic foundations, corporations, and private individuals. Some major sources of funding include the Lynde and Harry Bradley Foundation, the John M. Olin Foundation Inc., the Smith Richardson Foundation, and the F. M. Kirby Foundation.

Heritage and AEI, meanwhile, make no effort to hide the connections between their political agenda and the financial support they enjoy from organizations like the Scaife family, the Lynde and Harry Bradley Foundation, and Asian-based groups like the Korean Foundation and Samsung. The latter two groups support an agenda-driven discourse on issues such as Taiwanese independence, North Korean nonproliferation, and Chinese human rights abuses. Activist funding can cause think tanks to sponsor specific positions on issues of the day. While there is plenty of disagreement among members of AEI or Hudson on issues within the conservative camp, they proceed largely from a common ideological basis that keeps these disagreements within well-defined bounds.

Ideology and the Interns

Another way to measure the variance in ethos between these types of think-tanks lies, remarkably enough, in how they choose their interns. A crucial part of the Heritage application form is titled "Your Ideology." Here the applicant must first choose the title that best describes him or her: conservative, liberal, libertarian, moderate, moderate-conservative, multilateralist, neoconservative, or realist. Having thus labeled themselves, applicants have to tick whether they "agree" or "disagree" with a number of policy statements, such as "a strong Israel is vital to American interests in the Middle East," "the US should get approval from the United Nations before engaging in any military action abroad," and "free trade is beneficial to the United States." There is no margin for error here: to get a job at Heritage, the applicant must score 100 percent on this section.[13]

Brookings and CSIS do not brand their political identity from a choice of labels or describe their ideology. Selection is based purely on area expertise and curriculum vitae. Brookings, for example, does not use an application form, requiring only rèsumès, writing samples, and references that relate to the specific program of interest. At both Brookings and CSIS, the emphasis in the application process is on knowledge of specific regional languages or a relevant academic background. One graduate from the University of Pennsylvania who worked as an intern at CSIS told us, "I would have been laughed out of the building if I'd turned up saying that I wanted to work there because I believed in the right to drive SUVs or America's right to act without the UN." His particular work, on a project outsourced to CSIS from the State Department, was "all work-focused and policy-specific . . . not about my belief-system." In contrast, an intern at Heritage told us that he did everything he could to be accepted there because "it's the pinnacle of the conservative movement . . . because Heritage has the right ethos . . . because it stands for everything I believe in." Across town, another intern told us she chose Hudson because "it's conservative and so am I."

Institutions like Heritage and Hudson screen interns on the basis of a belief-system. Even some of the websites that interns told us they relied upon to pick the right institution stress that applicants must be careful to find the right place to match their views. As one website puts it, "Does the think-tank's philosophy match your own? If not, it could lead to an unhappy experience."[14] This difference in the experience of interns at places such as Hudson and CSIS underlines the distinction between two entirely different modes of operation in the national debate—one of policy research, and one of advocacy.

Bad Debate Sells

There is nothing wrong with advocacy. Legitimate partisan groups in a free political system may promote the agenda of their choosing. The problem for the think-tank system, however, is that advocacy has a greater impact on the national discourse than purely rational experts.

At the more informative events—the Wilson Center's panel on Hong Kong's economic relations with China, Cato's discussion of "loose nukes," and the Heritage presentation on black literacy—diverse views were brought to the surface and complex ideas were discussed with a minimum of political bias. But these events engaged their emotions and their audiences not nearly as much as the Big Idea conferences. The speakers were less entertaining, the subject matter tended to be bland, and the audience contributions less flamboyant.

The broader characteristics of America's mass information culture—the rush to simplicity, the emphasis on merchandisable sound-bites, and the primacy of the easy message over nuanced, dispassionate expertise—provide organizations such as Heritage, AEI, and Carnegie an opportunity to make a powerful impact on debate. By emphasizing information, independent research, and open debate, on the other hand, PPI, Wilson, USIP, and Brookings deny themselves bumper-sticker accessibility and entertainment value. The whiz and bang of sound-bite ideology sells far better than a bland, middle-aged, former government expert on the politics of energy competition in the central Asian republics. Small wonder that such topics fail to pack the room.

A SYSTEM COLLAPSED

It would be hard to conclude that the think-tank system has fulfilled its promise. It is a system in disrepair. Our chief complaint is that the enviable financial resources available to the think-tank system are not being brought to bear; they are failing *as a collective.* Nowhere is this more apparent than on the issue of Iraq. The final word on the Iraq war has, of course, not yet been written, but there is enough evidence already to suggest that it will come to be seen as one of America's greatest foreign policy blunders, likely on a par with the Vietnam War.

Here, organizations like AEI, Heritage, Hudson, WINEP, and the Center for Security Policy have much to answer for. Though they had well-identified views in favor of the Iraq policy, they failed to remain true to their intellectual mission of offering a platform for a debate on the merits. They have been led by the Administration's crisis narrative and framing concepts. This is wrong for an organization ostensibly in the ideas business. Heritage, for instance, demonized those who disagreed with it in a formal seminar where opponents of the Iraq war were described as "communist fellow travelers."[15] In effect, these organizations, together, fashioned a well-funded campaign of conferences, books, magazine articles, op-eds, and regular appearances on television and talk radio that relentlessly advanced a single Big Idea, namely that the Middle East could and should be transformed into democratic states, in which process the Iraq war was an essential first step.

Institutions like Brookings, CSIS, New America Foundation, Carnegie, and the CFR contributed to the problem in different ways. Just as substantial sections of the political elite favored the Iraq war, these institutions had every right to reflect this view. But it was far from the full story. Opinion in the country was mixed, with concern being expressed by conservatives, liberals, and independents alike. Within senior political, diplomatic, intelligence, and military circles there was considerable unease, some of it on the record.[16]

Brookings, for example, can certainly not be described as reflexively acquiescent to the Administration. The organization contains a spectrum of views. Yet the bulk of material specifically on Iraq being produced at Brookings in this period was coming from those, like Michael O'Hanlon and Kenneth M. Pollack[17] and others, whose international views had steadily evolved to accept neoconservative solutions.

In late 2001, for instance, O'Hanlon and Philip Gordon, another Brookings scholar, had been writing cautiously about Iraq, noting that "for now, the costs and risks of containment appear lower than those of attempting to overthrow Mr. Saddam."[18] As it became clear that the United States was moving toward war, the same two scholars, now joined by Martin Indyk, a former Ambassador to Israel, seemingly underwent a change of heart: "with sufficient American leadership, commitment and sacrifice, the military, diplomatic and nation-building challenges involved in regime-change in Iraq can all be met."[19] As the Administration's line grew harder, so did Brookings's.[20] Speaking about the fall of Saddam, Indyk said: "Wednesday, April 9, 2003, will be a day that will go down in history. You will probably remember and even tell your grandchildren what you did on this day."[21] A year later his tune had changed: "failure is not only an option but a likelihood."[22]

A review of the archives indicates that if some in the building were skeptical of the Administration's rationale for the Iraq war and the democratic transformation of the region, they were not writing about it. In this sense Brookings became a microcosm of the larger national debate. The discussion attracted those who were supportive of the patriotic consensus that dominated America's sociopolitical landscape, while the critical American seemed to have gone on holiday.

Brookings has continued to be a microcosm of the national debate. As the national political discussion gradually regained its balance and critical voices made themselves heard in the Congress and among the nation's editorial writers, so the critical voices at Brookings grew more pronounced. This would suggest that America should not expect its major research institutions to operate separately or externally from the broader dynamics and pressures of national debate at times of crisis. The post–9/11 period indicates that institutions such as Brookings are as much a product of the public space as they are a mechanism for its quality control.

This should not be the case. Any one of these eminent research institutions (really all of them) should have ensured that their programs included a rigorous examination of the Administration's reasons for war. This should have occurred not just through the occasional commentary of an individual scholar but on an institutional basis. That it did not is a matter of great wonderment.

In 2002, for example, the Carnegie Endowment for International Peace found time in its eighty-six events to discuss China six times, India four times, and Nepal and Kyrgyzstan twice each. But Iraq got onto the agenda only once—in November 2002 when the die was already cast.[23] That discussion was largely technical, concerning the possible ramifications of the use of weapons of mass destruction by Iraq, and begged the question of whether Iraq had such weapons in the first place. The next time Carnegie discussed Iraq was on February 3, 2003, when its main conclusion was that war seemed likely. In 2002 the New America Foundation staged seventy-three events, not one of which was dedicated to Iraq. CSIS did not hold a single event on Iraq in 2002. In January 2003 CSIS published a long analysis "A Wiser Peace: An Action Strategy for a Post-Conflict Iraq," which, while it anticipated many of the problems that in fact occurred, included the point that "it takes no position on whether there should be a war."[24] A month later, open-mindedness was gone. At a time of intense public consternation about the unfolding course of American policy, CSIS provided a forum for Senator John McCain to make the case for war.[25] In 2004 CSIS held seven events on Iraq. By then, the golden hour was long gone.

We mention the Council on Foreign Relations last because the failure here was the most egregious. Here is the national membership organization to which all Americans (membership is not open to nonnationals) of any standing in the foreign policy world aspire. It describes itself as a "nonpartisan resource for information and analysis."[26] No other venue is better suited to the airing of the full range of views about major decisions, most especially a war of choice in a strategically vital area of the world.

Yet the CFR stood mute on the matter of opposition. Search the articles of *Foreign Affairs* from the fall of 2001 to the spring of 2003, the period in which the Iraq debate was conducted, and you will look in vain for a single article that raises moderate skepticism, let alone fundamental questions, about the looming decisions. There were numerous articles setting out the case for war.[27] There were plenty of reviews of books that stirred the pot for war. But there was nothing that reflected the widespread disquiet in the country. As with Brookings, as soon as it was safe to criticize, criticism started to emerge—albeit counterbalanced by substantial articles defending the Administration's approach.[28] Perhaps the editors of *Foreign Affairs* will argue that nothing suitable was available. In that case, they should have commissioned something. It is clear from their subsequent writings that some CFR officers were disturbed by the course of policy.[29]

Again, this is an institutional failure. Certainly, the pressures to conform were immense. All the major institutions receive research grants from appropriated funds. Scholars did not fail to notice that certain institutions, like Carnegie, engineered the departure of internal critics; others, such as Cato, which stood out against the war, had to deal with sharp questions from their supporters. The task facing the rational center is not an easy one. But it is precisely at such times of stress that the think-tank voice must come through. It does not have to be self-sacrificial, but it should ensure that any flaws in the Big Idea of the moment are thoroughly examined.

The Iraq debate demonstrated a fundamental characteristic about think-tank Washington today: information and open debate struggle to compete in the public space with empty, slogan-based exchange that simplifies the variables and suppresses detailed discussion. The more a think tank can craft a simple, coherent message, the more its discourse prevails in an environment of complex ideas. Months after the 2004 presidential election, former Democratic candidate Howard Dean told Comedy Central host Jon Stewart that if politicians want to make an impact on the national discourse, "facts are not enough. You've got to have facts and a message." The rule, it seems, applies equally to the think tanks.

FIVE

An Unreliable Elite

Nonperformance among the nation's intellectual elite is not confined to the think tanks. A look at the nation's top universities shows that professors who are leaders in their fields and whose knowledge and analytical skills could be instrumental in helping the nation address complex policy challenges, often do not. Instead, as the nation grapples with approaches to radical Islam and probes for common ground that might form a bridge between the West and the cultures of the Middle East, some of the most prominent intellectuals have gained personal celebrity by playing to popular prejudice and Big Ideas. But pandering to the Administration's Axis-of-Evil, one-size-fits-all paradigm is just part of the story. Distinguished academics have bolstered their importance at public expense in other ways. Some have used fear, detailing the prospective nightmare of nuclear terrorism, for instance. Others have plucked the strings of nativism and xenophobia, exacerbating the immigration issue and frightening Americans with the seeming loss of their heritage to a flood of "unwanted immigrants."

Others, convinced that the US government is an irredeemably flawed vessel and the source of many of the ills plaguing the world, have taken a different tack. Theirs is an unstinting celebration of the virulent and, at times, paranoid left. These academics, while gaining great prominence on campuses and in the left-of-center press, have distanced themselves from the rational center, becoming morbid "hawkers" instead of problem solvers in the policy debate. And there is still a third category, the straddlers; experts in a particular field who use their prominence—often in good conscience—to criticize Administration policy in areas where they know little more than the rest of us. All of these intellectuals accept a Faustian bargain: in exchange for the easy celebrity found in the ambit of Big Ideas, they muddy the debate and diminish their reputations.

What follows is a look at how some of the nation's most widely known intellectuals, using the Administration's narrative as a foil, have enhanced their prominence. The common denominator is that each of them could have made a critical contribution to the rational center at an important time but instead compromised themselves by overstating their case, in hopes of wider recognition and celebrity.

THE DISTORTIONISTS

No three subjects set American nerves more on edge than nuclear attack, immigration, and Islam. A quick browse of any bookstore window or magazine rack, a stop at the video store, or a look at the week's TV specials reveals a stream of vivid nightmare scenarios of the coming Armageddon.[1] The scope for panic and sensationalism is enormous. Many Americans feel they are under attack not for what they do but for who they are.

Much of the anxiety fed by such apocalyptic scenarios is rooted in the Big Idea expressed by President Bush shortly after 9/11, "They hate us for our freedoms."[2] Faced with such a vague yet malignant threat, Americans need insight from those whose experience and perspective can accurately quantify the danger. During the Cold War the US devoted substantial efforts to understanding the other side. It needs similar efforts in the areas that disturb our lives today.

The nation, of course, has at its disposal a wealth of intellectual talent capable of doing precisely that. We discuss three such authorities here: Professor Graham Allison of Harvard University on nuclear issues; Professor Samuel Huntington, also of Harvard, on Islam and immigration matters; and Professor Bernard Lewis of Princeton University on the Middle East. The question we will ask of them is whether they have provided a rational context, and balance for the Administration's narrative in each area.

Americans thrive on an information culture accented by crisis. Each day they are assailed by sensation that roils the public discourse and gives scope to irrational policies. The nation relies upon the rational center to produce a different reality: one grounded in accepted fact, recognized data, and the historical record that provides a valid point of reference for the policy process. Academics feel competing pressures to inject themselves into the political discourse and yet maintain some detachment; it is a dilemma they need to solve, not ignore. If the most prominent members of the academic community are not providing balance, the community as a whole fails to realize its institutional promise.

Nuclear Attack

Suppose a Harvard professor with a named chair described a genuine plot, known to the CIA, in which Al-Qaeda terrorists planned to detonate a 10-kiloton nuclear device in central Manhattan. Surely this would get your attention. If he had gone on to list precise details of the devastation this would have caused, including some 1 million deaths and the destruction of Times Square, Radio City, and other familiar landmarks, you could be forgiven for being scared out of your wits. And suppose, for the benefit of readers not familiar with the geography of New York City, the same professor went on to list the effects such an explosion would have in San Francisco, Houston, Washington, Chicago, Los Angeles, and Charlotte.

You might be forgiven for asking why you had not heard about this at the time. The reason is that the threat was never real. At an early stage, the story turned out to be a false alarm based on reporting from a CIA source named "Dragonfly." The deaths and desecration were never more than figments of Dragonfly's imagination. At this stage you might feel that you had been told the story on false pretenses, in which the details were deliberately blurred in order to terrify you.

Unlike Dragonfly, we are not making this up. The supposed plot was served up by Graham Allison, the Douglas Dillon Professor of Government and director of the Belfer Center for Science and International Affairs at Harvard University, in his book *Nuclear Terrorism: The Ultimate Preventable Catastrophe*. Despite its title, more than half of the book is taken up with asserting that a terrorist nuclear attack is "inevitable," a concept that is hard to reconcile with "preventable."[3]

The 10-kiloton bomb with which *Nuclear Terrorism* opens is lifted almost verbatim from Allison's book *Avoiding Nuclear Anarchy*, written eight years earlier, in which the 1993 World Trade Center and 1995 Oklahoma City bombings were cited to make a case for impending nuclear disaster.[4] This case included the possibility that if the World Trade Center were destroyed, more than thirty thousand lives would be lost. This mode of argument—citing a recent terrorist event and then making the self-evident point that it would have been much worse had it involved nuclear weapons—seems to be a familiar template for the Belfer Center. For example, the May 2005 report "Securing the Bomb 2005: New Global Initiatives," written by Belfer scholars Mathew Bunn and Anthony Weir, makes just this point about the September 2004 school siege in Beslan, Russia.[5]

These scenarios are, of course, genuinely scary. But where we fault Allison is on his unwillingness to provide what a lawyer would call exculpatory evidence. For example, in *Nuclear Terrorism* he might have noted that eight years had passed since his earlier prediction of a nuclear detonation inside an American city without the event having taken place. Instead he took the opposite tack: in a presentation at the Center for Strategic and International Studies in Washington, DC, on April 1, 2005, a single possible nuclear detonation became two. One might also have expected Allison to point out that, contrary to his earlier claim that "leakage of weapons-grade fissile material from the former Soviet lands has already reached alarming proportions and is likely to get much worse,"[6] cooperation between the United States and Russia had actually improved on precisely this point. In fact leakages of weapons-grade material in volumes even remotely approaching those needed for bomb manufacture have simply not taken place. This would suggest that there were elements of stability in the system that the author had missed the first time around—or even that the system had been improved as a result of the concerns he and his institute had raised.

Allison's book is divided into two parts, one called "Inevitable" and the other "Avoidable." This could lead one to think that two scenarios are being presented, one in which a nuclear attack is inevitable and one in which, with policy changes, it can be avoided; but this is not how the case is made. Allison also quotes some unusual sources such as Tom Clancy in his novel *The Sum of All Fears* and public statements by investor Warren Buffett, whose views as concerned private citizens are entirely legitimate but whose authority on nuclear terrorism is not obvious.

Allison quotes the former Soviet general Alexander Lebed on the question of Soviet "suitcase" bombs, playing down the fact that such bombs would by now have most likely degraded beyond usability and in fact may not have existed in the first place. Nor does he mention that Lebed's credibility is severely compromised by his history of unsubstantiated grand claims. Miniaturization of nuclear devices presents significant problems for a terrorist. In general, the more reliable a weapon one wishes to build, the larger it needs to be. Given that a terrorist most likely will not be able to test any device before deployment, this raises a considerable risk of malfunction. Of course, mentioning this detracts from the drama. But that is the point: the function of the expert is to reduce hysteria and guide the public toward rationality.

If Allison genuinely believes a nuclear attack is inevitable, or at least highly probable, and is not just scare mongering, this conclusion would introduce a series of policy implications, none of which he addresses. If the probability of something happening is greater than 50 percent—for example, of a hurricane coming ashore in Florida during hurricane season—then the concept of prevention must be seen in the context of pre-event preparation and post-event responsiveness. This is an area where, as the chaotic response to the Hurricane Katrina crisis in August 2005 shows, serious governmental deficiencies exist. If a terrorist strike is really inevitable—Allison quotes Eugene E. Habiger, former commander, US Strategic Air Command, who offers the "categorical conclusion" that "it's not a matter of if; it's a matter of when,"[7] and the State Department's top counterterrorist officer has spoken publicly in similar terms[8]—then it is essential to prepare for the scenes of devastation outlined in Allison's nightmare scenario. Otherwise, one disaster could turn into a much larger one.

The possibility of such an attack raises enormous questions about the US response, both domestically and internationally. Other writers, such as Michael Ignatieff, have expressed fears that a terrorist nuclear attack would "entail the disintegration of our institutions and our way of life"[9]—and the same might be true on a global scale if the US retaliation knew no bounds. In expressing these concerns, Ignatieff, who is also a Harvard professor, draws on the research carried out by Allison and the Belfer Center. This reinforces the point, that leaders like Allison exercise seminal influence in establishing the nature of these phenomenon and how they are publicly presented.

The point here is not that the threat of nuclear terrorism is negligible or that Allison is wrong to write about it as an urgent problem. With his extensive experience in the arms negotiation field, he is precisely the kind of expert the public looks to for guidance. The choices that would face the nation in the event of nuclear attack are so serious that it is incumbent upon distinguished academics to plot the way forward dispassionately. In raising our alarm about the inevitability of this cataclysm, Allison is obligated to focus our attention on the real-life consequences that flow from it and what steps may be taken to ameliorate the effects. It is wrong to simply leave it as an unexploded grenade beneath the breakfast table while he moves on to other issues.

Islam, Identity, and Immigration

One of the striking sights for any visitor to Berlin in the 1970s was the number of flags on display in the western sector proclaiming allegiance to the Federal Republic of Germany. Crossing into the Eastern Sector and standing on the massive Alexanderplatz, one would see a similar display, this time asserting allegiance to the Soviet-controlled German Democratic Republic. Today, these manifestations of nationalism have disappeared. They have also disappeared in Japan, where a drive from Narita airport into downtown Tokyo will net perhaps one or two sightings of the Rising Sun flag. The United States, by contrast, experienced an understandable surge of nationalism following 9/11. Many Americans struck by this concluded that it was a matter of "us versus them" in which "they" had brought war on "us." The way to this conclusion was, in part, paved by another Harvard professor, Samuel Huntington, and his theory of a "clash of civilizations." When first published in *Foreign Affairs* in 1993, Huntington's article "The Clash of Civilizations?" attracted enormous attention.[10] Some of it was favorable, but many political scientists and historians criticized him for having generalized too far about parts of the world with which he was unfamiliar.

Huntington's thesis was that the fundamental source of conflict in the coming decades would not be primarily ideological or economic, but cultural. Until the end of the Cold War, he argued, the conflicts between nation states and ideologies of concern to us had largely occurred within Western civilization. But with the collapse of the Soviet Union, civilizational identity would become increasingly important. Future conflicts would be shaped in large measure by the interactions among the world's seven or eight major civilizations: Western, Confucian, Japanese, Islamic, Hindu, Slavic-Orthodox, Latin American, and what Huntington described as "possibly" African civilization. From these basic rules for the new world order, Huntington warned that the West would come into increasing conflict particularly with two "civilizational Others"—the Chinese (Confucian) and Islamic.[11]

The rubble from the World Trade Center had not even settled before Huntington's 1996 book (bearing the same name as the journal article but shorn of its modest question mark) became the dominant source for understanding the 9/11 attacks.[12] The *Washington Post*, *New York Times*, and *Wall Street Journal*; *Newsweek*, *Time*, the *New Republic*, *Foreign Affairs*, and *Atlantic Monthly*; the television and radio networks; and the tabloid press all explained America's sudden predicament in terms of Huntington's thesis, often by direct quote. Columnists, op-ed writers, cable-news editors, and talk-show pundits rushed to squeeze this new world into a grand paradigm, conflating "terrorism" and "Arab backwardness" to shorthand explanations of political violence that omitted any genuine political analysis of interests or contexts. The roots of this "new barbarism" were simply the product of whole backward civilizations and cultures.[13] The simplicity of Huntington's paradigm seemed to be the basis for its success in the confusion surrounding the attacks. The notion of an Islamic holy war against the West provided a dramatic concept that fast overtook detailed formulations of the issue in the public sphere. Dispassionate analyses of Muslim attitudes across a global mosaic of demographics that encompass some 1.2 billion people, over 20 percent of the world's population, over fifty countries, and over sixty languages were shrunken into the paradigm of an apocalyptic confrontation between two giant, static civilizations, with "the West" on one side and a monolithic Islamic peril on the other.

As Andrew Sullivan wrote in the *New York Times*, "this is a religious war."[14] The *New Republic* meanwhile ran a piece explaining how the nineteen hijackers had attacked America because they, along with the rest of the Muslim world, could not accept that women had gained their freedom in the West.[15] In an echo of what would soon become a White House mantra, the *Wall Street Journal* argued that a barbaric culture had declared war "not because of our policies but for what we stood for—democracy and freedom."[16] National Public Radio introduced *National Review* editor Richard Lowry as a Middle East "specialist," and he in-

structed its listeners that Muslims had a problem in telling the truth.[17]
Reuel Marc Gerecht wrote in the *New York Times* that the Middle East
was a brutal land of paradoxes and that today's bitterness derived from Islam's past military failures.[18] *Foreign Affairs*, the publication of the American Council of Foreign Relations, ran a special issue with the title "Long
War in the Making" and pieces arguing that the roots of 9/11 lay in
the medieval crusades, Mongol invasions, and seventh-century Arabia.[19]
The *Atlantic Monthly* published an article contending that events had
now vindicated Huntington and commended him for "looking the world
in the eye."[20]

Huntington himself joined the celebration of his foresight with a long
article in *Newsweek* in which he clarified this new era in all-embracing
terms. "Contemporary global politics," he wrote, "is the age of Muslim
Wars." With Al-Qaeda's attack on the East Coast, these wars "had come
home to America."[21] Since it was rooted in "the rise of Islamic con-
sciousness," Muslim violence "could congeal into one major clash of civilizations between Islam and the West or between Islam and the Rest."
Along with some sixty other prominent intellectuals, including Francis
Fukuyama, Michael Novak, and Daniel Patrick Moynihan, Huntington
signed a long statement issued by the Institute for American Values supporting the War on Terrorism on the ground that it defended American
values and the "achievements of civilization."[22]

In the period since 9/11 and the US invasion of Iraq, Huntington's notion of a "Clash of Civilizations" has enjoyed increasing popular and political support, not only in America and the Western hemisphere but
across parts of the Middle East and Asia. Events such as the Danish cartoon controversy and the London terrorist attacks of July 2005 were
hailed in a number of American and European media outlets as confirmation of a civilizational confrontation.[23] US and UK newspapers talked
of a "cartoon clash," while Tony Blair defended British Middle East policy in the months after the Underground bombings with phrases like "a
clash about civilizations." In April 2006, Osama bin Laden recaptured

the world's attention with claims of a "Zionist Crusaders' war on Islam" and a "clash of civilizations," made apparent by such events as international hostility towards the new Hamas-led government in Palestine, European willingness to publish depictions of the Prophet Mohammed, proposals at the UN Security Council for a Western peacekeeping force in Sudan, and, naturally, the war in Iraq.[24]

The publication of declassified excerpts from the US National Intelligence Estimate of April 2006 only added grist to the mill of many commentators, as it argued that "four underlying factors are fuelling the spread of the jihadist movement: (1) entrenched grievances, such as corruption, injustice, and fear of Western domination, leading to anger, humiliation, and a sense of powerlessness; (2) the Iraq jihad; (3) the slow pace of real and sustained economic, social, and political reforms in many Muslim-majority nations; and (4) pervasive anti-US sentiment among most Muslims, all of which jihadists exploit."[25]

The authors would like to offer a cautionary note, however, in a discussion that has been driven in the US public sphere to no small extent by an American media cycle with a disproportionate reliance on slogans and catchphrases as a way to feed the entertainment-demands of crisis, drama, and simplification.

The daily barrage of atrocities in Iraq has indeed mobilized widespread anger on the Arab-Islamic street and—as stated in the leaked National Intelligence Estimate—functioned to radicalize Muslim sentiment and recruit additional jihadists. Although the US-UK decision to invade Iraq was not driven by a "clash of civilizations," its aftermath and the botched attempts to rebuild the country have undoubtedly done a great deal to persuade significant sections of Muslim opinion that there just might be one. But this is precisely the point at which America's expert population must be able to step forward and prevent the discussion of a civilzational clash from becoming a self-fulfilling prophecy in the mind's eye of informed Western electorates. The Middle East policies of Washington and London seem to have created the very situation that Huntington first outlined in 1993, but this has happened for reasons set apart from those cited by the scholar himself. In other words, there is a great deal more to these circumstances than meets the eye.

For example, in the Danish cartoon controversy the issue for a number of European Muslims was less about what is permissible in Islam and more about how the cartoons appeared representative of broader trends in alienation and discrimination. Underlying this grievance in many cases was not the desire for separation from the host nation but the entitlement to enjoy greater respect and rights *within* it. Meanwhile in the Middle East, heavy press coverage in the official news media of countries like Iran and Syria, as well as de facto government authorization of public demonstrations, played a vital role in whipping up strong popular sentiments during the crisis. But the driving force behind these dynamics was political and national; governments and interested parties descended on the crisis as a way to further their regional and international objectives. If the cartoon controversy started in Denmark as an issue of religion, it functioned in the Middle East to advance political agendas among power-brokering groups and national governments. These are crucial factors wholly defied by slogans.

Similarly, the stated motivations of the London bombers provide an instructive example of how much the Iraq debacle has done to persuade certain groups that there *is* a clash between the West and Islam. They cited the obligation to protect Muslims and the Holy Land from a Judeo-Christian axis bent on invasion, occupation, and subjugation for the purpose of consumer-driven, oil-fueled global domination.[26] But these four young Britons from Leeds failed to inspire a pan-Islamic British uprising against the "military-industrial complex" at Downing Street. Rather, they did more to restimulate older multicultural debates about ethnic integration in British society that emerged in the 1980s after the Handsworth riots among Afro-Caribbean and South Asian communities. Mainstream Muslim leaders seemed ready to reject both the bombers and the tenets of British Middle East policy in equal measure.

Similarly, the conditions of Muslim resentment are variegated and fragmented. Some elements have formed largely through the prism of regional media outlets like Al Jazeera, which thrive off of and contribute to the sensation- and entertainment-value of anti-Western emotion and Polaroid-driven torture scandals. Others have been nurtured through the mobilization of organized public-relations machines that characterize the propaganda-rhetoric of Iranian and Syrian leaders. Skilful orators and flamboyant politicians in these countries might appeal to the greater sense of a Muslim identity ideal, but they operate in a regional balance-of-powers environment. The issues that regularly feature in this discourse relate more to questions of regional concern than civilizational identity, such as the presence of US troops, the alleged injustice of Israeli occupation and settlement, respective American support for these policies, a perceived US support for governments like those in Egypt and Saudi Arabia, Western reliance on the Middle East as a global gas station, and the perception of economic injustice inherent in the disparity of material wealth between the Transatlantic region and the Fertile Crescent.

Instead of a civilizational bloc of Muslim resentment, we see a complicated and interconnected matrix of bodies public and political, from warring Palestinian factions in disagreement over the decision to recognize Israel to the rival objectives of leaders in Iran and Saudi Arabia to the Iraqi insurgent groups that fight each other for the lion's share of national power as much as they fight to repel international forces. If a galvanized sense of Muslim identity plays a role in these scenarios, it is only one among a number of factors at once political, social, economic, and nationalist as much as they are pancultural or religious.

Immigration and Identity

As Huntington drew attention to the "us versus them" aspect of international politics, the "us" part of that formula was being drawn into a debate about immigration and American identity. And for many Americans, the perceived threat of terrorism became conflated with immigration, especially illegal immigration. The 9/11 terrorists were, of course, foreigners, but more generally, immigration raises the question of what "us" means. In May 2005 the police chief of New Ipswich, New Hampshire, a town of some five thousand residents incorporated in 1792, started arresting illegal immigrants for "unlawful trespass" on the grounds that they represented a "threat to our way of life."[27] This movement has proliferated across the country, including into Herndon, Virginia, a suburb of Washington, DC.

After the US experience in the Balkans during the 1990s, one might have expected leading American academics to avoid the "us against them" path. Perhaps some did, but Professor Huntington was not among them. He has entered the lists again with another volume: *Who Are We? The Challenges to America's National Identity.* In his introduction, Huntington acknowledges that he is adopting an approach that departs from strict scholarly rigor:

> This book is shaped by my own identities as a patriot and scholar . . . The motives of patriotism and scholarship, however, may conflict. Recognizing this problem, I attempt to engage in as detached and thorough analysis of the evidence as I can, while warning the reader that my selection and presentation of the evidence may well be influenced by my patriotic desire to find meaning and virtue in America's past and in its possible future.[28]

Were it written by a PhD candidate, this acknowledgement that evidence had been chosen to produce an outcome in line with the writer's personal predispositions would get the author an invitation to choose another line of work. Huntington's use of the word *patriotism* is also notable given the use that has been made of that word since 9/11 to chill debate. But let us give him credit for being frank about his approach and concede that it is perfectly legitimate for him to write as he pleases.

Yet his approach creates a problem. We are faced with a work that re-sembles academic inquiry but is more akin to out-and-out advocacy in which the facts are assembled to make a point. Huntington moves back and forth between these two genres in often confusing ways. For in-stance, in an elegant sleight of hand, he refines the original migrants to America from Europe not as "immigrants" but as "settlers." He uses his term to assert once-and-for-all rights for this group, a sort of perpetual primogeniture for the first generation of European arrivals and the cul-ture that descends from them—to which he gives the name "creed." This is consistent with his wish to ground American national identity in the Anglo-Protestant culture that sprang up around 1790.

The argument turns out to be circular. With primacy defined in terms of the settler culture, it follows that anyone arriving later than 1790 (or admitted to the full community after the passage of the Fourteenth Amendment in 1868) is a Johnny-come-lately who can become "Ameri-can" only by "adopting America's Anglo-Protestant culture."[29] Hunting-ton quotes, seemingly with approval, the common bumper sticker, "will the last American to leave, please haul down the flag?"

What *Who Are We?* delivers is a primer on ethnic tension within the US. Of course, the issue is a central one. As Huntington points out, when the US national soccer team cannot schedule qualifying games in Los An-geles against Latin American opponents for fear that the region's ethnic fan base will turn these into "away" games, something is out of joint. The lay public looks to the expert to clarify what that "something" is.

But, like his Harvard colleague Graham Allison, Huntington has waded into one of the most explosive issues in contemporary American politics and then reached for the gasoline. Instead of helping readers un-derstand why they feel as they do—whether they are established "Ang-los" struggling to deal with demographic change or more recent arrivals wondering whether accession to Anglo-Protestant culture is really their only option—Huntington has written a lengthy "op-ed" in which he de-fines American identity in terms that appear academic and scholarly but in fact are little more than a nativist defense of the dominant caste. There is no shortage of such views. Go into any country club and you will find an old codger on a bar stool complaining of the bad manners and dubious lineage of the new members.

Our argument is that this analysis falls short of what we should be expecting from Harvard professors or other experts. They should be looking at such matters in the round, both strengths and shortcomings. When they fail to reach this standard and still receive respectful reviews in *Foreign Affairs*, then we are prompted to issue distress calls on behalf of the rational center.

The Islamic Question

Many Americans will instinctively agree with Huntington's assertion that the 9/11 attacks "filled the vacuum created by Gorbachev with an unmistakably dangerous new enemy [that] pinpointed America's identity as a Christian nation."[30] The publishing industry quickly obliged those interested in amplifying their knowledge of the new enemy. Too much of the result, however, did a better job of playing into the dominant stereotype than of providing a better understanding.

One expert who might have offered a different perspective on the emergent consensus was Bernard Lewis, Professor Emeritus of Near Eastern Studies at Princeton University. The 9/11 attacks catapulted Lewis into the public eye. The *Wall Street Journal* called him "the single most important intellectual countering the conventional wisdom on managing the conflict between radical Islam and the West."[31] He was proclaimed the "doyen of Middle Eastern studies" by the *New York Times Book Review*,[32] "the great Islamic scholar" by the *Washington Post*,[33] and "arguably the most respected Islamic scholar in the West" by *Newsday*.[34] Vice President Dick Cheney, National Security Adviser Condoleezza Rice, Deputy Secretary of Defense Paul Wolfowitz, and Senior Presidential Advisor Karl Rove all consulted him.

Lewis enjoys outstanding credentials: a BA in Middle Eastern history from the University of London in the 1930s; fluency in Turkish, Persian, Hebrew, and Arabic; first-hand experience of the Middle East in the 1940s as an intelligence official for the British government; a successful career teaching at London's renowned School of Oriental and African Studies; and culminating in a distinguished position in America's Ivy League establishment. As a scholar Lewis has produced a detailed and profound body of work on subjects ranging from antiquity to the Mongol invasions in the thirteenth century; the rise and fall of Ottoman rule; the import of Western nationalism; ninteeenth- and twentieth-century British and French regional involvement; the failure of Islamic states to prevent the establishment of Israel; and the scientific, technological, industrial, and political revolutions that transformed the wealth and power of the West in relation to that of Islamic societies.

Furthermore, in his article "The Roots of Muslim Rage," which was published in the September 1990 issue of *Atlantic Monthly* (subsequently republished in the Summer 2001 issue of *Policy Magazine*), Lewis could plausibly claim to have foreseen the rise of Al-Qaeda and the series of attacks on American entities that culminated in 9/11.[35] This article traced what Lewis saw as a rising sense of Muslim humiliation at the hands of the West starting with the final repulse of the Ottoman Caliphate outside the gates of Vienna in 1683 and accelerating through the nineteenth and twentieth centuries. It gave birth to the concept of a "clash of civilizations," later borrowed and supersized by Huntington, and it drew attention to the different Christian and Islamic traditions regarding the separation of church and state. Specialists will take exception with some of Lewis's arguments—the failure to note Western complicity in the overthrow of Iranian Prime Minister Muhammad Mossadeq, and the description of the shah as "Westernizing"; the conflation of the terms *Ottoman*, *Arab*, *Islamic*, and *fundamentalist*; the shortchanging of the age-old debate within Islam between the ummah (or community) and ulema (or "wise men," specifically Muslim scholars trained in Islam and Islamic law)—but his conclusion is striking:

The movement nowadays called fundamentalism is not the only Islamic tradition. There are others, more tolerant, more open that helped to inspire the great achievements of Islamic civilization in the past, and we may hope that these other traditions will in time prevail. But before this issue is decided there will be a hard struggle, in which we of the West can do little or nothing. Even the attempt might do harm, for these are issues that Muslims must decide among themselves. And in the meantime, we must take great care on all sides to avoid the danger of a new era of religious wars, arising from the exacerbation of differences and the revival of ancient prejudices.[36]

These words draw on a theme that runs throughout Lewis's writing. In his 1966 work *The Arabs in History* he discussed the various paths that Arab Islamic culture might follow: submission to the West, the mirage of a lost theocratic ideal, or a recovery of a self-confident moderate identity. For the third path to be followed, he wrote, "the removal of the irritant of foreign interference is a pre-requisite so that they may succeed in renewing their society from within."[37]

So what happened between the writing of the *Atlantic* article and Lewis's interview with senior *Newsweek* editor Michael Hirsh in 2003 when he said, "I have no doubt that September 11 was the opening salvo of the final battle"?[38] Later he told C-SPAN, "In a sense, they've been hating us for centuries . . . You have this millennial rivalry between two world religions, and now, from their point of view, the wrong one seems to be winning."[39] America, he said, had two choices: "Get tough or get out." Getting out meant finding a substitute for oil "so the Middle East no longer matters. Leave them to their own devices."[40] Getting tough meant installing secularized, Westernized Arab democracies that would cast off the medieval shackles of Islam and enter modernity. Even these two choices were apparently too many: as Lewis emphasized to the Defense Policy Board just eight days after the attacks, only getting tough would avert still worse terrorism against America in the future. The whole region had to be transformed. The scholar's recommendation to

Vice President Cheney was reportedly simple: "Get on with it. Don't dither."[41]

Lewis soon became a media star, giving regular television interviews and publishing pieces with such titles as "A War of Resolve" and "A Time for Toppling," all the while emphasizing that the long-term roots of 9/11 lay in the great struggle between Christendom and Islam.[42] Elevated to the level of national wise man, Lewis was free to promote, almost without critical dissent, his notion that America must transform the Middle East if it wishes to be safe, that toppling Saddam Hussein's regime (never mind that it was one of the most secular regimes in the Arab Middle East) was the easiest route into this process, and that Westerners could expect to be received as liberators.

"One is often told," Lewis contended, "that if we succeed in overthrowing the regimes of what President Bush has rightly called the 'Axis of Evil,' the scenes of rejoicing in their cities would even exceed those that followed the liberation of Kabul." And if regime change seemed hazardous, he warned, "the dangers of inaction are greater than those of action."[43] This was certainly the view of the war's advocates, but most of them were not distinguished Middle East experts. Lewis could have used his years of scholarship and analysis to deliver some cautionary analysis. Still, his conclusions are his to draw.

Perhaps we can forgive the statements on cable television. After all, we have argued that this is a dysfunctional medium in which the apt phrase triumphs over substance. But why the sudden rush of books repackaging Lewis's scholarship in terms that can only be explained as commercial? Why, for example, was a book focusing primarily on Turkey's relatively successful transition to modernism entitled *What Went Wrong?* when it might as easily have been called *What Went Right?* Why does a "crisis" of Islam—to cite another quick post–9/11 title, *The Crisis of Islam: Holy War and Unholy Terror*—arise when confrontation with the West manifests itself but not when the object of the revolt is the Ottoman Empire? What went wrong in this case, we would argue, is that the imperatives of the moment won out over scholarship. The rational center failed to hold.

The failure to provide balance in the face of populist orthodoxy is not simply a matter for regret inside academic cloisters. It represents a significant weakness in the nation's foreign policy capabilities. As the US position in the world grows less unchallengeable, its need for finely calibrated policies rises. This fact brings with it a temptation to seek "policy relevance" by moving onto the policy makers' turf. This is not easy to resist—invitations to the White House or the Pentagon are substantial career boosters—but if resistance fails, then policy will suffer.

AMERICA HATERS: SAME GENUS, DIFFERENT SPECIES

Just as the lure of celebrity makes it difficult for preeminent intellectuals to maintain a balance between opinion advocacy and academic detachment when they are aligned with the political trends, so the temptations of celebrity pose different problems when they are outside the charmed circle. The sort of opposition such people face may be found in the crisp words of David Horowitz, President of the Center for the Study of Popular Culture: "When your country is attacked there can be no such thing as an 'anti-war' movement. Protesters against America's war on terror, are not peaceniks, they are America-haters and saboteurs, and they should be treated as such."[44]

The label "America haters" is an invidious one, for many critics of the current Administration are just as passionately patriotic as those who actively support it. Their patriotism does not rule out the prospect that the country has been tarnished by its current policies. But these critics hardly raise the level of debate when they adopt essentially the same tactics, namely calling into question the good faith of the Americans who support and implement those policies. They make themselves just as easily dismissible as anti-American foreign critics who range from serious scholars such as Jürgen Habermas to pop writers like Emmanuel Todd, whose virulent deconstructions of all things American top the best-seller lists in Europe and Asia.

Here, our discussion considers three examples: Professor Noam Chomsky of the Massachusetts Institute of Technology; Professor Chalmers Johnson, formerly of the University of California at Berkeley and San Diego; and Professor Paul Krugman of Princeton University who is also a columnist for the *New York Times*. Like the other experts we discuss in this book, they are here because of their professional distinction and because they have thrown themselves into the debate about the nation's critical foreign policy challenges. Our argument is that they and other liberal critics of American foreign policy, such as the University of Maryland professor Benjamin Barber or the late Susan Sontag, have fallen short of the standards needed in oppositional public intellectuals. Instead of bringing their authority and scholarly expertise to bear, they have become street fighters, comparable in some ways to entertainment polemicists such as Al Franken or Michael Moore whose audiences are much wider. They have sacrificed their standing. They attract a devoted following to the point where they connect almost exclusively with those who agree with them, thus antagonizing many others and providing an easy target for their opponents.

The ensuing loss to the national discourse is considerable. Conservative foreign policy analysts tend to concentrate on power relationships and free-market economics. Alternatively, when they look at social or cultural issues they do so from the point of view of the dominant strain. This too often leaves out or demeans a vast range of crucial factors in the interaction of nations—relating to culture, history, perceptions of justice and equity, and so on—that those on the liberal-progressive side of the continuum could and should inject into the foreign policy debate. Their failure to do so in a persuasive way provides a space for nonexpert counterextremism to flourish.

Noam Chomsky

In 1969 Noam Chomsky went to Oxford to give the John Locke lectures, one of the most distinguished lecture series in philosophy. Both of us were in residence there at the time. Chomsky was already a towering figure in what was then the relatively new discipline of linguistics, and he spoke to packed lecture halls. Since that time his influence within linguistics has only increased. He does not lack for academic critics, but there is little doubt that he has set new standards in this field.

For the general public, Chomsky was and is much better known as a consistent critic of US policy on almost everything. Government is not his primary expertise, but it is his primary passion. This is not a good mixture. In essence, he argues that the US has for decades been the world's leading terrorist state. Far from dismissing the rantings of Osama bin Laden, he treats them as serious explanations of why some parts of the world regard Washington as a terrorist regime. For Chomsky the shameful record is replete: Vietnam, Laos, Cambodia, Colombia, Nicaragua, Panama, Sudan, and Turkey are only the beginning.

Chomsky contends that Washington does more than simply acquiesce in the oppression of peoples in other parts of the world; it supports despots when doing so suits American interests. As a historical fact, there is some truth in this. Secretary of State Condoleezza Rice admitted as much in a speech at the American University in Cairo on June 20, 2005.[45] President Bush made much the same point in a speech in May 2005, when he described the Yalta agreement as following in the

> unjust tradition of Munich and the Molotov-Ribbentrop Pact. Once again, when powerful governments negotiated, the freedom of small nations was somehow expendable. Yet this attempt to sacrifice freedom for the sake of stability left a continent divided and unstable. The captivity of millions in Central and Eastern Europe will be remembered as one of the greatest wrongs of history.[46]

Yet, Chomsky takes the argument much further. Giving no place to real-world policy constraints, he asserts that the repression of peoples is itself a specific American interest and a distinct objective of American policy. He calls this the "threat of a good example," by which he means that a characteristic of American policy is to prevent the emergence of a successful non-American style of reform, for example, through land redistribution in Central America, which might act as a "good example" to other potential reformers looking for alternatives to the US model.[47]

No country, no matter how unimportant, is exempt from this treatment. In fact, it is the weakest, poorest countries that often arouse Chomsky's most intense interest. For example, when Grenada embarked on what he saw as a mild social revolution, Washington quickly moved to destroy the threat by invading the island. When a low-level social revolution began to develop in Laos, Washington undertook secret bombing to wipe out large sections of the population. American actions in Nicaragua and El Salvador during the Cold War apparently also sprang from this philosophy. The reason for all this, Chomsky says, is that the weaker and poorer a country is, the more dangerous it is *as an example.* If a tiny, poor country like Grenada can bring about a better life for its people, some other place that has more resources will ask, "why not us?" This prospect apparently terrifies Washington's "elite class."

For decades, says Chomsky, the dominant governing philosophy in Washington has been that if you want a global system "subordinated to the needs of US investors, you can't let pieces of it wander off." What the United States government seeks is "security for the upper classes and large foreign enterprises." If it can achieve this with formal democratic devices, fine, but if not, "the threat to stability posed by a good example has to be destroyed before the virus infects others." That is why even the tiniest speck poses a threat "and may have to be crushed."[48] With classical left-wing reductionism, Chomsky declares that the people running the U.S government are driven by their desire for a global empire of market share. They support corrupt and oppressive governments in places like the Middle East because access to oil at a stable price is absolutely fundamental to the United States and other national economies to sustain themselves and their global dominion. Thus, the Bush Doctrine of preventive war—

which Chomsky defines as great empire building—does not, in his view, represent a break with the past. He believes it has been the operating principle of American foreign policy for many years. Since the 1940s Washington has regarded the world in terms of sources of strategic power and material prizes and has been committed for decades to taking control over a core oil producer while placing a reliable military base at the heart of the world's major energy-producing region. Washington would prefer, for example, "an iron fisted Iraqi Junta" but for now must be satisfied to seek the second best thing—democracy.[49]

In Chomsky's world view, all that America does abroad is part of the great right-wing conspiracy. American foreign policy is in the hands of a sinister elite that holds a vested interest in maintaining the status quo around the world. Meanwhile, another favorite idea of Chomsky's is that resistance to this domination inside the United States is subdued by corporate elites who completely control the flow of information available in the public space.

In their inherent simplicity, these interpretations—framed by the notion of America as Evil—are sharply delineated. Theories that feature satanic powers such as an imperial Washington motivated by a thirst for world dominion are easy to grasp, so long as one is a member of Chomsky's ideological communion. But in his capacity as a scholar, Chomsky is rendering a disservice by creating an intellectual environment in which he overrides the details and facts of a reality infinitely more nuanced than he is presenting. There is, for example, a straightforward argument that the global economy—not just the US economy—depends on the foundation of secure access to oil from the Middle East and that the policies of the world's only superpower relate to a structural interest in ensuring that the global economy remains stable. By no means does this exhaust the range of interpretations of American policy. The point is not that the United States has never pursued a cynical, self-interested, or frankly destructive policy; but Chomsky's political ideas are precisely the sort of theories that, in his field of expertise, he would reject out of hand. They are not up to the standard of analysis one expects from an expert—even one whose expertise is far removed from the subject at hand.

Rather than understanding policy making as a layered and fractured process involving the competing voices of elected officials, career advisers, professional analysts, and various political actors from across the polity, Chomsky invariably interprets official policy as following the wishes of "the powerful" or "the elite," who routinely bomb and terrorize populations around the world in defense of their "elite interests."

There is an old joke about a poor Jewish tailor who says his favorite book is *The Protocols of the Elders of Zion* because "it makes us seem so powerful." Chomsky's scenario betrays a similar misunderstanding of the mechanics of policy making. The big secret of Washington is that there *is* no single elite able to plot world domination from the dusty reading rooms of the city's luncheon clubs. One government official described policy making like this: "you wake up in the morning, spend your whole day fighting to be heard, go to bed and start all over the next day."

But for Chomsky, the vaguely defined "they" are behind every policy. He refuses to acknowledge legitimate national security concerns or plausible sources of anxiety that might have swayed policy makers' decisions. It is ever the capitalist puppet masters. The extent to which the mistaken Domino/Containment Theory preoccupied government officials and evolved into a political neurosis that inexorably propelled America into Vietnam after 1954 is well documented. Yet, misguided assumptions, anxieties within a prevailing political culture, and systemic failures that can lead to mistaken policies never appear in Chomsky's analysis. American global domination is the simple motivation behind every policy.

Though his name is more widely recognized than that of any other intellectual in the world, Chomsky's critique fails to contribute to the debate of America's crucial challenges. Like his analogue Gore Vidal, his calls go unheard. The great irony is that the reason for his failure is that he has adopted exactly the extremist simplicity that he criticizes in his opponents.

Chalmers Johnson

The case of Chalmers Johnson is a little different. Johnson is a foreign policy specialist with deeply anchored expertise on China and Japan. As the United States feels its way toward a new posture in East Asia, his voice should be among the most prominent. Instead, he has taken himself out of the mix, primarily because he has allowed himself to be dismissed, however absurdly, as an enemy of America. Let us look at his background.

Chalmers Johnson is a former US Navy officer whose first visit to Japan, in 1953, began a lifelong engagement with East Asia. He served for many years as a professor at the Berkeley and San Diego campuses of the University of California, taking charge of Berkeley's Center for Chinese Studies at the age of thirty-six. In retirement he cofounded the Japan Policy Research Institute, a small foundation located outside San Francisco, of which he remains President. Unlike Chomsky he comes from a conventional anti-Communist Cold War background; he once saw the "Communist revolution in China as a dangerous, deeply disturbing development." He supported the Vietnam War and records that he was "irritated by campus anti-war protesters."[50]

Johnson established his academic reputation on Asian affairs with his 1962 book, *Peasant Nationalism and Communist Power*, and his 1983 book, *MITI and the Japanese Miracle*. His 1973 book, *Autopsy on People's War*, is still quoted by military analysts struggling to make sense of the Iraqi insurgency. But he is far better known for three recent books: *Blowback: The Costs and Consequences of American Empire* (2000), *The Sorrows of Empire: Militarism, Secrecy, and the End of the Republic* (2004), and *Nemesis: The Crisis of the American Republic* (2006). We will talk mainly about the first two.

In *Blowback* the Clinton Administration comes in for unremitting criticism on a charge that may surprise many conservatives, namely that it was overly aggressive on the military front. This charge derives from a personal epiphany by Johnson, who writes that his support for the Vietnam War arose because he "knew too much about the international communist movement and not enough about the United States government and its Department of Defense." Based on this, he develops the thesis of "blowback," which states that the "malign acts of 'terrorists, drug lords, rogue states and illegal arms merchants' often turn out to be the blowback for earlier American operations." Simply put, a "nation reaps what it sows."[51]

The *reductio ad absurdum* of this theory, which is regrettably the point Johnson inhabits, is that nothing bad occurs in this world unless it is America's fault. Of the genocidal Pol Pot in Cambodia, for example, he writes that "without the United States government's Vietnam-era savagery he could never have come to power."[52] The point here is that he uses an over-the-top word like *savagery* to suggest a direct US causal link to genocide. He attributes coresponsibility for the killing during the 1980 Kwanju Uprising in Korea to American military and diplomatic figures such as William Gleysteen, General John Wickham, Richard Holbrooke, and Warren Christopher and states that US policy in Central America "has created genocidal conditions." The 1993 attacks on the World Trade Center in New York were caused by the Gulf War and American ties to Israel. With regard to economic matters, he approvingly quotes a description of Richard Nixon's 1971 abandonment of the Bretton Woods fixed exchange system as the "single most destructive act of the postwar world. The West has returned to the monetary barbarity and instability of the 19th century."[53]

The Sorrows of Empire picks up where *Blowback* leaves off. Here, the target is the Bush Administration. Having made the case in *Blowback* that the Clinton Administration's retaliation to the 1998 bombings of the US Embassies in Kenya and Tanzania meant that "future blowback possibilities are seeded into the world," Johnson makes the corollary assertion: placing responsibility for 9/11 on the fact that the "United States was something other than what it professed to be, that it was, in

fact, a military juggernaut intent on world domination."⁵⁴ Johnson rein-
terprets American foreign policy since the declaration of the Monroe
Doctrine in 1823 as purposefully and designedly imperialist—and does
so with a virulence that carries him far beyond such earlier proponents
of this approach as Charles A. Beard and William Appleman Williams.
The CIA is now "just one of the secret commando units maintained by
our government."⁵⁵ All US agencies, including the Agency for International Development and the United States Information Agency, abet the
imperial project by supplying a "veritable army of colonial administra-
tors."⁵⁶ Globalization is just another name for the exploitation of the
poor by American pharmaceutical corporations.

There is, of course, a constituency for these views. But it does not include those who will simply not recognize the embittered description of
their country in Johnson's analysis. As a result Johnson's hard-earned expertise goes to waste. Not only that, he opens the door to opportunistic counterattack from the most illiberal elements in American society, who take
delight in tainting moderate foreign policy critiques (such as those offered
by Anatol Lieven's *America Right or Wrong*, Michael Scheuer's *Imperial
Hubris*, or Stephen Kinzer's *Overthrow*) with extremists like Johnson.⁵⁷

Paul Krugman

Paul Krugman is an economist of established reputation who achieved
tenure at the Massachusetts Institute of Technology while not yet thirty
years old. He is the author of several standard texts on international economics. In 1991 he was awarded the John Bates Clark medal, given every
two years by the American Economic Association to the best American
economist under forty. He is now a professor of economics at Princeton.

A distinguished economist with a gift for vivid writing is a rare treasure.
But in hindsight, one might suspect that Krugman has long felt the temptations of popular punditry. In his 1989 book *Foreign Direct Investment in
the United States* (with Edward Graham), which provided an oasis of calm

amid the hysteria about Japanese investment in the United States, he issues a warning against popular books that "contain a remarkable absence of serious analytical discussion" but instead draw on "anecdotes and *a priori* judgments rather than a systematic analysis of the data." He cautions that "popular treatments of foreign direct investment have sometimes seemed to suggest that a wholesale takeover of US assets is occurring."[58] In another 1989 book, *Exchange-Rate Instability*, he criticizes analysts who eschew the "usual ideas of careful analysis and rigorous evidence."[59]

In many ways, Krugman's comment perfectly foreshadows his own trajectory. His next book, *The Age of Diminished Expectations* (1990), represents a deliberate new direction for him. In the preface he talks about three kinds of economics books: "Greek letter," by which he means dense technical argumentation for the profession; "up and down," or business-book analysis of the vicissitudes of the market; and "airport," which he derides as "usually fun, rarely well informed, never serious."[60] Yet the last is the path Krugman chose.

Except for two undergraduate textbooks, coauthored with Robin Wells and published in 2004 and 2005, Krugman has become a populist. *The Age of Diminished Expectations* was followed in rapid succession by *Pop Internationalism, Peddling Prosperity, The Accidental Theorist, Fuzzy Math: The Essential Guide to the Bush Tax Plan*, and *The Great Unraveling*. Some of these books recycled material already published in *Slate* or *Fortune* magazines or in the *New York Times*, where he became a twice-weekly columnist in 2000. All of them have sold very well. His columns in the *New York Times* are often among the paper's most e-mailed.

It is not for us to question a particular academic's choice of writing style or venue. But as we seek in this book to identify some of the reasons why an expert-based foreign policy discourse is so hard to achieve, we feel justified in drawing attention to the dangerous bargain Krugman has struck when he moves from economics, on which he writes with real authority, to foreign policy, where he is simply an unusually articulate and well-positioned lay citizen.

Between early 2003 and mid-2005, the subject of Iraq was never far away from Krugman's thoughts. Of some 124 columns published between March 2003 and July 2005, 94 concerned Iraq, not far short of one per week. Of course, Iraq was the dominant foreign policy issue of the time, and Krugman's mandate from the *Times* clearly includes the issue. We quote the concern raised by the *New York Times* public editor Daniel Okrent: that Krugman "has the disturbing habit of shaping, slicing and selectively citing numbers in a fashion that pleases his acolytes but leaves him open to substantive assaults."[61]

Let us look at some examples. Here are some lines from Krugman's column of September 21, 2004:

It [scaling back expectations] also means accepting the likelihood that Iraq will not have a strong central government—and that local leaders will end up with a lot of autonomy. This doesn't have to mean creating havens for hostile forces: remember that for a year after Saddam's fall, moderate Shiite clerics effectively governed large areas of Iraq and kept them relatively peaceful. It was the continuing irritant of the US occupation that empowered radicals like Moktada al-Sadr.

So what's the answer? Here's one thought: much of US policy in Iraq—delaying elections, trying to come up with a formula that blocks simple majority rule, trying to install first Mr. Chalabi, then Mr. Allawi, as strongman—can be seen as a persistent effort to avoid giving Grand Ayatollah Ali al-Sistani his natural dominant role. But recent events in Najaf have demonstrated both the cleric's awesome influence and the limits of American power. Isn't it time to realize that we could do a lot worse than Mr. Sistani, and give him pretty much whatever he wants?

Yet we're still doing it. Ayad Allawi is, probably, something of a thug. Still, it's in our interests that he succeed.[62]

Opponents of the Bush Administration's Iraq policy find such comments refreshingly sensible. But let us look more closely. Here is Krugman, the credentialed economist, writing about the intricacies of Iraqi Shiite politics. He draws distinctions between moderates and radicals; he throws his support to one leader and then another; he endorses a federal style of government. The reader is entitled to ask where the factual knowledge to support these judgments comes from.

To take another example, from May 16, 2005: "In other words, the people who got us into Iraq have done exactly what they falsely accused Bill Clinton of doing: they have stripped America of its capacity to respond to real threats."[63] Here, we see economist Krugman writing about America's military posture.

And on November 25, 2003, Krugman had this to say about President Bush:

> He was a stock character in 19th-century fiction: the wastrel son who runs up gambling debts in the belief that his wealthy family, concerned for its prestige, will have no choice but to pay off his creditors. In the novels such characters always come to a bad end. Either they bring ruin to their families, or they eventually find themselves disowned. George Bush reminds me of those characters—and not just because of his early career, in which friends of the family repeatedly bailed out his failing business ventures. Now that he sits in the White House, he's still counting on other people to settle his debts—not to protect the reputation of his family, but to protect the reputation of the country.[64]

This suggests that Krugman's writing about Iraq is driven by a personal distaste for President Bush. Krugman makes no apology for this. He writes: "How important is civility? I'm all for good manners, but this isn't a dinner party. The opposing sides in our national debate are far apart on fundamental issues, from fiscal and environmental policies to national security and civil liberties. It's the duty of pundits and politicians to make those differences clear, not to play them down for fear that someone will be offended."[65]

There is nothing wrong with Krugman the journalist writing about Iraq policy, the character of the President, or any other subject. But in doing so, he is striking a dangerous bargain that jeopardizes his standing as an expert. When he leaves economics, where he can assert an advantage over his readers in both information and analytic expertise, and ventures into the foreign policy field, where he enjoys no such advantage, he deflates his own authority. Once he is forced to rely not on expertise but on personal opinion, his biases and prejudices—in this case, a relentless hostility to the Bush Administration—become clear.

The difficulty is that Krugman is not simply a guy solving the world's problems from the back of his pickup truck. He is an expert with a real capacity to present the dense complexities of economics in terms that make sense to lay readers. But his Faustian arrangement with the media has put that capacity at risk. His expert commentaries on economic issues—many of which are excellent—are now perceived as an extension of his wish to attack the Bush Administration. In essence, he has committed precisely the error he warned against in *Pop Internationalism*:[66] he has become a "policy entrepreneur," for whom the ideological thrust of his argument is more important than a dispassionate sifting of the evidence. Only Krugman is responsible for this situation, but we are all losers by it. The lure of celebrity has captured another scalp.

Readers may object that we are, in the first instance, trying to limit the celebrity of prominent pro-Administration intellectuals such as Huntington and Lewis whose ideas have become fashionable; and in the second instance that we are trying to reign in the left and house-train passionate pundits so that they tone down their attacks. We accept both charges. In fact, we *are* doing both these things, but for a good reason. Our concern is that as the center of gravity of American foreign policy moves toward the East, we can ill afford to lose Chalmers Johnson's expertise or his passionate insistence on US adherence to international law. His warnings about growing anti-American hostility in Korea and Japan are worth considering—or would be if they were delivered with greater respect for their audience. Noam Chomsky usefully reminds us that there is another universe of perceptions out there about American actions and intentions. The dangers of empire he points to are not negligible. Paul Krugman has much to offer on the economic consequences of ill-considered foreign policy adventures. Yet all this is being lost either in a storm of invective sown by these writers themselves or in an unseemly scramble for celebrity where their credibility is squandered and their contribution to the national policy debate is marginalized.

The point applies equally to Samuel Huntington, Bernard Lewis, and Graham Allison, whose contribution to the foreign policy debate has also been compromised. As the nation struggles to balance its concerns about privacy and civil liberties with the need to prevent another terror attack, and to allocate resources for recovery in the event of an attack, we look to people like Allison for clear and rational analysis, not alarmist scenarios. Moreover, who more than Harvard's Huntington or Princeton's Lewis can help to fashion balanced and constructive responses to the challenges raised by radical Islam? This is of vital concern. The supply of seasoned expertise to the foreign policy debate is every bit as essential as the supply of engineers or computer scientists to our graduate schools.

The posture these men have taken is particularly disappointing because, while they have advanced their own celebrity, they have abetted the Big Idea in ways that marginalize even their own remarkable expertise—ranging from a knowledge of Farsi and the intricacies of Middle Eastern history, to the optimum steps for nuclear decontamination, to the intricacies of development economics. The national discourse, which could have benefited greatly from their suggestions on, for example, how the question of democracy-building in Iraq might have been approached differently, was denied that expertise. Moreover, on talk shows and in public debates, they lent the weight of their prodigious reputations to the Administration's flawed rationale so that lesser voices, speaking truth to power, were drowned out. This is cause for reflection; it is true institutional failure.

SIX

Elites and the Use of Force

On July 29, 2004, Senator John Kerry accepted the Democratic Party's nomination for President with the words "John Kerry, reporting for duty." The rapturous acclamation he received gave his party hope that it had finessed the decades-old suspicion among voters that the Democrats are not to be trusted on security issues.

The hope proved stillborn. But the fact that Kerry—who has both experience in sharp-end combat and an understanding of war's limitations as national policy—chose to play up his martial side illustrates the potency of one of the more important Big Ideas of our time: namely, that America's advantage in foreign policy lies in its military power and willingness to use it. This notion has bred a substantial literature—by no means confined to conservative writers—on what is called the "Revolution in Military Affairs" and the expansive options this prowess in war fighting opens for the United States. Among significant elements of the high-ranking elected and appointed government officials, military power is not seen simply as a matter of self-defense or a last resort but as an instrument for recasting political cultures and governments around the world to accept American values and governing principles and to protect American interests. As the 2005 National Defense Strategy put it, the

United States needs to be "postured . . . for extended conflict and continuous transformation."[1] This approach was confirmed in the 2006 Quadrennial Defense Review released in February 2006. The Republican and Democratic Parties and the national security elite, whether left or right, dissident or mainstream, have generally come to accept this view.[2]

That the new high-tech military has transformed the way the United States conducts its foreign policy was evident in both the Balkan and Iraq wars, and it features prominently in thinking about Iran and more distant scenarios involving China. Of pressing importance, however, is a question largely unaddressed, namely whether our expectations about the utility of military force are dangerously unrealistic. In this chapter, we consider whether America's recent difficulties in Iraq, for example, result from the imperfect execution of an essentially sound idea (this has been the position of many Democratic elites[3]), and whether, by putting their trust in a Big Idea, American policy makers are condemning themselves to repeated disappointment.

Federal expenditure figures underline the priority attached to maintaining the US advantage. The fiscal year 2006 federal budget request to Congress represented a 41 percent increase over 2001 and a 4.8 percent increase over 2005. When supplemental requests are factored in, the military budget for 2005 comfortably exceeded half a trillion dollars. The comparative numbers are even more telling. In 2001 the *difference* between spending on the military (including international military assistance) and all other civilian forms of international activity (such as diplomacy, international aid, humanitarian relief, and information) was just under $300 billion ($311.44 billion for the former and $11.52 billion for the latter). For 2002, the year immediately following 9/11, the difference rose to $436 billion. For 2010 the Office of Management and Budget projects it to be $477 billion. Over the two George W. Bush terms (spending for the fiscal years 2001–2008), we estimate the cumulative excess between spending on the military side of America's international posture and the civilian, diplomatic side to be more than $3.5 *trillion.* This trend continued in the 2007 defense budget, which foresaw spending close to $600 billion. As the proportion of nonsecurity spending in the federal budget continues to shrink, this divergence is set to increase not only in nominal cash terms but as hardwired percentages of national spending. These figures are a stark contrast to US allies such as Britain and France. Both countries have relatively large militaries, but military and civilian spending are more evenly balanced. The US approach is closer to that of China, which also devotes a disproportionate share of international spending to its military.[4]

The public is not troubled by the absolute size of the defense budget, even when other discretionary spending has to be held back in compensation. Despite unusually fulsome recourse to supplementary appropriations, there is little subterfuge on this issue. Neither as a candidate well before 9/11 nor as President has Bush made any secret of the importance he assigns to defense spending. His solid credentials on this issue assisted his re-election. The public also seems unworried about these allocations between military and civilian *international* spending. In polls conducted by the Pew Research Center for the People and the Press, the present level of defense spending wins solid majorities. Spending on diplomatic and foreign aid attracts minimal support. By a ratio of nearly three to one, Americans believe that the use of force is likely to be more effective in fighting terrorism than nonmilitary approaches like poverty alleviation.[5]

This predisposition in favor of military force is relatively new. In an address to a duly respectful audience assembled in the majestic reception room of one of Washington's most exclusive private clubs, Henry Kissinger underlined the change since his time in office. He noted that the hardest foreign policy challenge he faced as Secretary of State had been to create a political consensus around the use of military power.

That was then. Today, an alternative discourse favoring military force is apparent among both liberal and conservative foreign policy elites. It is particularly marked among the civilian leadership, who are often more aggressive in their advocacy of force than the professional military. Secretary of State Madeleine Albright's question in 1994 to then Chairman of the Joint Chiefs of Staff Colin Powell, "What are we saving this superb military for, Colin, if we can't use it?" has been repeatedly cited as an example of the civilian embrace of war.[6] It is only a slight exaggeration to say that, in complete contrast to Kissinger's day, the modern debate is about when and how we should "lean forward." Were he in office today, Kissinger would find that the cautionary example of Vietnam has lost its persuasive power. Today's watchword is "Munich," with all its connotations of not doing enough soon enough. There is literally no part of the planet—which the Pentagon calls the "global commons"—for which there is no US military contingency plan. Space is the final frontier, and even that is filling up rapidly with programs such as the US Strategic Command's Global Strike.[7]

This commitment to the use of military force has not come about by accident. It arises from the decisive influence of three Americans, the late Albert Wohlstetter, Andrew Marshall, and the late Admiral Arthur Cebrowski. The first two are supreme examples of the "defense intellectual," while the last put their ideas into operational effect when he led the Pentagon's Office of Force Transformation from 2001 until shortly before his death in November 2005. *Defense intellectual* is a made-in-America profession that has arisen from the Pentagon's practice of outsourcing its strategic thinking to civilian research institutions. Despite their enormous influence, these men are hardly household names. So who are they?

Albert Wohlstetter was born in New York in 1914 and died in Los Angeles in 1997. Trained as a mathematician, he became one of the principal intellectual forces behind US nuclear strategy, first at the RAND Corporation, which he joined soon after its founding in 1949, and later at various universities, most notably the University of Chicago. In 1985, along with his wife, Roberta, he received the Presidential Medal of Freedom from President Ronald Reagan. He is memorialized by the eponymous Wohlstetter Auditorium at the American Enterprise Institute, itself the home to so many proponents of modern "neo-war" theorizing.

Andrew W. Marshall was born in 1921. In 1949 he was one of the founding members of the RAND Corporation, where he overlapped with Wohlstetter. He was one of the pioneers of the emerging discipline of "systems analysis" but was also one of the first to recognize its limitations. At present he directs the Office of Net Assessment in the Pentagon, a job he has held since 1973, when the office was established. Its purposes involved taking an "even-handed look at both sides" in balance-of-power comparisons with the idea of providing "side-by-side, head-to-head, and major systems comparisons, as well as data on trends, qualitative factors, and examinations of key asymmetries."

Arthur Cebrowski was born in Passaic, New Jersey, in 1942. He was a 1964 graduate of Villanova University, after which he entered the US Navy. Following thirty-seven years of naval service, he was appointed in 2001 as director of the Office of Force Transformation, a post he held until its disbanding in September 2004. In the Pentagon's description, the purpose of this office is to "link transformation to strategic functions, evaluate the transformation efforts of the Military Departments, and promote synergy by recommending steps to integrate ongoing transformation activities." For anyone who has ever witnessed one of the PowerPoint presentations by Cebrowski or one of his disciples (much their favored format) there was no mistaking that that "transformation"—meaning the claimed change from a twentieth- to a twenty-first-century mode of warfighting—was the concept of the day. Its uncritical application in Iraq exposes what can happen when framing concepts shut down debate.

The policy influence of these men reaches much further than these lapidary entries. To start with Wohlstetter, the achievement for which he is normally given credit took place while he was still at the RAND Corporation, when he authored a paper that brought about a review of the basing policy of the Strategic Air Command. This led to a decision to base the bombers deep in the US heartland on well-protected sites, effectively ensuring that the United States would be able to survive a first-strike nuclear attack from the Soviet Union and still be in a position to retaliate. Among the results was a strengthened deterrence that made nuclear war less likely. As a theorist concerned with enhancing the survivability of US nuclear weapons systems, he later became one of the earliest champions of strategic missile defense.

But Wohlstetter's greatest influence lies elsewhere. From the mid–1970s he was among the first to realize the potential of emerging technology in the field of targeting accuracy. Working with a concept called "circular error probable" (CEP)—the radius of a circle within which 50 percent of a specified munitions system, such as a missile, will fall—he understood that as the radius of the circular error decreases, so the confidence that the target will be destroyed increases, eventually reaching 100 percent. This led him to champion a concept called "discriminate deterrence," which anticipated that war-fighting below the level of global engagement would be fought with lower-yield nonnuclear weapons made as effective as their high-yield nuclear predecessors through their much greater accuracy. This idea laid the groundwork for the precision wars now being fought by the United States.

Upon this groundwork, Marshall then built the intellectual super-structure. In the words of a Congressional Research Service study:

Since the late 1980s, Andrew Marshall . . . has probably been the main catalyst inside the government examining the potential for a Revolution in Military Affairs (RMA). It is Marshall's hypothesis that today we are in a period equivalent to that immediately after the end of World War I in which the technologies, doctrines and organizations which were to win World War II were just being formed. Marshall's office has taken the lead in financing studies on the history of military innovation in the pre-World War II period—innovation which led to such things as carrier strike aviation, amphibious warfare, and Blitzkrieg—and in sponsoring its own war games and other RMA studies today.[8]

The hypothesis this study spoke of led to an immense blossoming of military technological inventiveness, organized by the Pentagon's Defense Advanced Research Projects Agency (DARPA) and put into doctrinal ef-fect by Admiral Cebrowski in the form of "network-centric warfare," which allows the substitution of "information for mass."[9] Wars can be fought with fewer large platforms, like ships and planes, and fewer contract troops. As a result the United States established a dominant lead in two critical areas of modern warfare: the use of information technology (IT) to link together all the fighting platforms in a particular space and thus give commanders a real-time overview of the battlefield, and increasingly accurate munitions that can be delivered under all weather conditions from remote firing positions.

The first capability, which is "C4ISR" in military jargon—for command, control, communications, computers, intelligence, surveillance, and reconnaissance—is designed to more or less abolish the "fog of war," at least as it occurs on the battlefield. The second minimizes the risk of collateral damage and loss of American lives. While the first Gulf War demonstrated the effectiveness of these munitions against a conventional army deployed in the open desert, the real proof came in the Balkan wars. During those campaigns, a B–52 was able to take off from its base at Whiteman Air Force Base in Missouri, fly across the Atlantic with the aid of in-flight refueling, drop a 1,000- or 2,000-pound payload of Joint Direct Attack Munitions from an altitude of 35,000 feet (far above the range of enemy anti-aircraft batteries) into downtown Belgrade with a CEP of 40 feet, and return to Missouri with the crew barely aware that it had been in a war zone.

CEP has now been complemented in the targeteering phase by a new measure, "desired mean point of impact" (DMPI). It is now estimated that a US weapon can hit its DMPI with a deviation of a meter or less. Effectively, this means that there are no two bricks one on top of the other that US weapons cannot dislodge—any time, anywhere in the world, and in any weather. The introduction of highly lethal "unmanned aerial vehicles" (UAVs) like the Predator and Global Hawk have further enhanced the US capability to inflict damage at zero risk to American lives.

The reaction among the military to the Revolution in Military Affairs is instructive. Of all the spheres of government activity, the military may be the branch most addicted to the slogan of the moment. In the late

1990s *jointness* was all the rage, meaning that the four individual services and their weapons systems had to strive to work together. In 2006, *transformation* was the buzzword, although it is giving way to a new one, *effects-based. Transformation* means that all decisions on organization, doctrine, training, and platform acquisitions have to proceed beyond "legacy" ways of doing things and advance to the next generation. Both ideas are subsumed under the rubric of the IT-based Revolution in Military Affairs.

These fads work their way seamlessly into the military vocabulary. Military personnel talk the talk, insert the concepts into their ubiquitous PowerPoint presentations, and affix new badges to weapon systems in accordance with the slogan du jour. Beneath this facile approach, however, it is notable that there is an active debate and an immense bibliography among the uniformed military and at the service colleges about the exact meaning of the claimed Revolution in Military Affairs. While it is generally accepted that advances in IT, especially in munitions targeting and battlefield command and control, have delivered an immense battlefield advantage to US forces, there is less certainty on whether these advances represent a true revolution in the American ability to win *wars.*

The debate has intensified since the start of the second Iraq war, where, all other difficulties aside, questions have persisted about the effectiveness of the vaunted C4ISR assets to deliver the needed intelligence picture.[10] It has, however, to a great extent, escaped the attention of the civilian leadership and the foreign policy elite. Rather, they have seized on Wohlstetter's notion of "discriminate" war to assert that, in the future, wars fought on the basis of America's new capabilities need not be massive affairs involving overwhelming force, need not entail large-scale civilian or American casualties, and can be predicted to achieve quick victories using only the existing all-volunteer force, without the need to revive the draft.

By shrinking the dimensions of war, this vision makes war more economical, reduces the risk to civilian leaders, and gives a new proportionality to war-making. Political scientists such as Princeton's Michael Walzer have proposed an updated theory of "just" wars, the key element of which is that the means must be proportional to the ends.[11] For example, while accurate targeting depends on accurate intelligence and thus does not eliminate error (the destruction of the Chinese Embassy in Belgrade in April 1999 is an egregious example) it does allow political leaders to argue with a reasonable degree of conviction that such mistakes are truly unintentional. Even in the case of civilian deaths—as happened in the Balkans and continue in Afghanistan and, to a much greater extent, Iraq—decision makers can still assert with fairly clear consciences that these remain proportional to the greater good that the military action is intended to accomplish.

While campaigning for President in 1992, Bill Clinton, a former war protester, became one of the first civilian leaders to make this argument when he called for air strikes on Serbia. Richard Holbrooke, a possible Secretary of State had Kerry won the presidency, was among the earliest advocates of bombing against Serbia (and he, too, like his Republican successors, did not put much emphasis on getting UN approval). In a May 2003 *Vanity Fair* interview by Sam Tannenhaus, during the run-up to the invasion of Iraq, Deputy Secretary of Defense Paul Wolfowitz spoke about how Wohlstetter's technological vision had made war easier:

> Albert Wohlstetter was one of the first people, most influential people, to understand what a dramatic difference it would make to have accurate weapons. And that in particular what he was really interested in was the ability . . . to use conventional weapons in ways that people, that only nuclear weapons could be used, to be able to get out of the nuclear mindset kind of things.
>
> But going back much earlier, Albert, starting in '73 or '74 put together something called the New Alternative Workshop or New Alternative Panel. I think it was Workshop. To look at the implications of new technology. But the ones that interested him the most were the ones that

promised great improvements in accuracy. And as a result he was the first intellectual figure to recognize that the Tomahawk cruise missile which was being developed by the Navy primarily as a nuclear delivery system was much more significant as a conventional delivery system because it could give you very accurate weapons with ranges of what we have now, 600 miles or more.

If it hadn't been for Albert, I believe the Tomahawk cruise missile would have been traded away in the SALT II talks in 1976. So it was a matter of considerable personal satisfaction to watch those missiles turning right angle corners in the Gulf War in 1991 and demonstrating that this stuff really could do what Albert Wohlstetter had envisioned 15 years before.[12]

The new "American way of war" uses technology instead of manpower to deliver the traditional American format of decisive force. Max Boot, a conservative analyst at the Council on Foreign Relations, sees the United States fighting an unending series of small wars based on advanced technology. This is not, for Boot, simply a way of achieving military victory but a means of producing a global "empire of liberty."[13] Robert Kaplan (at one point among George Bush's favorite authors), writing in the *Atlantic Monthly*, sees a global mission for the US military of offering security and advice on good governance.[14]

On the liberal side, in his book *Virtual War: Kosovo and Beyond*, Michael Ignatieff of Harvard University (now a member of the Canadian Parliament) writes enthusiastically of the bombing of Belgrade; indeed he wishes it could have been carried out with less restraint: "The paradox is that greater ruthlessness—going downtown on the first night and taking out the grid—might have been more effective, and in the end, more merciful." He writes that the Balkan wars returned "war in the West to its position as the continuation of politics by other means."[15] For this, Ignatieff received great kudos from Boston University's Alan Wolfe, an academic with impeccable liberal credentials who also argues strongly for the use of military power.[16]

Thus, what began as a technological and tactical transformation has morphed into a compelling idea: America's technological superiority enables its military to impose solutions more rapidly and effectively than can be achieved through diplomacy. Why cajole the timid Europeans or horse-trade with third-world dictators when you can achieve the objective with the ever more accurate Predators? Robert Kagan's thesis that Americans are from Mars and Europeans from Venus—indeed that Washington's readiness to assert its interests militarily distinguishes the United States from the limp-wristed Europeans, who have lost the will to fight—enjoys wide support.[17]

Among Democratic and Republican elites differences on the utility of military power are negligible. Fewer than half of the Democratic Senators voted against the bill authorizing the use of force against Iraq. Every Democrat whose political ambitions extended beyond the Senate floor voted in favor. Former Secretary of State Madeleine Albright's openness to thinking in military terms has already been mentioned. In fact, she is not noticeably less belligerent than Vice President Dick Cheney. In 2005 she founded a new organization, the Security and Peace Initiative, which declares on its website that it is aimed at "restoring American leadership" through "vigorous military action."[18] Although he now disavows his support for the Iraq war, Peter Beinart of the *New Republic* finds it difficult to break away from embracing the new military technologies that, seemingly, expanded the universe of achievable foreign policy goals. He argues that Democrats have to regain their "comfort with military power."[19] Perhaps so, and this underscores our point. Beinart's argument fails to address the limited context in which military power can be decisive in today's insurgent conflicts. The *political* dimensions of this problem are seen in bold relief when one considers the dilemma facing Senator Hillary Clinton, who, on Iran, seems more aggressive than Donald Rumsfeld. While her public positions over two decades would suggest otherwise, her prospective presidential candidacy in 2008 has compelled her to support military action to thwart Iran's nuclear program in hopes of solidifying support among security-conscious Democrats and "undecideds," and to blunt an expected Republican attack on her discomfort with military power and how it is used.[20]

In the case of Iraq, liberal newspapers like the *Washington Post* found themselves urging the nation to war as vociferously as Rupert Murdoch's *New York Post*—and even today it has not joined journals such as the *New York Times* and *New Republic* in any sustained soul-searching. Instead, it continues to assert itself in the justification of the necessity of the Iraq war. In making the case for war and in supporting premature claims of victory, there was a difference in tone between the liberal-inclined Brookings Institution and the conservative American Enterprise Institute, but there was less difference between them than one would expect in terms of substance. With occasional exceptions such as David Rieff, few liberals who supported the Iraq war have reproached themselves publicly. Most liberal advocates of the war have said only that they would have fought it better.[21]

Not for them the "Sherman-like razing of infrastructure" advocated by former CIA analyst Michael Scheuer.[22] Rather, according to Kerry, liberals would be "more effective, more thoughtful, more strategic, more proactive, more sensitive."[23] They would be less unilateral in tone, embrace a collective approach to security, and be more subtle in execution and less in league with the oil and defense industries.

But their approach is much the same as the conservatives': America's high-tech expands the range of achievable foreign policy goals; it is what the United States does best; and American policy makers should use it in transforming global trouble spots. Far from being agents of treason, as some conservative commentators allege, the liberal elite, represented by organizations such as the International Crisis Group (that got its start with funding from the liberal financier George Soros), is more than comfortable with the culture of military force. They have updated the Catholic concept of "just war" to make it an enabling rather than a constraining doctrine. They would even suggest that *not* to use military force in certain circumstances of humanitarian stress (for instance, in

1998 in Rwanda and more recently in Darfur) constitutes a moral lapse.[24] Even the United Nations—an organization founded on the principle that war is a scourge—has gotten into the act, with its evolving doctrine of "Responsibility to Protect" implicitly predicated on a willingness to use military force.[25]

For this reason, those questioning the entrenched wisdom of the Big Idea have a hard time gaining traction. The case of retired West Point graduate and Vietnam veteran Andrew Bacevich is instructive. His book *The New American Militarism: How Americans Are Seduced by War* offers a powerfully argued case against this culture as a "misbegotten crusade."[26] Nonetheless, it explicitly accepts the very premises on which this culture is built, namely that we are fighting World War IV and that the primary relationship between the United States and the rest of the world can be cast in military terms. Interestingly, he dates the beginning of this war to 1980 when, following the Iranian revolution and the Soviet invasion of Afghanistan, President Carter was driven to enter a "great contest" to re-impose America's will on the Middle East. Given that Bacevich dreads the possibility of an American defeat in this war, he finds himself in the same uncomfortable place as opponents of the Iraq war: disagreeing with the Administration's policies yet arguing that he would do much the same thing, only better. It takes a British general, Rupert Smith—who commanded forces in Zimbabwe, Northern Ireland, Iraq, and the Balkans—to lay down for the civilian political leadership the true parameters they should bear in mind when deciding upon war.[27] Smith is especially instructive in the crucial interaction between ends and means and in noting the fluid relationship between these two variables.

While the establishment has been in lockstep—either from conviction, opportunism, or intimidation—there is a growing realization now evident in the editorial columns, among the research institutions, and within the uniformed military that military power can advance the policy agenda only so far. Reality is a harsh teacher, and as the lessons of Afghanistan and Iraq are absorbed, it is clear that military supremacy does not necessarily belie a civilian security or the hoped-for creation of a civil society. New thinking is placing US military prowess more firmly in a wider operational context where it becomes one of several elements in the attempt to build civil societies where the cultural and security preconditions are adverse.

In his book *Taming American Power* Harvard professor Stephen Walt points a way forward. Although he too defines the question in terms of what the United States should do with the "unprecedented opportunity" afforded by its power, he develops a useful argument that this power is not in fact as all-encompassing as some claim and that it does not constrain foreign options as much as might be expected.[28] Walt's approach challenges the Big Idea that US military prowess can bring stability and pluralism to global trouble spots. His analysis of the counterbalancing capabilities available even to militarily insignificant states is especially illuminating. Walt's words highlight the need for radical new thinking on the subject of the American military. It is desirable that this goes beyond mere adjustment at the margins. The good news is that much of this new thinking is already underway inside the US military college and research institutions. Now, a wider audience needs to participate. There are seven questions requiring answers:

1. Is Our Understanding of Military Power too Narrow?

In terms of raw capability to destroy targets anywhere in the world, the United States is irresistibly strong. There is no reason to waste any time debating this point. The more interesting question is what use we make of this capability. Have we, for example, simply defined military power in the terms most favorable to ourselves—the ability to prevail in any firefight and thus produce a crushing victory of the sort we enjoyed in Iraq in March and April 2003? This is certainly the American "way of war" as it has been historically practiced and recently updated.[29]

But we need to look at what this definition excludes in terms of outcomes: the adverse effects of public opinion both domestically and internationally, including sharpened frustration at home and increased resistance to US initiatives within world bodies from the United Nations to the World Trade Organization; the alternative uses for the $350 billion spent on the Iraq war through June 2006; and the capacity of adversaries to adapt, resulting in diminished regional stability. Ironically, on the latter point, while there were no demonstrable Al-Qaeda operations in Iraq before the war, there is a significant and growing concentration in Iraq of groups connected to anti-American violence that is now described by that organization as the "main front." Advocates of the current paradigm need to rethink their definition of *victory*.

At this critical point in the policy process it is important that rational center institutions—the editorial writers, research centers, and the academy—act to produce a constructive definition of *success* that acknowledges the concerns cited above and places the military element in perspective.

2. Why a War on Terror?

In a memo of October 16, 2003, to the chairman of the Joint Chiefs of Staff, Defense Secretary Donald Rumsfeld asked:

> Are we capturing, killing or deterring and dissuading more terrorists every day than the madrassas and the radical clerics are recruiting, training and deploying against us? Does the United States need to fashion a broad, integrated plan to stop the next generation of terrorists? The United States is putting relatively little effort into a long-range plan, but we are putting a great deal of effort into trying to stop terrorists. The cost-benefit ratio is against us! Our cost is billions against the terrorists' costs of millions.

If the cabinet official presiding over $3.5 trillion more spending on international affairs than the combination of all other government agencies can have doubts about the cost-benefit ratio, then all of us should. In essence, Rumsfeld is pointing to a numbers game. If ten terrorists are recruited for every one killed, the math is against us. If through war-fighting, we turn 1.2 billion Muslims against the United States, once again the math is against us. The last time the United States adopted a "broad, integrated plan" to face a foreign challenge—during the Cold War—it succeeded without a single hostile sortie being flown by NATO.

3. Does Technology Really Transform War?

Despite all the celebrated C4ISR assets available to minimize the fog of war, there have been continuing reports from Iraq that the fog persists. As Staff Sergeant Kevin Saber put it, "I have no idea who I am up against . . . We're just riding around, waiting to get hit."[30] Sgt. Sager's uneasiness seems to be well understood by the uniformed military strategists who have written on the dangers of "asymmetric war" or "fourth generation war"—namely the tactics historically used by the weak, starting with David, to negate the advantages of the strong. Three years into the US occupation of Iraq, the most prominent road in the country—the road from the airport into Baghdad—was also the most dangerous, with the US Secretary of State being forced to don a flak jacket and helmet on her way to the airport from the US Embassy on October 5, 2006. Nearly 70 percent of US combat fatalities and 75 percent of injuries in Iraq come from roadside bombs.[31] When the enemy's main weapons are the impro-vised explosive device and the suicide bomber, the technological wonders of the F–22A Raptor are of little utility. The Administration's answer is that these are strictly military problems: all the United States has to do is employ different tactics and introduce new technology on the battle-field, and all will be well again.

But it is worth asking what real advantage military predominance has delivered to American hands. Proponents of force argue that so long as force is applied properly and with the appropriate follow-up, the advan-tage it provides is overwhelming. Yet, the ability to project decisive power when necessary is, as we have seen, only one part of the complex process of building civil societies. As the late House Speaker Sam Rayburn used to say, "any mule can kick down a barn door, but it takes a carpenter to build one."

4. Are We Discouraging or Encouraging Nuclear Proliferation?

For a decade the United States has confronted North Korea and, more recently, Iran over their respective nuclear programs. The military option has never been off the table, either during the Clinton Administration or especially under the Bush Administration, which for six years set aside Clinton's diplomatic component. The result has been a deadlock in which both Iran's and North Korea's nuclear programs have advanced and North Korea has detonated a nuclear bomb. One reason for this is that American saber rattling provides a perverse incentive to both countries (and any others watching the drama unfold) to accelerate their nuclear programs. As one commentator put it, if you were a dictator watching American actions in North Korea and Iraq, you might well conclude that pretending to have nuclear weapons is not safe. Having them is much safer.[32] Current policy thus encourages nuclear proliferation. It may be time to consider something else.

5. Do Our Military Policies Contribute to Anti-Americanism, and Should We Care?

A former Korean foreign minister recently told us that while he personally was committed to a strong United States–Korean relationship, he believed that the US insistence on seeing the problems of the Korean peninsula in predominantly military terms, giving little weight to popular aspirations for peacefully reuniting the two halves of the country, might eventually turn the Korean people against the United States. This is a small but typical example of a massive problem: the use of military power without adequate and convincing diplomacy can easily result in diminished support for the United States.

America's friends want it to act in a predictable manner, deploying the range of problem-management and problem-solving tools used by the rest of the world. To the extent that it is willing to do so, it can avoid the increasing alienation and animosity of other nations and proceed in its exceptional way to fashion a compatible global order.

6. Is China Primarily a Military Problem?

Here at last is the classic state-on-state confrontation for which the US military is properly prepared. Interdicting a possible Chinese invasion of Taiwan is an entirely appropriate use of American military power. It is a clear and definable mission. But the open question about China and the United States is whether the two countries must inevitably become enemies. By thinking predominantly in military terms, the United States makes this outcome more likely.

7. Is American Exceptionalism Defined by War Fighting?

This question reflects a debate as old as the Republic: should American values be an example to the rest of the world, or should America seek to impose these values where they do not exist? Today, that debate has become—unnecessarily and illogically—enmeshed with a sort of dream palace of American military power. The United States has the ability to exert its will anywhere in the world, but can it *force* other cultures, with very different histories and traditions, to embrace democracy, free markets, free expression, and the secular state?

None of these questions have simple answers. But they all have bearing on the role and utility of military power in American foreign policy. Achieving the correct balance between military power and the other instruments of foreign policy is a challenge to which the rational center has a critical contribution to make.

SEVEN

Insurgency

This is another type of war, new in its intensity, ancient in its origin—war by guerrillas, subversives, insurgents, assassins, war by ambush instead of by combat; by infiltration, instead of aggression, seeking victory by eroding and exhausting the enemy instead of engaging him . . . [It] preys on economic unrest and ethnic conflicts. It requires in those situations where we must counter it, and these are the kinds of challenges that will be before us in the next decade if freedom is to be saved, a whole new kind of strategy, a wholly different kind of force, and therefore a new and wholly different kind of military training.[1]

These words have a distinctly contemporary feel, but they were spoken over forty years ago, by President John F. Kennedy to the 1962 graduating class at West Point. They provide a foreword to the widespread institutional failure within US policy circles, to effectively address the problem of insurgency in the early twenty-first century. Entranced by the idea described in the previous chapter, that military technology has transformed America's foreign policy options by providing military short-cuts to seemingly intractable diplomatic problems, leaders within the Administration, in Congress, in the military, and the media have discounted the possibility that the United States could face a meaningful military challenge in the decades ahead.

Thus, they were slow to acknowledge the growing insurgency in Iraq. In October 2003 an unnamed senior military officer was quoted in *Time* magazine as saying, "Look around. We're not facing some kind of organized guerrilla force. What's happening is that peace and stability are taking hold, and the more they do, noncompliant forces are becoming more desperate and radicalized." Yet as the insurgency became more effective, some leaders tried to ban the use of the word.[2] The seriousness of the insurgent threat was chronically underestimated in Washington, with Vice President Dick Cheney declaring on CNN in June 2005 that it was in its "last throes."[3] This was just before one of the deadliest spells in the insurgency, which in early 2006 brought Iraq to the edge of civil war. At this writing, in October 2006, the insurgency is out of control with many analysts believing Iraq has entered civil war. Moreover, contrary to the triumphalist literature of 2003–2004, which asserted that the American invasion was largely uncontested, it now seems that if the insurgency was not planned in advance by the Iraqi military, it was activated by groups sympathetic to Saddam's regime just after the invasion began.[4] It was this ongoing misunderstanding of the implications of asymmetric warfare, where the advantages of a high-tech military are reduced and at times eliminated, that led to a fatal underestimation of the enemy and eventually to the President's premature "Mission Accomplished" declaration in May 2003.

Three years later we stand beneath a banner that reads "Mission Misunderstood." This points to a definitional problem that has inhibited our analysis of insurgency for some time. Decision makers in the United States have defined the insurgents in Iraq the way they did the Viet Cong, as a small, cowardly minority that is brutal, totalitarian, and evil. The assumption in their definition has been that these violent "dead-enders," to use Donald Rumsfeld's phrase, are separate and alien from the communities in which they operate; that their criminal behavior is intolerable, that merchants, schools, and religious institutions see them as disrupting community coherence, not facilitating community progress.

Such definitions and denunciations, while comforting those who make them, induce planners to ignore the crucial logistical support—food, transport, shelter, medical aid, communications, and intelligence—that insurgents obtain from the community around them. Put another way, these denunciations mistake the plane on which the struggle for "hearts and minds" takes place and ignore the overwhelming burden of being the occupying force. Thus, the concept of insurgency must be reconsidered to give greater scope to the depth and spiritual resources it can bring to bear.

It must not be assumed that since the United States is on the side of the good, that insurgencies are unpopular movements. Nor can it be assumed that insurgencies pose merely a technical challenge that can be managed by deploying what the Pentagon calls a "stability operations" component or what the State Department calls "reconstruction and stabilization" capabilities from the tool box for what has come to be known as "post-conflict stabilization."[5]

A substantial body of evidence suggests that both of these assumptions are flawed. It is in uncovering these fallacies that we see the greatest role for the rational center. If next time around the United States is to cope more successfully, it needs to have a deeper understanding of the phenomenon and move away from slogans such as "clear and hold," now used in Iraq,[6] where tactics expand to become strategy.

To address these issues in a fresh manner, there are two egregious misconceptions that the rational center should examine and correct. The first is that the United States has, as a matter of government policy, not supported insurgencies in the past. The second is that a contemporary democracy can subdue an insurgency. We may dismiss the first by referring readers to the Iran Freedom Support Act, which passed in Congress in September 2006 and foresees support for an insurgency in Iran. So the notion that insurgencies are intrinsically evil must be set aside—not only in respect to this instance, but to a number of others we shall come to.

On the second point, namely the odds of democracy defeating an insurgency in today's media and political environment, they are not good. In fact the chances are less than two in ten. These unfavorable odds apply not just to the United States but also to any of its like-minded democratic allies. In Vietnam, Rhodesia, and Nicaragua the authors saw the evidence close up. From 1973 to 1980, for example, the Rhodesian Central Intelligence Organization showed the British authorities list after list of the "terrs" (terrorists) they were killing. The British believed them. Then, without warning, the "terrs" swept the national elections in 1980 and were in charge. In Iraq, unless the United States cares to adopt Chinese practices, which are discussed below, the odds of defeating the insurgency while the United States remains in the capacity of an occupying power are essentially zero. Once again, this is not because of unique American mistakes. No democratic nation—given inherent political and legal restraints, a free media, and the growing power of world opinion—would stand a chance.

AMERICANS AS INSURGENTS

We begin with the measured prose of Colonel Douglas Lovelace, the Director of the Strategic Studies Institute, writing in a monograph prepared by the Army War College: "The United States, particularly the Army, has a long history of counterinsurgency support."[7] In most respects this is a straightforward and commonsense observation. It conveys the familiar notion of the United States assisting duly constituted authority (deemed "good") against insurrectional anarchy (deemed "evil"). This appears to be how the United States see itself in Iraq, where even liberal magazines like the *New Yorker* and the *New York Times Magazine* offer adulatory references to the tactics imported from US counterinsurgency experience in El Salvador during the 1980s.[8]

But as ever, this concept suppresses more than it explains. It hides the more complicated reality that the United States has regularly sided with the insurgents (in 1953 in Iran, in Afghanistan in the 1980s), sometimes brought them into being (Nicaragua in the 1980s), and sometimes approved the results insurgencies have achieved (the African National Congress in South Africa in 1994 and the Kosovo Liberation Army in Serbia in 1998). At least once, in the American Revolution, the Americans themselves were the insurgent power. American insurgents like Davy Crockett are the heroes of popular ballads. Support for insurgencies is not confined to US Administrations but can be found in both right-leaning and left-leaning religious and civic organizations. In southern Sudan, for example, Samaritan's Purse, an Evangelical Christian movement led by Franklin Graham, has openly sided with the antigovernment rebels. The International Crisis Group, which has close links to the New York financier George Soros, was in sympathy with the Kosovo Liberation Army in the 1990s.

In other words, playing the insurgent is not an unfamiliar American role. During the height of the Contra insurgency in Nicaragua in the 1980s, one of the authors met Joe Fernandez, then the CIA station chief in San José, Costa Rica. Fernandez could have written the definitive book on American insurgency tactics: finance, leadership, use of external safe havens, intimidation of the local population, media relations, and so on. Of course, his experience was gained prior to the Iran-Contra scandal. The same is true of those in the Nixon Administration who were more deeply involved than they might care to admit in the overthrow of Chile's President Salvador Allende.[9]

Many Americans, including military figures, find it uncomfortable to think of themselves as insurgents.[10] Perhaps they see insurgency as something Mao Tse-tung and Fidel Castro did. So they revise the story as did Cheney, who, in a complete reversal of the historical record, compared the Continental Army (an insurgent force pitted against the occupying British) with the US military in Iraq (an occupying force pitted against an insurgency).[11] In a broader effort to camouflage American support of insurgencies, politicians and the military have used names like "unconventional war," "fourth generation warfare," "low-intensity warfare," "small wars" (oblivious to their ironic use considering the etymology of the Spanish word *guerrilla*), and "regime change."

Plainly put, insurgency is simply one of many military technologies. Pro-insurgency tactics are a standard part of US military study. The Marine Corps maintains a "Small Wars Center of Excellence" at its base at Quantico, Virginia. The Center manages to finesse the fact that *inter alia* it is in the pro-insurgency business by defining its interests as: "operations taken under executive authority, wherein military force is combined with diplomatic pressure in the internal or external affairs of another state whose government is unstable, inadequate, or unsatisfactory for the preservation of life and of such interests as are determined by the foreign policy of our Nation."

The Marine Corps' *Small Wars Manual*, dating from 1940, still—rather remarkably—counts as the standard reference work for the study of insurgency. The Army War College is another important location for the study of insurgencies, and, to its great credit, it has published monographs severely critical of the counterinsurgency tactics in Iraq.[12]

It remains, however, that, unlike the cutting-edge analysis surrounding the strategic and, particularly, nuclear battle space advanced by Albert Wohlstetter, Andrew Marshall, and Arthur Cebrowski, the US has lagged behind European militaries in refining counter-insurgency thinking and capabilities. US analysts and commanders were slow to absorb the lessons of the British in Malaya and of the French in North Africa.

In certain instances the United States has presented itself as a quasi-insurgent challenger of the established order. In a speech at the American University in Cairo, Secretary of State Condoleezza Rice said, "for 60 years, my country, the United States, pursued stability at the expense of democracy in this region here in the Middle East—and we achieved neither. Now we are taking a different course. We are supporting the democratic aspirations of all people."[13] It is quite true that the speech was calibrated to avoid explicitly advocating armed struggle. Nonetheless, the assertion that the United States had in the past overemphasized stability tilts the nation toward the side of those who use extraparliamentary means (otherwise known as "street power") to oppose a status quo of which America disapproves. We have already seen examples of this in the democratic "revolutions" in Ukraine, Georgia, and Lebanon, where the United States put itself on the side of mass demonstrations. In Washington there is no shortage of people who take this sentiment to the next stage by advocating that the United States arm what are perceived to be prodemocracy insurgencies, for example the "freedom forces that can bring down the regime" in Iran.[14]

PAST INSURGENCIES

With insurgency a part of the nation's past and a likely part of its future, one would expect a more supple understanding of the phenomenon in Washington and among military commanders. One would certainly expect insurgency warfare to be widely taught at the military academies.

It is not that America's leaders were unaware of the historical context. Having first banned the use of the word *insurgency* or derided the insurgents as "dead-enders," Defense Secretary Donald Rumsfeld later grew more realistic. As he put it on June 26, 2005, "insurgencies tend to go on five, six, eight, ten, twelve years."[15] Some last much longer. Indian nationalists cite the Sepoy Rebellion of 1857 (known in British imperial history as the Indian Mutiny) as the first shots in the war that eventually drove the British from India in 1949.

The greater problem arises from the notion we mentioned earlier—the belief held in Washington that defeating an insurgency is primarily a technical matter in which the right tactics will produce the right result. This is perhaps an unexpected manifestation of American Exceptionalism: American leaders are in essence declaring themselves immune to the law of averages with regard to insurgencies. This law suggests that the odds against victory are high. The reason insurgents (including the United States) undertake insurgencies is that they are highly effective. They are, one might say, the perfect antidote to a high-tech military like the US.

Among the reasons for this success rate are the many ways an insurgency can win without having to triumph in set-piece battles. In Iraq, for example, the insurgency made its point by raising the cost of infrastructure projects, impeding transportation, limiting public assembly, and demonstrating that the Administration could not secure the environment, which has had a range of follow-on negative effects. The Administration's insistence on Sunni representation in the new Iraqi government underscored its acceptance of the insurgency's strength. This seemed to have been further acknowledged by a succession of redeployments around Baghdad in hopes of containing the violence as well as a spirited debate in the US about the number of troops that are needed. So, while there are exceptions, we note that democracies perform very poorly against insurgencies. Israel has managed a succession of insurgencies rooted in the West Bank and Gaza over the decades—but not without debilitating human, psychic, and monetary cost.

Table 1 provides a selective list of insurgencies in which Western powers have been involved since World War II. This is not to suggest that insurgencies are exclusively a modern or Western phenomenon. They are not. But the instruments of war-fighting that are available to authoritarian governments may not be appropriate for a democratic polity subject to media scrutiny and the vicissitudes of public opinion. Americans are unlikely to want to engage in the sort of insurgency war that Uruguay fought in the 1990s, which delivered victory against the Tupamaros but also delivered Uruguay into the hands of a military government.

Table 1 makes three points:

1. Insurgencies are rather common. At least seventeen are going on today.
2. US involvement and has been for, against, and in-between.
3. The failure rate of insurgencies is low. Since World War II, with hardly any exceptions, they have been successful against occupying democratic powers.

Table 1 Insurgencies: Successful and Otherwise

Successful Colonial Insurgencies

Location	Dates	Defending Entity	Insurgent Entity	US Involvement
Aden/South Arabia	1962–1967	UK	Liberation movement	None
Algeria	1954–1962	Algerian government, France	Liberation movement	None
Angola	1961–1975	Portugal	Liberation movements	Opposed
Cyprus	1955–1959	UK	Liberation movements	None
India	1942–1947	UK	Liberation movements	None
Indochina	1945–1954	France	Liberation movements	Opposed
Israel	1947–1948	UK	Zionist movements	Supported
Mozambique	1964–1975	Portugal	Liberation movements	Opposed
Namibia	1966–1988	South Africa	Liberation movements	Mediator
Northern Ireland	1969–1998	UK	Liberation movement	Mediator
South Africa	1958–1990	South Africa	Liberation movements	Mediator
Tunisia	1952–1954	France	Liberation movements	None
Zimbabwe	1972–1979	Rhodesia	Liberation movements	Mediator

Successful Postcolonial Insurgencies

Location	Dates	Defending Entity	Insurgent Entity	US Involvement
Afghanistan (Soviet occupation)	1979–1989	USSR	Liberation movements	Supported
Afghanistan (Taliban)	2001	Taliban	Liberation movements, US forces	Supported
Cambodia	1966–1975	Cambodia	Opposition movements	Opposed
Chile	1970–1973	Chile	Opposition movement	Supported
China (CCP/KMT)	1945–1949	Republic of China government	Chinese Communist Party	Opposed
Congo	1964–1997		Civil war	Opposed
Cuba	1952–1959	Cuba	Opposition movement	Opposed
Eritrea	1961–1993	Eritrea	Opposition movements, Ethiopia	Opposed
Guatemala	1954	Guatemala	Opposition movement	Supported

continues

Successful Postcolonial Insurgencies *continued*

Location	Dates	Defending Entity	Insurgent Entity	US Involvement
Haiti	1990	Haiti	Opposition movement	Supported
Haiti	1994	Haiti	Opposition movement	Supported
Haiti	2004	Haiti	Opposition movement	Supported
Indonesia (East Timor)	1975–1999	Indonesia	Liberation movement	Opposed, then mediated
Iran	1953	Iran	Opposition, US, UK	Supported
Iran	1979	Iran	Religious opposition	Opposed
Iraq	1991–2003	Iraq	Opposition movement	Supported
Israel (Intifada)	1987–1993	Israel	Opposition movement	Opposed
Kosovo	1998–1999	Serbia	Liberation movement	Supported
Laos	1954–1962	Laos	Opposition movement	Opposed
Lebanon	1975–1990	Lebanon	Factional forces	Supported, then opposed, then mediated
Mozambique	1975–1994	Mozambique	Opposition movement	Opposed, then mediated
Nicaragua (Sandinista)	1978–1979	Nicaragua	Opposition movement	Opposed
Nicaragua (Contra)	1981–1988	Nicaragua	Opposition movement	Supported
Panama	1989	Panama	Opposition movement	Supported
Somalia	1982–1994	Somalia	Ethiopia, Opposition	Opposed
Vietnam	1953–1975	Vietnam, US	North Vietnam, Opposition movement	Opposed

Ongoing Insurgencies

Location	Dates	Defending Entity	Insurgent Entity	US Involvement
Chechnya	1991–	Russia	Opposition movement	Opposes
China (Xinjiang)	1990–	China	Insurgents	Opposes
Colombia	1966–	Colombia	Opposition movement	Opposes
Cuba	1959–	Cuba	Exile movements	Supports
Iran	1979–	Iran	Exile movements, Insurgents	Supports
Indonesia (Aceh)	1976–	Indonesia	Liberation movement	Mediator
Iraq	2003–	Iraq, US	Insurgents, Militia	Opposes
Kashmir	1947–	India, Pakistan	Insurgents	Mediator

continues

Ongoing Insurgencies *continued*

Location	Dates	Defending Entity	Insurgent Entity	US Involvement
Liberia	1999–	Liberia	Rebels	Mediator
Nepal	1990–	Nepal	Rebels	Opposes
Philippines (Mindanao)	1968–	Philippines	Separatists	Opposes
Spain	1959–	Spain	Separatists	Opposes
Sri Lanka	1972–	Sri Lanka	Separatists	Opposes
Sudan	1984–	Sudan	Rebels	Mediator
Thailand	1967–	Thailand	Rebels	Opposes
Turkey	1977–	Turkey	Separatists	Opposes
Venezuela	2002–	Venezuela	Coup plotters	Supports

Mediated Insurgencies

Location	Dates	Defending Entity	Insurgent Entity	US Involvement
El Salvador	1979–1984	El Salvador	Insurgents	Opposed
Mozambique	1975–1992	Mozambique	Rebels	Opposed
Peru	1980–1992	Peru	Insurgents	Opposed
Sudan	1955–1972	Sudan	Rebels	Supported

Unsuccessful Colonial Insurgencies

Location	Dates	Defending Entity	Insurgent Entity	US Involvement
Angola	1975–2002	Angola	Rebels	Supported, then mediated
Kenya	1952–1960	UK	Liberation movement	None
Malaya	1948–1960	UK	Liberation movement	None

Unsuccessful Noncolonial Insurgencies

Location	Dates	Defending Entity	Insurgent Entity	US Involvement
Bolivia	1966–1967	Bolivia	Cuba, Insurgents	Opposed
China (Tibet)	1949–1959	China	Liberation/Opposition	Covertly supported 1951–1972, then opposed

continues

Unsuccessful Noncolonial Insurgencies *continued*

Location	Dates	Defending Entity	Insurgent Entity	US Involvement
Dhofar	1965–1975	Oman, UK	Insurgents	None
Greece	1945–1949	Greece	Opposition movement	Opposed
Philippines (Huk)	1945–1954	Philippines	Insurgents	Opposed
Uruguay	1967–1971	Uruguay	Insurgents	Opposed

Unsuccessful Insurgencies against Foreign Occupying Democracies

Location	Dates	Defending Entity	Insurgent Entity	US Involvement
Greece	1945–1949	Greek Government	ELAS	significant covert support
Malaya	1948–1960	Malaya, Britian Commonwealth	Malayan Races Liberation Army (MLRA)	none
Philippines	1942–1955	Philippine Government U.S. Government	Huk pro-Communist	assist, support, advised helped mediate

Point three is the most striking. But before we address it, we offer a few brief observations about points one and two. These make it clear that insurgencies and American involvement in them are both rather routine events. Some military writers have suggested that insurgencies represent the flip side of globalization. Such modern developments as globalized communications and Internet-based explosives expertise have taken away governments' "monopoly on violence" and given insurgents readier access to the means that facilitate their aims.[16] Analysis of these movements is thus best conducted within the general context of war studies and political science. To confuse insurgencies with terrorism—which is simply one of the instruments used by insurgents—is to add a distracting layer of emotion.

LOOKING FORWARD

As the United States confronts the Iraqi insurgency and anticipates future ones (in which it could well be on the insurgent side), it is worth considering history's lessons. British imperial history is especially replete with examples to suit practically any point of view. Those looking for encouragement that insurgencies can be defeated are often drawn to Malaya.[17] Here a twelve-year insurgency (1948–1960) was defeated on the battlefield, and the British were able to depart Malaya claiming success. On the other hand, the forced British withdrawals from Palestine, India, Yemen, and Oman give hope to insurgents. Analysts in the United States often note the defeat of the Huk pro-Communist insurgency in the Philippines (first formed in 1942 to fight the Japanese occupation) as an example of a successful counterinsurgency cooperative effort involving both the US and the Philippines, and the post–World War II defeat of Communist guerillas in Greece. They also acknowledge the French and American defeats in Vietnam and the Israeli and American withdrawals from Lebanon. Revisionist histories arguing that US counterinsurgency tactics in Vietnam were actually working, such as Lewis Sorley's *A Better War*, have attracted a readership among senior US commanders in Iraq.[18]

Picking and choosing particular historical instances is both fascinating and dangerous. What succeeds in one context fails in another. An example is the British tactic of concentrating the population and restricting food distribution, which was effective in Malaya for denying the insurgents access to food and shelter but ineffective when, as "strategic hamlets," it was tried in Vietnam. The United States successfully supplied weapons to insurgents in Afghanistan but unsuccessfully in Angola. And all these activities took place before the days of media intrusiveness.

As the historical data mining enterprise progresses both at universities and military colleges, the key aspect to focus on is the complete absence of success in defeating insurgencies when democratic governments are the foreign occupying powers. This is an arresting fact given the number of countries that have tried it: Britain, France, the United States, Israel, Belgium. Totalitarian powers have not fared much better in the 24/7 media age. The Soviet Union was expelled from Afghanistan by the insurgent mujahideen and, reconstituted as Russia, it has been forced to disgorge all its former occupied territories and client states.

THE EXCEPTION

Returning now to the third conclusion from the chart, the one exception to this list of failures is China in Tibet.[19] Even this is subject to caveats. Although Tibet is ethnically and religiously distinct from Han China, it is now almost universally recognized as being part of China. Even those who contest this legal status concede China's long historical involvement in Tibetan affairs. So it is not absolutely clear cut that China counts as a foreign occupying power. Still, at the time of the 1950 invasion by the People's Liberation Army (PLA), Tibet enjoyed many of the attributes of an independent state, having expelled the Chinese Administration after the fall of the Manchu dynasty in 1911 and run its own internal affairs under Britain's benign eye from Delhi. The Dalai Lama headed a government called the Kashag. It appealed for help against the Chinese invasion—though the Chinese naturally reject this term. In the mid-1950s the CIA offered help to Tibetan rebels with the objective of wresting Tibet away from China. Operation Mustang continued from 1961 through 1974, but it was discontinued as United States–China relations warmed.

When the hot stage of the insurgency—the Khampa, or Kanding, revolt—broke out in 1955, leading eventually to the Dalai Lama's flight from Tibet in 1959, the Chinese responded with a conventional military counterattack, destroying monasteries and killing ordinary Tibetans on a grand scale. But, what happened in the years afterward is of greater interest. China flooded Tibet with PLA troops and then with hundreds of thousands of Han Chinese immigrants, which enabled it to establish unchallengeable control of local commerce and administrative structures.

With security thus ruthlessly established and Tibetan culture circum-scribed, monitored, and diminished, China moved on to "post-conflict" management: an active civil program of modernization, which has in-cluded road construction, schools, sewers, and a Beijing to Lhasa rail-road, all designed to win over the civil population. Even as special efforts were made to woo the aristocracy, Tibet was presented as a Buddhist theme park at the roof of the world for Chinese tourists. This further di-minished the cultural base from which resistance could arise and so re-flected China's close attention to suppressing both the military and cultural aspects of potential insurgency. And, finally, Beijing has made conciliatory gestures, saying it looks forward to the day when Tibet would be an autonomous region of China, nominally ruled over by the Dalai Lama.

Thus, China imposed a set of policies, aimed not just at controlling the insurgency but at asserting a Han Chinese cultural hegemony over Tibet. Textbooks were rewritten, the teaching of Chinese was made standard in Tibetan schools, Tibetan religious practices were suppressed, and millions of ethnic Chinese were resettled in Tibet.

Practices such as these attract regular criticism in the State Depart-ment's annual report on human rights. The 2004 edition contained ten pages of detailed critique. Both chambers of Congress regularly pass res-olutions condemning Chinese behavior in Tibet. There is an active non-governmental campaign, often involving celebrities, demanding that China cease these practices. Among students of counterinsurgency at America's military colleges it is not easy to find any who praise Chinese tactics in Tibet or recommend that the United States should learn from them. The word *genocide* is occasionally heard.

The point is a simple one: Chinese practices in Tibet are anathema to the United States and are simply not available to a democratically elected government answerable to a free press. An Israeli political scientist put it this way: "democracies fail in small wars because they find it extremely difficult to escalate the level of violence and brutality which can secure victory."[20] Yet, this premise may be mistaken. As our table shows, failure against insurgencies is not confined to democracies. Colonial governments, military governments, totalitarian governments, and illegal governments have all taken their turn and failed.

In a welcome reassertion of rational-center policy thinking, the Pentagon, in July 2006, published a trial draft of a new Army Field Manual for counterinsurgency detailing the extraordinary difficulty modern democracies face when confronting insurgencies. The main authors, Lieutenant General David H. Petraeus and retired Lieutenant Colonel Conrad C. Crane, both practitioner-experts with plenty of experience in Iraq, make two essential points: first, that many of the egregious errors made by the United States in the early stages of the Iraq campaign could have been avoided with a closer reading of the recent histories of insurgent wars; and second, that the US political system, with its aversion to risk and competing demands, may not be capable of maintaining "a long-term commitment to insurgent or civil wars costing hundreds of billions of dollars and thousands of men."[21]

In challenging the notion that American military power can overcome remote insurgencies that possess limited resources, they recast the challenge of fighting this kind of war. The new manual stresses, for example, that

> these kinds of wars are "protracted by nature." They require "firm political will and extreme patience" . . . "considerable expenditure of time and resources" and a large deployment of troops ready to greet "hand-shakes or hand grenades" without mistaking one for the other.
>
> Successful operations require Soldiers and Marines to possess . . . a clear, nuanced and empathetic appreciation of the essential nature of the conflict . . . an understanding of the motivations, strengths and weaknesses of the insurgent "as well as . . . knowledge of the culture and leadership."[22]

Their latter point approaches a domestic political "third rail," namely, the point Marine Colonel Thomas Hammes makes in his book *The Sling and the Stone*, that often the insurgents confronting the United States have "legitimate grievances."[23] The incongruence of the United States, the default defender of human rights, taking arms against those with legitimate grievances is among the most difficult aspects of counterinsurgency to be absorbed by modern democracies and often (Johnson in Vietnam, Bush in Iraq) leads to reversals for the political leadership. And it is here that the rational center must assert itself as these conflicts take shape to be sure the confrontation is not defined in black and white, as freedom fighter versus terrorist—with all of the accompanying moral presumption. Rumsfeld, like Napoleon in Spain in 1808, found that however much one may deny the very existence of an insurgency, or define it as a tiny collection of malcontents, or demonize it, none of this represents an effective policy for countering it. The rational center must move deliberately as the next insurgent situation arises—and it surely will—to define the conflict in a palate of grays, with emphasis on limiting cultural and religious clashes—the handmaidens to civil war—underscoring the massive, long-term commitment involved, and not falling silent in the midst of the fevered patriotism that seems always to provide the context for these events.

EIGHT

The Intelligence Dilemma

In the past few years it has become plain to even the most casual observer that relations among the intelligence services, policy makers, and politicians have become dysfunctional. Since 9/11 both the British and the American intelligence services have found themselves pressed into serving the Big Idea known in US policy circles as the "Middle East Project" and more generally as "Freedom on the March." Where policy is normally based on intelligence, instead, the intelligence process and its findings, its judgments, and its estimates were, in important instances, crafted to support a policy, which, we now see, was misconceived.

Intelligence and Big Ideas—ideas designed to mobilize sentiment, project national values and models of governance, or rally the nation to respond to crisis—do not mix well. The intelligence process is more the province of the rational center. It is painstaking, detailed work that yields nuanced judgments and at times provides less guidance than policy makers would like. Often, intelligence products are accurate as far as they go but do not or cannot fully capture the situation at hand. And it must be added that the intelligence services are no strangers to failure.

The belief, held by many in Washington and London, that the intelligence services can be reformed from the top down—so that analysis is based only on facts that are verified several ways and on sources that are fully vetted, so that the product presented to policy makers is necessarily more accurate—is unfounded. Knowing what intelligence can reliably provide and how easily the process can be corrupted by political objectives is the first step in developing a better system.

THE NEEDLE IN THE HAYSTACK

In late June 1985 Bill Casey, director of Central Intelligence under President Ronald Reagan, heard that Oleg Gordievsky, the KGB officer turned British spy, had arrived in London after having been smuggled across the Finnish border in a car trunk. He could hardly contain himself. He invited himself to London and, within twenty-four hours, was probing Gordievsky for his secrets on the Soviet Union.

Casey hastened to London for several reasons. One of them has received little attention, but, in the torrent of demand for intelligence reform in Washington after 9/11 and the Iraq war, it needs greater emphasis. Casey's precipitate haste reflected the fact that Gordievsky was one of an extraordinarily small class: he was a genuine Soviet spy under American or British control, not suspected of being under Soviet control, and he had substantial access to secret information. The irreverent name given to such sources was "two-legged," to distinguish their product from the intelligence produced from technical sources like communication intercepts. The archives containing the hard numbers, of course, are not open. But sources suggest that this class numbered not more than ten and possibly less than five. If one looks more widely over the whole of the former Warsaw Pact countries, the number of truly dependable sources under full control was in the order of twenty to thirty at any one time.

Let's remember the circumstances under which Casey operated. During the Cold War years—from 1949, when the World War II alliance with the

Soviet Union finally crumbled, until 1989, when it became clear that the Soviet Union was no longer a going concern—the combined US and British intelligence services went all-out to recruit Soviet spies. The intelligence services in other NATO nations were doing the same. Budget was a nonissue. Political caution was not a restraint. Identification of potential targets was straightforward—the Soviet bureaucratic order of battle had a fixed address. Even access was not unimaginably hard. There were large US and UK embassies in the Soviet Union. Every hour of every day, Western intelligence officers somewhere in the world were sparring with their Soviet opposite numbers at cocktail parties in Buenos Aires, tennis matches in Seoul, or steamer trips on Lake Geneva. There was a flow of regular business that brought Western and Soviet officials together.

"Non-official cover" officers, often called NOCs, operated without the benefit of diplomatic cover in Moscow and the other Warsaw Pact capitals. Among the gambits designed to entice well-placed officials were extravagant offers—for example in the form of national lotteries or travel packages they had won. Others were invited to New York or Hollywood to help write screenplays on topics with which they "happened to be" familiar, in the hope that they might provide valuable information or be recruitable. The approaches were infinitely variable. Moreover, the cultural divide was not unbridgeable. Western case officers grew up reading Tolstoy and listening to Tchaikovsky; their Soviet counterparts could discuss Austen and Hemingway. More worldly subjects like ice hockey, soccer, and alcohol provided other topics of conversation. Beyond this, the West had all the advantages in terms of ideology, money, and glamour.

And yet the results were terribly thin. Moreover, general lessons were few; each of the important cases was quite distinct, involving different services, different kinds of information, and having very different conclusions. Of the better-known high-profile defectors, GRU (Chief Intelligence Directorate) Colonel Oleg Penkovsky, said to be the CIA's best human asset in the USSR, and GRU Lieutenant Colonel Oleg Gordievsky both provided extraordinary information on Soviet intentions, strengths, and policy positions. Former KGB General and Counter Intelligence Chief Oleg Kalugin, now a US citizen, has written an interesting book but was never a defector despite what many think. And many in the counterintelligence community remain at a distance, still unsure of him.

Viktor Cherkashin was chief of the "counterintelligence line" in Washington. He served as one of the deputies to the resident or chief of the KGB Station and gained notoriety for writing a book about FBI spy Robert Hanssen and CIA spy Aldrich Ames. He has an American son-in-law, but lives in Russia as a retired KGB officer. Kanatjan Alibekov defected from the Soviet biowarfare headquarters, Bio-Preperat, and provided hitherto unknown information about the status of Soviet biological warfare capabilities, transforming the focus of the Cold War endgame. And Colonel Ryszard Kuklinski, a Polish military officer who was a CIA penetration of the Warsaw Pact, supplied information about Soviet/Warsaw Pact military war plans for Europe for some nine years. His work is contained in a book (supported by the CIA) called *A Secret Life*.

In a lower key, the performance of British intelligence at the time of the constitutional conference on Rhodesia in 1979 allowed the British government to make a series of highly risky decisions based on an authoritative, intelligence-based understanding of the underlying positions of the other participants. In 2004 American and British intelligence officials combined to negotiate successfully with Libya's Muammar Qadaffi on giving up his nuclear ambitions.

But the fact that these stories can be listed on a few pages and summarized in short paragraphs makes the point. The true intelligence successes of the Cold War were few and far between. The known cases are already documented—and the list is in single figures. Perhaps there are others but a chronic curse of intelligence is that even the apparently knowledgeable see only a part of the whole. The profession is built on compartmentalization. Nonetheless, in the case of these unsung successes, they and their case officers have been usually and commendably discreet.

The Soviets, for their part, did not fare much better. After the early successes of the immediate post–World War II generation—Klaus Fuchs,

Julius and Ethel Rosenberg, and Kim Philby—recruitments became much harder. George Blake, Aldrich Ames, and Robert Hanson may have had star quality, but, once again, the numbers were low. And certainly, none of the Soviets' efforts prevented their system from going out of business.[1]

Why were there so few successful recruitments when one considers the benefits available to a prospective recruit—fame, money, prestige, security, release from tyranny, and so on? The options seem so favorable, so one must ask why potential targets have often remained so obstinately resistant to these blandishments. Take the case of Juan Miguel González, father of Elian, the young Cuban boy discovered at sea off the coast of Florida in November 1999. When he came to Miami in 2000 to collect his son, it was obvious to most Americans that his and his son's best interests lay in staying in America. There is no doubt that very significant sums of money were on the table. The general assumption was that Juan Miguel would succumb to these temptations. Yet the pull of family, the prospect of becoming a Cuban icon, an apparent faith in Cuba's socialist values and in "the Revolution," were more powerful than most Americans imagined—and he chose to return to Havana. The lesson is that the luster of the American Dream is not, at least in the eyes Mr. González, sufficient to overcome the lure of Cuban celebrity.

The odds in the terrorist world are even more intimidating. In every important facet—contact, visibility, ideology, culture—Western case officers are significantly more handicapped now than they were against the Soviet Union or in the developing world. As far as is known, only one Westerner has cracked the code of gaining personal access to Osama bin Laden other than as a journalist. And even journalists have had scant success.[2]

That one, of course, is John Walker Lindh, a young, not overly gifted youth from Mendocino County outside San Francisco. Despite the fact that he transported himself to Pakistan, let his hair grow long, adopted a revolutionary posture and at least some rudimentary Arabic—in fact, enough to snag a couple of sit-down sessions with America's Public Enemy

Number One—he did not emerge a hero. Instead, he is serving a sentence of twenty years in a federal penitentiary for a feat that no CIA or other American intelligence office has come close to emulating.

THE PERSISTENCE OF FAILURE

It is commonly held that if we can fix intelligence, we can fix our security. Nothing could be further off the mark. Intelligence is not "fixable" in the way that word is commonly understood in corporate America. Failure, consistent grinding failure, is the norm. It is much harder than hitting a baseball, where a 30 percent success rate is considered top quality. It is more like medical research where a hard-working, highly motivated career can go by without making a single breakthrough.

Only infrequently can human intelligence be proved right or wrong by either "technical means" or "open sources." Because the validity of each asset's reporting is a serious and continuing issue, the United States uses several procedures in tandem to try to increase the level of certainty for policy makers. One of these is a "production review," which is a thorough examination of the intelligence production from a particular person viewed over a period of time and in comparison with parallel reporting. A second is "vetting." Beyond background checks, this includes operational testing to determine if an asset is controlled or is a fabricator. And handlers put assets through further tests to determine their reliability, integrity, and discretion. With it all, an asset's reporting can be inaccurate or misinterpreted; ambiguous information can be made to support a political agenda; or a source, such as "Curveball," who was instrumental in the 2003 decision to invade Iraq, may be a fraud.

Among the reasons human intelligence is so difficult to assess is that no matter how well an asset is vetted, and no matter how diligent the continuing checks and inquiries to ensure the assent is not controlled, assets provide inaccurate information for many reasons. They may not know the answers to the questions being posed and fabricate so they don't disappoint their handlers and forfeit future payments; they may not wish their handlers to know they have lost access to the target of the operation; they may have misled themselves and accepted rumor as fact; or they may simply get it wrong because they were misled.

And yet, that human intelligence is indispensible was underscored by Ray Cline, a former deputy director for Intelligence at the CIA who, in an age of technical wizardry, reminded one of the authors that "You can't photograph a man's intentions."[3] Moreover, beyond the complications inherent in managing human assets, the nature of intelligence information itself is problematical. No matter how many times an executive is warned that the views and analysis he is reading are little more than a snapshot of the issue at hand and lack the depth and context of a policy document, for example, such cautions are often overlooked. This is particularly vexing for those involved in the unwieldy and layered process of developing the President's daily briefing, called the President's Daily Brief (PDB). They are acutely aware that the short paragraphs they generate are simply a version of the reality at hand. To be sure, they attempt to make it the most accurate, straightforward version possible, but it doesn't arrive without caveats and is a *version* nonetheless.

All of this came together in the fiasco surrounding the determination by the US and British governments that Iraq possessed weapons of mass destruction (WMDs).

In conversations with one of the authors in Washington and London, senior officers of both the CIA and MI6 reveal similar difficulties in assessing the available human intelligence and verifying it by "technical means" or "open sources."[4] The claim that Saddam Hussein had WMDs[5] was not simply a fabrication to move both nations to war. The reason both intelligence services came to this conclusion was that the SIS (Secret Intelligence Service) and CIA had developed assets with access among Saddam Hussein's generals and ministers.[6] And here is where it gets tricky. Key regime figures made it clear at meetings and in personal asides in the build-up to the war that Iraq still possessed WMDs. It was a very sensitive topic and understood not to be discussed among the senior military staff. Generals commanding certain parts of the battle space believed that while they did not have WMDs under their command, units of the Special Security Organization closest to the regime, and under the direct control of one of Saddam's sons, did retain a WMD capability. The British thus concluded that, based on the confirmation of their well-placed senior sources in the Iraqi General Staff, Saddam had WMDs.

The irony is that the regime's whispers to its generals may have been designed to leak—but not to the British or the Americans. Saddam's purpose was to warn off the Iranians, who he thought would attempt to take advantage of his weakness when the Coalition invaded—which he believed was a virtual certainty. Moreover, once Saddam saw that the Coalition believed he had WMDs, he could not reverse himself with his generals and still maintain their loyalty and commitment to the battle ahead, so he was confined to a posture leading to a war he knew he would lose. Senior CIA officers, though not the Director or Deputy Directors, who ordinarily would have been included among the recipients of cable traffic on the developing crisis, were not included. What they saw they describe as "inconclusive." One told one of the authors: "we assumed they must have more than this—they had to."[7] In their compartmentalized world, they assumed the issue was so sensitive that information was being "stove-piped" directly to the Director and his immediate staff and then to the White House. The checks and balances, experts, and country-desk officers were all excised from the process by the powerful political currents swirling around the CIA.

Neoconservative activists both inside and outside the Administration, emboldened by the view that the British information was correct, caused Washington not to accept the findings of the UN inspectors and other open-source information. The Administration believed it had to proceed on a "worst-case" basis; moreover, its political discourse had prepared the nation for war, and it could not present an uncertain trumpet.

With Iraq we have the anatomy of a colossal intelligence failure that features many of the most perplexing aspects of the business. Asset management, compartmentalization, and the intrusion of political agendas combined in a perfect storm.

In this sense, therefore, the intelligence business is one where failure is a salient characteristic, not just regarding Iraq—as seen most recently and most visibly—but over the long haul. However, as a counter to those who might argue that, if this is true, it would be better to shut the business down altogether, it is accurate to say that intelligence collection has important definable benefits. Beyond winning the lottery, the major breakthroughs—the Gordievskys or the Alibekovs, which can provide decisive advantages on vital issues—the careful sifting, analysis, and assessment of information from multiple unofficial sources reduces, on balance, the margin of error on programmatic and budgetary decisions in Washington by adding to what is known about the issues at hand.

Thus, the essential questions are how to improve the analytical product, how to ensure the policy maker correctly perceives the strengths and liabilities of the information provided, and how to structure intelligence reform to win that lottery twice a decade rather than once. Implicit in this is tamping down expectations of change. Intelligence is not like writing computer code to fix problems like Y2K—bring enough resources to bear and stay at it long enough and the job will get done. It is instead a delicate endeavor undertaken in a world bounded by human frailty and limitation.

THE CENTRAL THESIS

Here, it is legitimate to ask whether a profession based on failure can usefully counter these threats. To answer this, let us start by looking at the central thesis of intelligence, specifically that what you see is not what you get. The story behind the story is more important than the story on the surface. Public domain is not as good as private domain. The off-the-record comment is closer to the truth than an on-the-record comment. An official UN inspector going through the front door will get snowballed; a secret source with a fancy nickname communicating via a "dead drop" will get the truth.

The British Foreign Office issues "guidance" telegrams on a daily basis to all British embassies around the world. These contain the "line to take" on issues of the day. They used to have a cascade of formulations for explaining British policy. This would start with the official vanilla line that was usually beyond bland. Then the formulations would proceed through successive categories beginning with "for use with trusted contacts," then proceeding to "if pressed," then proceeding to "if called a liar," and finally to "if called a bloody liar." In each case slightly fuller, apparently more credible information would be provided. The diplomat's art lay in maintaining dignity as he or she proceeded through the cascade. The assertion of the intelligence officer is that he takes you to the truth palaces beyond the "bloody liar." The claim of intelligence is that it makes you the ultimate insider—and, of course, there are no restraints on governments against trading on this sort of information.

But what is the precise nature of this insider information? Unlike the world of stock tipping and horse nobbling, it is not easy to pin down. Spy fiction illustrates the point. One of the aspects of John Le Carré's many books, especially those set in Soviet contexts, is that his great descriptive and imaginative gifts seem to come up short when it comes to talking about the actual intelligence received by or purloined from George Smiley and the others and smuggled across borders with such fantastic ingenuity. We are always assured that it is the "crown jewels," but what exactly is meant by that is left to the imagination. The "minutes of the East German cabinet" are once referred to in reverent tones. Documents of this sort do, from time to time, come into the possession of an intelligence service. After the initial backslapping for an intelligence coup, those whose job is to process them are soon hard put to justify the translation costs, so turgid were the minutes and so unenthusiastic was the reaction of the foreign office recipients.

The key point here is that just because something is classified does not mean that it is right—or even interesting.

THE MEANS OF PRODUCTION

This brings us to the unsurprising fact that the *means* by which intelligence is pursued and obtained are often a lot more exhilarating than the end product itself. To put this another way: what is special about intelligence is the means by which it is produced. Consider the case of Penkovsky. He dropped documents photographed by a microcamera into a passing baby carriage pushed by the wife of the British Moscow Station Chief. More current examples would be to use exotic technology to tap into a mobile phone, to use vast computer time to mine telephone records for abnormal calling patterns, or to apply a back-door key to a global e-mail system. The advanced capabilities of American special forces are often mentioned in this context. In January 2006 the Russian intelligence service put on display some communications gear disguised as a rock found in a Moscow park that was allegedly used by British agents.[8]

It is crucial to understand that, of themselves, these means say nothing about the quality of the intelligence. People can lie and mislead on the telephone. They can send e-mails designed to be intercepted and then to deceive. Intelligence officers may be reluctant to believe it, but, after going through five hours of ingenious countersurveillance following a detailed preset pattern to reach a safe house by midnight, the agent they meet there may still lie or be under the control of the opposition, or, perhaps more likely, have incomplete or conflicting information.

Thus it is the thrill of the chase that lures the bright, energetic new recruits who pour their energies into operating an Islamist charity in

Tangier or Bradford, or pulling the strings behind a radical madrassa in Lahore or Jaipur. This is not surprising. We have heard much advocacy from bodies such as the 9/11 Commission and the Robb-Silberman Commission about the need to shake up the intelligence agencies, about the urgency to find new ways "to get boots on the ground."[9] These are the new ways.

Back Office Skills

Alongside the glamour jobs, it is also essential to get the fundamentals of the intelligence business right. These are what we call the "back office skills," and they have to do with ensuring that the intelligence product is understood for what it is and evaluated alongside the totality of information available. This sounds obvious, but in practice it is often not the case.

The first back office skill lies in instructing the ultimate decision maker—be it a president, a prime minister, or a generalissimo—that it is an illusion to think of intelligence as a sort of universal shortcut. Confronted with all the surface confusion of a region like the Middle East, the temptation for top decision makers is to see their intelligence agencies as a FedEx service delivering philosopher's stones that unlock the unfathomable mysteries in front of them. This is where the seasoned intelligence officer needs to say "I would add, sir . . . "

There is indeed a case to be made that as a matter of policy the top decision makers should never be shown raw intelligence that is the product from the field before it has been assessed and checked. In fact, the information presented to policy makers is almost always finished. It is rare that a policy maker knows the identity of the source or sees raw reporting, but it does happen—and for all the wrong reasons. The titillation factor for both intelligence officer and President is simply irresistible. In the British system, terrorist-related intelligence is now required to be, as the *Economist* reported, "on several desks in Whitehall [including, very often, the Home Secretary's], sometimes within minutes, rather than hours, of its gathering."[10] The point here is that intelligence must be part of a total information package to be most effective; context is essential.

Part of today's mythology is that even if Washington was wrong on Iraq's WMDs, so was everyone else. This is not correct. The heads of the UN inspection teams, Rolf Ekeus and Hans Blix, were saying at the time that they were unable to find any signs of WMDs, even when they visited map coordinates provided by American intelligence. As Swedes, they were easy targets for the conservative blogging community who christened Blix "Hans the Timid" and drew attention to what they called his "unsurpassed record of failure in dealing with Saddam Hussein."[11]

But, as it turned out, the reason that the UN inspectors were having such a hard time finding WMDs before the invasion had nothing to do with their nationality and everything to do with the fact that there were none, which is to be explained in part as the successful outcome of the United States's own policies on controlling imports and restricting Iraqi access to sensitive materials.

What went wrong is that evidence from the high-visibility part of the spectrum—that is, the routine activity of the UN inspection teams in Iraq—was given less or, indeed, no weight when compared to evidence from the dark end. This goes back to the point made earlier that what is special about intelligence is not the information itself but the means through which it is produced. The backstory still needs to be checked against the front story. Open-source material is valuable. It and intelligence do not exist in independent universes. Sensibly, the Robb-Silberman report recommends the creation of an Open Source Directorate inside the CIA.[12]

So, in reforming the intelligence process in the hope of a better understanding of outside threats, whether from the Islamic world or elsewhere, intelligence production is an important part of the puzzle. But not the only part we have to consider. Retooling the means of production and throwing new resources into the pool does not mean your problems go away.

THE ETERNAL VERITIES

Having established these ground rules about the nature of intelligence, we return to the notion that this is an ancient art. During the Cold War it was practiced with an institutional and systematic approach not seen before. The techniques learned from that time still help to differentiate good intelligence from bad. These include: special pleading, fabrication, disinformation/hostile control, and the human factor. Each warrants some discussion.

Special Pleading—or Self-Interested Sources

A high priority for human intelligence is to understand the "real thinking" or "intentions" of the leadership elites in designated countries and organizations. A recent report by the CIA's National Intelligence Council, "Global Trends 2020," expands this to a need to understand emerging elites as well.[13] This raises an interesting question: do these elites in fact know what their "real thinking" is, and, if so, how do they record this? On paper, as in the voluminous correspondence of Ronald Reagan? Or in conversation, as in the record of President Lyndon Johnson's telephone calls collected in the LBJ Presidential Library? In other words, assuming that leadership elites do have identifiable "real thinking," what is the format to which it is consigned and in which it can be purloined? Usually, the sought-after record does not exist or is so ambiguous as to be meaningless. Bin Laden and Zarqawi have given us the benefit of regular videotapes, but even so, as Professor John Gaddis observes in the January 2005 issue of *Foreign Affairs*, "we know so little of Osama bin Laden's intentions or those of his followers."[14]

In the absence of useful or accessible documents, therefore, we end up talking to the people concerned, or to people who have talked with the people concerned and presumably can report their thinking. The problem is that all of these sources have biases, particular worldviews into which they fit their impressions, or frankly manipulative agendas, and too often they tell powerful people what they want to hear.

Margaret Thatcher had a keen eye for detail. When a report contained language with which she agreed—let us say, "what my country needs is a multiparty system based on free market principles"—she would note in the manuscript, "exactly! MT." In the American system, similar kudos applied if a report was featured in the Presidential Daily Brief or excerpted in the National Intelligence Digest. Naturally, these accolades get passed down the line and eventually make their way back to the source—who, in the instance cited above, was Zimbabwe President Robert Mugabe, simply gaming the system.

Thus, even in well-established intelligence relationships, sources, particularly those with a stake in the outcome, have a tendency to calculate the angles. This does not mean that intelligence services should not be in touch with people like Ahmed Chalabi or Manucher Ghorbanifar. But the product should not be called *intelligence*.

Fabrication

In a word, agents make things up. Even worse, case officers make things up. One of the authors was once discussing an unusually fascinating interpretation of African politics with a colleague. He commented that he had not yet read the material on which the colleague based his analysis. "You will," came the cheerful reply, "I just haven't found a source to tell me this yet." He was acting with the best of motives and was probably in his own right the most authoritative source on this particular subject. Yet the danger is clear.

In the United States, case officers are promoted based on their recruitments and their ability to obtain restricted or secret information requested by the consumer of the information—usually the policy maker. The problem here is the process. Case officers often meet assets in less than desirable locations, in the wee hours of the morning, with only limited time, and with pressure rising in all dimensions. The case officer often converses with his asset in a language learned in the classroom, and in which he is not fluent. He may not fully appreciate the caveats supplied by his source and, since he is a "generalist" usually with a liberal arts education, may have only tangential knowledge of the technical matters—missile gyros, for example—being discussed. All of this invites vital information to be "lost in translation."

Further, his report may be nuanced to avoid flat statements on which he later might be found wrong. That said, he reports what he thinks he hears, or perhaps wants to hear, and he is not unmindful that his consumer is seeking information to support a policy direction. In these circumstances it takes a strong-willed case officer to report information that would contradict the "state of play."

Fabrication also comes in other guises. Viktor Cherkashin explains in his book how the KGB deceived two of its officers who it knew were being controlled by the FBI and CIA.[15] Both officers were provided inaccurate information that they fully believed to be true and that they immediately passed to their US case officers. The information flowed to CIA headquarters and was judged to be correct because it had been reported by two sources who were known to be "validated." What was validated, in fact, were KGB suspicions; the KGB officers were lured back to Moscow, tried, and shot.

Similarly, there are constraints on how tightly the case officer may be able or willing to squeeze the source on the question of access. Access to political subjects does not necessarily give one access to battlefield intelligence. The vital concept here is access. This is especially true if coercive means are involved in eliciting information. Coercion cannot produce real access, although the person being questioned will often suggest that it does. If there is not an intimate connection between access and information, the latter—however fascinating and on the money it may be—is unreliable.

Disinformation

During the Cold War the debate about the integrity of sources operating inside the Soviet Union never stopped. This was not just among the professionally or temperamentally paranoid; it was also an endemic feature of all Soviet analysis. There was probably not a single piece of Soviet-related intelligence exchanged between the Americans and British about which at least one expert had not raised doubts. Indeed, a whole genre of reporting arose that was known to be sourced from agents under Soviet control but was deemed useful because it threw light on "what the Sovs want us to know." Even in the case of so impeccable a source as Oleg Gordievsky, distinguished academic analysts believed that the celebrated RYAN intelligence involving Politburo fears of a Western nuclear first strike was a classic piece of disinformation. It was orchestrated by the then Soviet leader Yuri Andropov to consolidate his power and to influence Ronald Reagan to moderate his posture toward the USSR, with Gordievsky being the unknowing vehicle for transporting this to the West.

Whatever the facts here, the danger is one of neglecting the critical counterintelligence function. Even if one does not believe that Al-Qaeda has the capabilities of the KGB, we should be wary of thinking that interrogation reports and cell-phone intercepts are free from disinformation, the third verity in this pantheon.

Human Factor

Even in days of increasing domination of the collection process by technology, the human factor is ever present. An example of the human factor would be the competitive urge both of individuals and of agencies as institutions to place themselves at the center of the policy process. "Policy relevance" is what intelligence professionals call it. The practical effect is that if a top decision maker lets it be known what he is after, he will get it from one part of the machinery or the other. Over Iraq, when the Pentagon was dissatisfied with the CIA, the Office of Special Plans inside the Pentagon was called into being to present a case more favorable to war.

CONCLUSION

None of this is to suggest that the Cold War was somehow the *belle époque* of the intelligence business that set the standards for all time. In many ways, as outlined above, it was an era in which, despite the input of many millions of person-hours, the output was derisory. Intelligence officers who learned their craft in those days must recognize that the challenges facing today's generation are radically different, notably in the nonstate, highly franchisable, culturally alien, perpetually mobile nature of the target.

Nonetheless, if it were possible to distill one overarching conclusion from earlier experience, it is that it would be a great mistake to give much credence to the notion that we can legislate a "new dawn" in the US intelligence system. Once the reform music has stopped playing and the new incumbents of exalted titles move into the grand offices, the challenges will remain pretty much the same, the available methods not much different, and the eternal verities still in place. No Act of Congress or Presidential Order can rescind these.

Professor Richard Posner—ironically, an esteemed judge of commercial law and a stranger to the intelligence world—gets it right when he observes that the 9/11 Commission promoted a "bureaucratic re-organization that is more likely to be a recipe for bureaucratic infighting, impacted communication, diminished performance, tangled lines of communication and lowered morale than an improvement on the previous system."[16]

Our argument would be to move in the opposite direction. Rather than thinking *supersize*, think *elite*. Shrink the CIA to a size where it is no longer trying to do everything but concentrating quietly and discreetly on what really matters. And even then don't expect too much. Don't pivot policy or the nation's security around intelligence. This is simply another way of guaranteeing further nightmares as discussed in chapter 5.

Beyond this, a more practical recommendation would entail greater focus on the need for users to be aware of both the range and the limitations of intelligence. There is nobody better able to conduct that education than the intelligence officer. This should be a key part of the intelligence officer's activities, to be conducted with pride about what good intelligence can achieve and humility about what it cannot.

There is nothing mold-breaking in these ideas; but that is the point—un-American and contrary to the prevailing wisdom though it may be. Intelligence is an old—one might even say, mature—profession. We are not starting *de novo*. The lessons of the past have value, if we are to get the intelligence service we need.

NINE

The Acid Test

Some years ago, as the New York Yankees prepared for yet another World Series, their legendary catcher Yogi Berra admonished his teammates not to "make the wrong mistake." While it was never clear how much of Yogi's cleverness was intentional, there is a sharp lesson in these words: some mistakes are much worse than others. In American foreign policy, "the wrong mistake"—the far-reaching and perhaps catastrophic error—would be a China policy built on a Big Idea and laced with passion. Perhaps we can avoid it, but the record is not encouraging.

For nearly two centuries, China has been a mystery for Americans: enigmatic, complex, and an open invitation to misunderstanding. Some Americans, from nineteenth-century missionaries to John Foster Dulles, have sought to "save" China, while others have sought fortunes there. Today, a rising China challenges American economic supremacy, and in time it will challenge American military preeminence in East Asia. To protect its interests and to maintain global stability, the United States has no greater strategic imperative than to fashion an effective, rational, and consistent policy toward China in the decades ahead. This is an inherently different challenge from that posed by Vietnam or Iraq. There is no room for error.

At mid-century, in the early days of the Cold War, America believed that its exceptional prosperity, values, and freedoms were being subverted by a grimly determined Communism, and it responded with the Red Scare, a Big Idea that filtered into the political discourse until it eventually defined the era. Joseph McCarthy's notion of monolithic Communism led to the delusion that the Korean War was meticulously planned in Moscow and Beijing, when in fact Kim Il-Sung had made some twenty-four trips to Moscow and Beijing to plead for support for his plan to invade the South.

A decade later, China experts had been so thoroughly expunged from the nation's policy councils that veteran diplomat Averell Harriman, taking office as Assistant Secretary of State for Far Eastern Affairs in 1961, described the bureau as a "wasteland" whose best people had been "blown like leaves all over the earth."[1] George Kennan believed that the Red Scare had destroyed any semblance of rational policy toward the region. "No matter how alluring the opportunities of the service might be . . . few young men would desire to enter if their careers might be blasted at any moment by a dismissal having no connection with efficiency and depending upon the capricious winds of politics."[2] With so many of the nation's talented China experts removed from positions of influence, the great upheaval of the Cultural Revolution, which transformed China in the 1960s, was perceived largely in stereotypes. The yawning expertise gap invited celebrity intellectuals like Walt Rostow to advance fashionable nonsense like his Stages of Growth theory, which ignored the forces of nationalism and misread local history, including the animus towards China evident throughout Southeast Asia. As the United States drifted toward war in Vietnam, the misshapen concept of monolithic Communist aggression also informed the Domino Theory. Senior policy makers in Washington downplayed the postcolonial, nationalist aspirations of the Vietnamese people, choosing to believe the assault on South Vietnam, like the 1950 invasion of Korea, was planned and supported by Beijing and Moscow. McCarthy's legacy so dominated the institutions of public debate that US recognition of China would remain off the national agenda for another decade.

Today, while the generation gap in the policy community is largely repaired, China poses a greater challenge to the American way than ever before. The two nations are deeply interdependent: the United States relies on China to help contain inflation by purchasing Treasury debt and by exporting inexpensive products for sale in US markets. China needs American dollars to fuel its export-driven economy. Without American demand for its products, there is little question that China would fall into chaos as unemployed workers filled the streets. China is a nation riven with internal tensions that result from rapid growth and social dislocation. Yet, there is a faction in the United States that remains instinctively suspicious of Chinese objectives, regarding them as a trenchant challenge to American interests, and convinced that military confrontation is inevitable. Such thinking is gaining traction in certain influential think tanks like the American Enterprise Institute, and should it dominate it could become a self-fulfilling prophecy.

The question we must ask, given China's ambitions and its heightened competition with the United States for oil, grain, and other commodities, is whether a rational, constructive policy of engagement can be sustained in Washington and Beijing. Can we protect American growth and jobs and resolve trade disputes through multilateral institutions such as the World Trade Organization (WTO)? Are both nations politically willing— and able—to sacrifice some growth to prevent imbalances from accelerating in the global environment and sustain diminishing resources? Can China be persuaded to cease using its currency as a trade weapon? If not, both nations will be driven to nationalist positions that carry the prospect of confrontation. To meet this challenge successfully, we must correctly gauge the pressures China faces today and link internal developments to international policies. We must exert pressure where it will benefit American interests but avoid unnecessary confrontation. We must clearly understand the hard pragmatism of the Chinese leadership and their emphasis on trade and investment to achieve their regional and global ends. Most importantly, we must appreciate how this Administration's apocalyptic admonitions about a world stained by terrorism have served to make Beijing's optimistic emphasis on economic growth and a better quality of life in the future more persuasive to those in Southeast Asia, Latin America, and Africa.

Clearly, if a future Administration is as inept and cynical in dealing with China as the Bush Administration is in dealing with the Middle East, it could mean the end of the United States as the world's leading power. America has already lost credibility as the global voice of reason and finds itself unable to assemble a coalition of allies sufficient to address the clearly dangerous nuclear ambitions of North Korea and Iran, or to contain the more conventional ambitions of Hamas and Hezbollah. More broadly, Beijing's predictable, interest-driven policies, abetted by its expanding economy, have made it first among equals in East Asia, where just a decade ago Washington was widely thought of as an honest broker and preferred partner.

It goes without saying that China's ruthless and farsighted leadership will use its economic and military power and growing geopolitical influence to turn any misstep caused by a righteously irrational US foreign policy to its benefit. For this reason alone, we must not again let US policy toward China be driven by Big Ideas: it is not a monolith but a vibrant, complex society with multiple, often conflicting, interests that is embarked upon a difficult transition and facing a range of internal challenges and external pressures—and it could not be of any greater importance to the American people and the West.

SOME INTERNAL REALITIES

No one can tell how China will evolve in the next half century. Perhaps the present leaders will retain their privileges and power; perhaps disparities in income and ideological disputes will bring chaos; or perhaps today's market-authoritarian model of governance will gradually give way to greater freedoms—even a pluralist state. What is certain is that the system is experiencing an array of new pressures that compel it to act in particular ways on the international scene. We may expect, for example, that to sustain its growth and maintain its domestic stability—which means ensuring jobs for the millions of workers leaving state industries for the private entrepreneurial sector—China will act aggressively to secure energy contracts with potential suppliers throughout Latin America and Africa regardless of their human rights policies, proliferation policies, or territorial aspirations—and remain silent when these issues arise in the UN Security Council. For the same reasons, China will seek every possible trade advantage and modify its policies only reluctantly under pressure from the WTO and bilateral partners who are prepared to take action to end Beijing's predatory practices. Moreover, the United States may expect that China will not increase the value of the yuan until it threatens specific and credible action such as tariffs on Chinese imports. Finally, China may be expected to find common cause on select issues with others attracted by the growth potential of "market authoritarianism," such as Russia.

While the examples below are hardly an exhaustive list, they suffice to show that China's behavior in the world, its approach to geopolitical questions, human rights, and trade, will almost certainly be affected by internal conditions not wholly under the leadership's control.

Trapped in Transition

In a nation that is a sea of distinct and competing peoples, the question "what is it to be Chinese?" lies at the center of China's present social torment.[3] The very nature of Chinese society seems to be in play; how this question is resolved will determine which segments of society benefit from modernization, the role of the Internet in Chinese life, and even where the boundary lies between public and private space.

Contrary to the view held by many Americans that the Chinese move as one unit, for many in China there is a vacuum at the center. They feel there is no coherent, broadly held view of the nation's values and priorities or a correct path to realizing them. The chief political struggle is between those proposing ideological solutions for China's current problems—sometimes called "the New Left"—and promarket forces advancing pragmatic solutions. Conflicts over growth-generated social pressures, polluted air and water, conflicting claims to the land, a spectrum of views on rights, and competing visions of the future all cloud the way forward. It is this growing void that has nurtured groups like Falun Gong and, to a lesser degree, the Democracy Movement, which has forced the authorities to recognize the critical importance of fashioning and guiding civic culture. China's leaders realize that if they want to avoid the chaos caused by these new and powerful centrifugal forces, they must rebalance the relationship between the Party, the people, and the ubiquitous consumer culture. But time is not on Beijing's side.

One reason is that globalizing trends and greater mobility mean that information is widely shared, alternative lifestyles are more widely available (and accepted), and Western notions such as "freedom of expression" and "privacy" have gained some acceptance in the public debate. The power of consumerism as an architect of the new Chinese identity is enormous. Yet the market-authoritarian model offers little guidance on appropriate ways to accumulate and enjoy money. Many, though certainly not all, people hide their wealth, not knowing if it is hazardous to be perceived as well off.

Many of the most pressing issues in China's transition, however, arise from new fissures in the social fabric surrounding the transition of workers from state-owned industries to the many private enterprises located in the cities. This reflects a broader demographic trend that has seen China's urban population increase by 13 percent since 1990 so that now 40.5 percent live in cities—a figure expected to rise to 60.5 percent by 2030.[4] Overcrowding has left millions of workers without adequate housing, or salaries to replace those previously subsidized by the state.

Lenient residence requirements have brought homelessness; Shanghai now has soup kitchens.

Thus, the pressures of modernization challenge both the leadership and the people. Communism, as a theory of state, competes with a resurgent consumerism on the eastern coast, which is increasingly divided from the heartland. The prosperous cities on the coast see globalization and economic liberalization bringing them into a modern, industrialized world; the rural countryside sees a Party detached from its socialist roots, rampant corruption, livelihoods evaporating as communal land is sold, and the breakup of families. And among the engines of division is the ever more powerful Internet, to which we now turn.

Democracy and the Internet

Beyond the hubbub of working life there is a separate reality inhabited by China's 111 million Internet users, who exchange opinions and information on everything from rural corruption to Shanghai housing prices and manners in the office. Absent is any detailed discussion of the mechanics of democracy and its applicability or inapplicability to China. This omission is not, of course, by choice: the authorities refuse to permit such discussions.

Confrontations over the spread of information are not new in China, where today there is a patchwork of permitted and forbidden topics. What is new is the presence of an "angry young online"—a growing semidissident community that challenges the Party's "China story." According to one Chinese Internet surveillance official, "the people who get their information from the web are the most active sector of society— 80% of web users are under 35."[5] The censors admit that technology, not politics, is setting the pace for change. The Internet has emerged as possibly the most important influence on public opinion, not only accelerating the communication of news and information within China but also relaying news of unfolding events from the worldwide Chinese diaspora.

The Chinese authorities' faltering efforts to control free expression on the Internet raise the question of how they have managed pressures for reform in other areas. The answer is found in the subtle administration—sometimes benign, other times coercive—of the space where social pressure and dissent have arisen.

The Shifting Boundary between Private and Public Space

The authorities have responded to changes in behavior and custom in several ways, sometimes intervening and other times choosing to ignore new trends. For instance, though China has succeeded in reducing the rate of population growth, the authorities believe that for this success to continue it must remain a secret. If people knew that the fines and sanctions are now rarely imposed, they would have more children. Thus, progress depends on what the authorities don't do: they neither punish violators nor admit that they have ceased to do so.

Sexuality in China today is less regulated than it once was. The authorities seem to believe that greater sexual openness on the Internet helps to release tensions and so do not object. Some of the most popular websites are run by women who describe in detail their many lovers and sexual exploits—a form of expression that would have been forbidden just three years ago.

Outside of cyberspace as well, limits on expression are being challenged more regularly. The resolution of these challenges seems to depend more on tactical compromise than principle. For instance, the weekly magazine insert *Freezing Point*, a section of the official China Youth Daily, was closed for publishing an essay on January 24, 2006, in which a historian, Yuan Weishi, criticized "dangerous nationalist distortions in Chinese history textbooks." Following a public outcry, the magazine was reopened a month later but with milder content and, in a compromise, the responsible editors were moved to the research department.[6] This also would not have occurred three years earlier—the magazine would never have resumed publication. But in 2006 the Party, fearing alienation in these contentious times, was compelled to respond to the public protest. A more arresting example of self-expression was an exhibition of modern sculpture in Beijing that included real body parts in the display. Here, the authorities' apparent lack of interest raised Western eyebrows, but the exhibition provides another example of what the Cambridge Sinologist Anne Lonsdale calls "little bubbles rising to the surface"[7]—and illustrates the delicate distinction between what is officially permitted and what is quietly tolerated. There is an emerging public space in China that must be carefully negotiated but that contains significant areas that are free of government restrictions or guidance.

Privacy

The Chinese notion of "privacy" is likewise evolving. Privacy as Westerners know it is largely absent. In public toilets, people squat elbow to elbow to defecate. Patients in hospitals receive medical procedures in full view of those visiting other patients.[8] There is little inhibition about casual inquiries into intimate topics. The Chinese word for privacy, *yinsi*, implies secrecy, conspiracy, and illicit behavior.

But the way the media, and particularly the Internet, portray questions of privacy in the West has shifted the boundaries between what is "rightfully" in the public sphere and what is private. In a variation of "political correctness," Chinese have become newly sensitive about data mining intrusions.[9] Employees object to their companies' intercepting their e-mails. Those receiving public services now increasingly query the authorities on the questions they are asked in applications for water, electric, and trash removal services.[10]

This is a change from a few years ago, when the public willingly gave information to a state that provided housing, employment, food rations, and travel. Women complied willingly with state procedures for monitoring their menstrual cycles to insure they did not have unwanted pregnancies. Today, however, the increasingly diverse, self-sufficient, and curious population in China's coastal cities, with access to ever-wider sources of information, is creating a new sense of self that implicitly challenges the authorities to conform to global norms regarding personal privacy.

The Future of the Communist Party

One school of thought in the United States asserts that the centrifugal forces at work in China will eventually force a split into three or four new countries: a cosmopolitan eastern coast; a less progressive rural and industrial interior; a far hinterland comprised of the arid northwest and Muslim areas; and Tibet. The likelihood of this actually happening, however, depends on a number of things centering on the strength of Chinese nationalism and its "anti-splittist" theme, whether a new national identity can be crafted, the economy, the future of the rule of law, the viability of the Party, and Beijing's management of rural protests surrounding the use of land and compensation for property seizures. At the center of the last issue is the question of who, exactly, owns the land—a question thought settled by the 1949 revolution. The answer—even the fact that the question has been raised—says much about the state of socialism in China today.

At the National People's Congress (NPC) in March 2006, these pressures boiled over into ideological confrontations on the direction and implications of China's economic development. The disparity in income and benefits between urban and rural populations and increasing rural violence provided the backdrop for the nearly unprecedented clash. Perhaps not surprisingly, the latter centered on the Achilles heel of China's transition, the ambiguity enshrined in the 2003 constitution over land ownership. A proposed law, developed over the past eight years but rejected by the delegates, would have codified property rights to allow the sale of communal land for commercial purposes. A coalition of leftist activists objected that the law failed to confirm that socialist property is inviolable, a concept that had been at the heart of China's socialism. The confrontation is emblematic of a wider issue—and it is not over.

Critics charged that those who drafted the law had copied "capitalist civil law like slaves" and given equal protection to "the rich man's car and the beggar man's stick." Writing in *Business Watch*, a state-run journal, the Marxist economist Liu Guogaung commented that "if you establish a market economy in a place like China, where the rule of law is imperfect, if you do not emphasize the socialist spirit of fairness and social responsibility, then the market economy you establish is going to be an elitist economy."[11] Free-market advocates responded that the sources of social unrest—like the high cost of education and medical care, land seizures, pollution, and poor public safety—were problems of inefficiency and government corruption, not shortcomings of the market.

While President Hu Jintao told the Party delegates that the nation must "unshakably persist with economic reform," he also made a point of praising Mao and underscored his support of Party education centers and the recently revived "self-criticism" sessions designed to revitalize the socialist spirit, particularly in the countryside.[12] The question of the status of property ownership remains very much alive, however, as Hu's government intends to place it before the Party delegates again, this time with greater preparation, realizing that a resolution of this central question is a precondition to China's continued economic progress.

If the National Peoples Congress of 2006 were an artist's canvas, the transition would be displayed in primary colors. And though President Hu painted a clear picture, he was challenged by the need to build consensus, which meant blending and balancing a number of clashing elements. In this case it meant reconciling China's socialist past with the potential of a market-driven future.

Today's Party is a very different creature from the compelling system that once oversaw a vast system of farming communes and work camps and ordered millions of people to build backyard blast furnaces to make steel. Though its influence is felt in every corner of the country, the Party struggles to remain relevant. With the failure to provide a viable Chinese "identity," the Party has been left largely to react to events. Beyond Beijing's inner circle (and perhaps within it), few can articulate the Party's long-term goals. With 69 million members, just 5 percent of the population, the Party has neither endorsed the "New Left," reflecting Mao's egalitarianism, nor expanded freedoms. "Egalitarianism," for all its nostalgic appeal, suggests a discredited "old thinking" and recalls the stagnation of the state-industrial and collective production model. On the other hand, though elites, intellectuals, and bloggers talk broadly about democracy, others are suspicious of the potential for chaos should the masses take the idea seriously. Moreover, it is clear to all that the market has lifted the general quality of life without democracy. So, like Godot, democracy is talked about—some expect it—but there is no way to know when, or if, it will show up.

The Party's failure to produce a compelling rationale for its leadership or provide a social adhesive has left the impression that its primary missions are to respond to emergencies and retain its own power and privileges. This is not to suggest that the Party has become irrelevant. Rather, it suggests the Party has become one of several important institutions affecting China's priorities and direction. It is not the source of innovation and productivity that has propelled China's remarkable growth nor, crucially, is it thought to have protected the interests of the rural population forming its base. But the greatest threat to its continuing viability has been the failure to address the growing numbers seeking greater meaning in their lives, including the Falun Gong, Christian, and Buddhist communities.

In the more developed parts of the country, an important challenge to the Party, particularly in the area of economic development, is the law. Where the Party was once first among equals in adjudicating disputes and establishing precedents for future commercial developments, more recently it is being replaced by the courts. To illustrate how this is playing out consider the drama of "Beer Street" in Shanghai, where residents turned to the law to fight a tacky commercial project on genteel Qinghai Road. At issue was not just whether the Beer Street development would be stopped, but what rules would apply and who would make the decision.

The residents' committee pointed to irregularities in the planning process and petitioned the local Party office to that effect. Older residents among the group believed the Party would protect the neighborhood—others believed the local Party cadres were in league with the developers who had promised kick-backs. And so, for this small corner of Shanghai, the system itself was on trial.

Eventually, a uniquely Chinese solution emerged, emblematic of the contradictions and pressures of transition. The local authorities agreed to permit the bars to open for three months, thus saving face for local officials and the developers. After that the bars would be closed. What is significant is that in this instance the people turned to the law (or the threat of it). They intended to set a precedent that would strengthen both the law and their position relative to the state. The solution reflected the conundrum of China's halting progress in this vexing area where tradition and custom clash with externally imposed notions of "due process." While the Beer Street residents' appeal was inconclusive, it demonstrated the developing relationship between the Party and the law in China and how it is being tested in the public space.

This case revolved around the toxic interface between development, the Party, and corruption. Other cases that push the boundaries of free expression or touch on matters embarrassing to the leadership, however, have been dealt with more harshly. Two come to mind. First is the case of Zhao Yan, a Chinese researcher for the *New York Times* who had been held by authorities since 2004 and was sentenced in 2006 to three years for fraud after originally being accused of leaking state secrets—allegedly, when Jiang Zemin would resign from his top military post. The second involves a blind rural activist, Chen Guangchen, who exposed state policies of forced abortion and sterilization in eastern China and was sentenced to fifty-one months in prison. In Chen's case, his lawyers were accused of theft and detained the night before the trial and then released an hour after it concluded. According to the *Washington Post*: "His supporters say the charges were trumped up to retaliate against him for preparing a class action lawsuit that embarrassed local family planning officials last year."[13]

Thus the progress of the rule of law has been uneven and depends, somewhat, upon the area of society being addressed. In many cases where there has been progress, it may be attributed to globalization and China's burgeoning foreign trade. It derives from pressure on the export and investment communities to accept the rules of the WTO, to enter contracts in which profits and liabilities are calculated by international accounting procedures and standards, and to accept the adjudication of international courts.

This said, it is the rural poor whose disaffection continues to inject a cautionary note. Many of them believe the Party no longer protects them against powerful commercial interests and perhaps has abandoned them entirely. In 2005 there were some 87,000 different protests, many of them violent, over land disputes, extortion, and other acts of malfeasance—up from 78,000 in 2004 and 58,000 in 2003. The element common to nearly all was the demand by locals for a greater voice in decisions that affect them, curbs on corruption, and limits on the Party's seeming arbitrary power to dispose of disputed land. Framing these emotional issues is the growing divide between the booming cities and a disconnected countryside, a world left behind. These feelings are reflected in the numbers: since 1985 nearly all the population growth has occurred in the cities, which means the population of the coastal areas is expanding at four times the rate of the interior.[14] The authorities take these trends seriously and have raised rural incomes by cutting taxes and subsidizing grain production, yet urban incomes continue to outpace rural incomes. Moreover, the differences are greater than the data suggest because urban governments and companies often provide health, education, housing, and retirement benefits not available in the countryside.

Perhaps more than any other issue in rural China, the land issue that disrupted the 2006 NPC has challenged the Party's legitimacy. Peasants expect the Party to protect their claim to the land and to ensure they are fairly compensated if the communes sell it for commercial development. The outcome of this contest will be a critical indicator of China's future as a socialist state. It will confirm that the government gives priority either to advancing socialism or, by allowing communal land to be sold for profit, to advancing capitalist development. This in turn will affect China's reaction to a range of commercial and financial issues that will have broader implications. Acknowledging how serious these pressures are, Chinese Premier Wen Jiabao offered an unusually blunt assessment on January 20, 2006, in Beijing. He said, "Land conflicts, fluctuating crop prices and backward conditions in the countryside are threatening China's stability and . . . China's ability to feed its 1.3 billion people." These problems will challenge the Party more deeply than even the prodemocracy movement that was crushed by the military in 1989 in Tiananmen Square.

Will Market Authoritarianism Work?

For half a century Western-oriented analysts, including may Americans, have believed that market economies inevitably lead to democracy. Typical of this school of thought is Mao Yushi's work:

> Since 1978, along with the emerging dual-track economy, China's politics also has been changing into a dual track system—the in-system and the out-system track . . . The in-system consists of politics combined with the public sector—State owned enterprises, the Party, the government and the military. On that track things more or less remained the same. The out-of-system track is politics combined with the private sector. Remarkable changes have been taking place in this newly emerging track. The nonpublic sector is relatively freer: no party rule, no government rule except observation of the laws, no coercive inculcation of ideology, and no political campaigns . . . From past experience, it can be expected that the out-of-system track will expand, taking the place of the other track . . .

Economic reform has expanded personal freedoms: people are freer to choose an occupation, to move from one job to another, to travel abroad, and to speak more openly . . . Lawyers have become more popular and some court trials have begun to allow visitors.[15]

The assumption here is that the market mechanism generates greater personal freedoms and is accompanied by less government control. These conditions, US policy makers believe, generate pluralist structures such as interest groups and civic associations that, in time, become political parties.

In China, however, choice in the marketplace of consumables has meant only limited choice in the marketplace of ideas. Those who believe that a vibrant market inevitably brings pluralism and democratic participation will be chastened to learn that the market-authoritarian model of governance driving China's expansion has done the opposite.

China's leaders understand that their longevity in office depends on continued economic progress. They calculate, probably correctly, that the story of China's economic miracle must dominate the story of repressed speech, local corruption, and the dissatisfaction of the Net-informed younger generation.

Should the leadership succeed in creating a new broadly accepted Chinese identity associated with growth and prosperity brought by the market-authoritarian model, it would have significant implications for US democracy promotion policies. This would certainly be the case if Beijing sought to export the market-authoritarian model as a template that invited others to apply their national versions of socialism or socialist principles. Among other things, it would demonstrate to authoritarian or quasi-authoritarian nations that one can capture the power of the market without surrendering public space to opposition political actors. Russia (which already calls this "managed democracy"), Cuba, Egypt, and the nations of Central Asia would have a dynamic alternative to the American model.

Americans should not be misled into thinking that consumerism and the Internet will guarantee democracy in China. They will not. Even with a weakened Party, socialist values are broadly accepted—circumstances Beijing can easily manage. As long as the United States remains willing and able to import its products, China's export-driven economy will continue to solidify its market-authoritarian governance. Change in China will come, but it will be varied and nuanced. The central question is, will increased wealth, a better quality of life, and a consumer identity that values material possessions lead to the formation of interest groups that could lead to pluralist political expressions—and eventually political parties? Or can the market-authoritarian model satisfy the people's material and perhaps spiritual aspirations while avoiding the evolution of interest groups and political pluralism?

Conflict and Common Interest

The new consumer identity, tensions between the Party and the law, and the Internet (now a prime social mover) will affect how China behaves on the international scene—sometimes in obvious, predictable ways, but often more subtly. By influencing China's foreign policy, these domestic trends will also influence US-China relations. It is a complex picture best painted in shades of gray. China's slow but steady acceptance of WTO rulings, apparent sensitivity to charges of "currency manipulation," and some progress on curbing arms sales to troubled regions all play into US-China relations. Each suggests moderate progress on contentious issues that juxtapose values and profit. Unless seen in the context of broader US objectives, reversals in one or another of these could trigger passions that alter the current balance. The key, of course, is to retain both equilibrium and the capacity to change the equation at any point that US interests, and particularly US security interests, are seriously challenged.

This is where the American attraction for Big Ideas may hinder the successful conduct of foreign policy. Any of several issues—the above-mentioned trade, currency questions, or more vivid issues such as Taiwan, secret missile sales to Iran, territorial disputes, even perceived personal rebukes such as we saw at the White House during Hu Jintao's visit in 2006—could unbalance the relationship and give nationalistic and jingoistic voices in both countries an excuse for provocations. The debate in the United States over China policy must move beyond depictions of a cunningly rapacious monolith to quantify China's military and trade challenges so that the policy discourse on China is anchored by fact and driven by a strict assessment of American interests. Four issues, in particular, invite the United States to make the "wrong mistake," with consequences that could adversely affect the quality of American life They include a confrontation over Taiwan at a time and in circumstances of Beijing's choosing; inadequate attention to China's strategic acquisition of energy and commodities; misinterpreting China's relationship with Iran and North Korea; and the absence of agreement on environmental policies by both nations to slow the production of greenhouse gases and the abuse of freshwater aquifers, which could lead to confrontations over water and grains.

CHINA IN THE WORLD

For three decades, China's foreign and defense policy has been remarkably pragmatic and relatively free of ideology. To see this, one need only look at China's relations with its neighbors. After two wars with India in the late 1950s and early 1960s, relations are peaceful; there are peaceful relations with Vietnam and Russia after conflict on both borders two decades ago. China has avoided military conflict with Taiwan and Japan and has taken calibrated actions in the North Korea nuclear crisis. This is an admirable record of realistic management on a wide range of foreign and security challenges. It reflects a carefully crafted and distilled set of policies that integrate an assessment of global trends, the balance of power, resource requirements, and trade relationships.[16] The question for American policy makers is, have China's perceptions of the global environment, trade, and security challenges changed materially in the past decade? And if so, how will the United States be affected?

According to the Pentagon, China sees itself as "a developing power whose natural resources, manpower, nuclear-capable forces, seat on the UN Security Council, and growing economy give it most of the attributes of a great power." Its objective is "to achieve 'parity' in political, economic, and military strength with other great powers" and the leadership believes its current trajectory will make it a "medium sized" power not later than 2050. In regional terms, China wants to be the preeminent Asian power, by which it means other global powers could not act in the region "without first considering Chinese interests."[17] The 2006 Pentagon Report on China makes the point that "the pace and scope of China's military build-up already place regional militaries at risk. Current trends in China's military modernization could provide China with a force capable of prosecuting a range of military operations in Asia—well beyond Taiwan—potentially posing a credible threat to modern militaries operating in the region." With the notion that "geography is destiny" Chinese military strategists suggest that with control of Taiwan, China could move its "defensive" maritime perimeter further seaward and improve Beijing's ability to influence regional sealines of communication.[18]

China's leaders believe that in an era generally characterized by peace among the great powers, economic power is the most important element in a nation's strength. Their priority, therefore, is sustained economic growth through investment in technology, domestic resource development, and gaining access to global resources. Military power is considered important mainly to ensure that economic expansion remains on course, to protect the nation's regional interests, and to prepare for a future global role. *Persuasion* is also valued: Beijing believes that improved relationships in the political, diplomatic, and trade areas are essential for the nation's development.[19]

Over the past decade, however, and particularly since 2004, there has been a debate within the leadership over whether the international environment is essentially benign, whether the trend really is toward multipolar power, and whether global conflict can be avoided. Party leaders believe the United States intends to contain the growth of Chinese power, restrain Moscow's re-emergence as a global actor, and retain its dominant position in Asia. They also believe the new United States–Japan Defense Guidelines encourage Japan to assume a broader role in the region. A re-militarized Japan, along with the expected deployment of a US regional defense missile system, could challenge China's nuclear deterrence and complicate its policy toward Taiwan.

The Pentagon concludes: "Beijing believes it will be difficult to develop a special relationship with Washington that would fundamentally moderate any US intent to 'contain' China or that would encourage the United States to cooperate with China in offsetting Japan's growing power."[20] These concerns are reflected in a palpable nationalism often taking the form of anti-Americanism[21] seen in the press, on the Internet, in Party statements, and among the military and other influential circles. The most prominent themes are US militarism or "hegemonism" and US interference in China's internal affairs, namely Taiwan. Both charges have been unremitting over the past decade: Beijing points to the transit of two aircraft carrier battle groups, the USS Independence (CV–62) and the USS Nimitz (CVN–68) in March 1996, sent in response to People's Republic of China (PRC) missile tests designed to disrupt Taiwan's first direct presidential elections. The charge of militarism surfaced again following the US attack in May 1999 on the Chinese Embassy in Belgrade (which may or may not have been an accident).[22] The next month the People's Daily, the Party's newspaper drew a comparison between the United States and Nazi Germany, saying they were "exactly the same" in "their self-centeredness and ambition to seek hegemony."[23] And Chinese rhetoric, matched by an outpouring of neoconservative analysis and scholarly concern in Washington, reached new heights when, on March 31, 2001, a US Navy EP–3 reconnaissance aircraft collided with a Chinese interceptor off of Hainan Island resulting in an extended negotiation for the return of the plane's twenty-one person crew.[24]

The discourse centering on American "perfidy" matured in the late 1990s when several developments pointing to a rising Chinese nationalism sparked concern among a group of American analysts in Washington known as the "Blue team." The term, adopted by William Triplett, a respected former China analyst at the CIA and former staff member of the Senate Foreign Relations Committee, was taken from the Blue team–Red team war games conducted by the Pentagon in which the United States was identified as the Blue team. They had been stimulated to act by what they believed to be an unacceptably lax attitude on the part of the Clinton Administration toward China's growing military capabilities. Particularly disturbing was the decision in March 1994 to terminate the Coordinating Committee on Multilateral Export Controls, the office designed to limit the flow of militarily capable technology to the Soviet bloc and the PRC. What followed were decisions allowing several hi-tech US firms, including AT&T, Loral Space & Communications, Hughes Electronics, and IBM, to export to China a range of telecommunications and computing technology that alarmed many in the Pentagon and Congress. Their charge was that technology exported by these (and other) American multinationals and purchased by the Chinese would be used to modernize and extend the capabilities of the Chinese military, particularly:

- to enhance the capabilities of the PRC's nuclear-armed ICBMs (intercontinental ballistic missiles) and other missiles;
- to manufacture weapons of mass destruction; and
- to enhance PRC intelligence capabilities.[25]

They thought these technologies could well be used against US forces sometime in the future. Moreover, there were cases in which research and development costs for the technologies in question had been borne by the US government.

One might ask how the China debate degenerated into such vitriolic personal exchanges so quickly, where motives and loyalty were routinely challenged; how had China so easily become the pivot on which the national security debate would turn as Bill Clinton sought a second term?

Relations with China deteriorated sharply after the brutal repression of prodemocracy demonstrators at Tiananmen Square on June 4, 1989. Hundreds had been killed and more injured—including a protester captured on grainy black and white film being run down by an army tank. The world recoiled at the raw force used by a seemingly remote and determined leadership willing to turn its back on a relationship that had been nurtured over three decades by presidents from Richard Nixon to George H. W. Bush. Though a decade later, Washington and Beijing would be described by some as "strategic competitors" and others as "strategic partners," many believed they had seen the real China at Tiananmen Square, where a hot summer morning in June revealed a cruel and trenchant adversary.

Peter Rodman—a prominent defense analyst, advisor to Henry Kissinger, and Assistant Secretary of Defense in the George W. Bush Administration—observed that Tiananmen shattered a "domestic consensus . . . used to sustain China policy over . . . three decades."[26] Even though President G. H. W. Bush secretly dispatched his National Security Advisor, General Brent Scowcroft, a close friend and consummate diplomat, to re-establish continuity in the relationship, the mold had been broken, relations were adrift. One couldn't help but think of Humpty Dumpty.

As if flipping to their default position, Americans were disgusted with the Chinese. Candidate Bill Clinton touched a deep chord when, during the 1992 presidential election, he referred to "the Butchers of Beijing." The crowds' throaty response made it one of the most compelling parts of his stump speech. Others, with vested interests in the US-China relationship—business groups, farm groups, and protrade members of Congress—bided their time; they wanted the former status quo ante, and they were willing to wait until a new Administration settled in before pushing for it. Thus, with Clinton's election, though there were multiple interests and many emotions, the understanding between Washington and Beijing had to be constructed anew.

The Clinton presidency saw the Blue team emerge as a counterweight to the powerful pro-China high-tech export lobby. American exporters, not unlike those in prior generations, saw Chinese purchases of everything from Boeing aircraft to IBM and Cray supercomputers, AT&T telephone switching, and fiber-optic technology as a boon to their bottom line.

The Blue team, combining old "cold warriors" and conservative social activists, now boasted such luminaries as William Kristol of the *Weekly Standard*; former CIA Director James Woolsey; author Robert Kagan; Congressmen Dana Rohrbacher (R-CA) and Ben Gilman (R-NY); authors Richard Bernstein and Ross Monroe; Richard Fisher, an influential staffer for then Congressman Chris Cox (R-CA); and many others at think tanks, publications, and foundations. All found China's policies objectionable and agreed that China's modernizing military posed an inevitable threat to US interests in East Asia—and particularly to Taiwan—and that "conflict with China was probable, if not inevitable."[27]

Among the issues that helped to reinforce suspicion about China's motives was the transfer of authority and control of the Panama Canal to the Government of Panama on December 31, 1999. There had been strong objections—voiced mostly by Republicans, and particularly by Ronald Reagan during the 1980 presidential campaign—about the Carter Administration's decision to proceed with the transfer in 1979. But in the deepening anti-Chinese sentiment of the late 1990s—stemming from charges of espionage, influence peddling, human rights abuses, and unfair trade practices—the Panamanian decision to grant Hutchison-Whampoa, a Hong Kong company with close connections to the PRC, permission to operate the ports at either end of the canal, beginning in January 2000, caused a national convulsion. The charge was that the Chinese now controlled the canal and could, at will, close the critical route from the Atlantic to the Pacific to the US Navy. Washington was at great pains to emphasize that Hutchison-Whampoa did not own but simply operated the ports on behalf of the Panamanian government, but this was dismissed as a technicality by the Blue team, particularly after President Clinton said: "I think the Chinese will in fact be bending over backwards to make sure that they run it in a competent and able and fair manner . . . I would be very surprised if any adverse consequences flowed from the Chinese running the Canal."[28]

The Blue team and its supporters imposed its definition of the issue on the national discussion, calling it the "Panama Canal Giveaway." It was an inviting platform. Phyllis Schlafly, a conservative social activist, injected her Eagle Forum into the national security debate with a report called "Red China: Gatekeeper of the Panama Canal," using the issue to generate both political and financial support through a direct-mail campaign directed at the conservative "base."[29] The Senate Foreign Relations Committee held hearings to be told by Admiral Thomas Moorer, a former Chairman of the Joint Chiefs of Staff, that:

> Any one who has been involved in logistic planning where the time of transit from sources of supply to the deployed forces is so critical, knows the danger faced when choke points are controlled by unfriendly forces . . . Control by a hostile power of the approaches to the Canal and the anchorages that would interdict the timely transit of those ships could require taking the facilities by force at a high cost in American lives.[30]

Blue team activists effectively utilized the Panama Canal issue to anchor anti-Chinese suspicions among analysts and commentators across the issues spectrum with considerable political impact. Gary Bauer, President of the Campaign for Working Families, is one example. A passionate anti-abortion activist and a candidate for President in 2000, Bauer mixed warnings about China's intentions in the canal and objections to China's joining the WTO with vivid images of Chinese forced abortions in his political speeches.[31] Human rights activists across the board were involved, even including the Friends of Tibet, who touched still another part of the polity by emphasizing the deplorable treatment of Tibetans and Uighurs whose religious practices were banned and basic rights denied.

The post-Tiananmen suspicions toward China achieved a new intensity in early 1996 when "FBI officials working in the National Security Division discovered through a 'technical penetration' . . . that the Chinese had implemented a plan to influence American politics, including Congress and the White House.[32] In fact, the FBI, with the assistance of an administrative worker in the communications office of the embassy, had planted an electronic device in the code room that intercepted messages from Beijing and, unbeknownst to the Chinese, transmitted the information to US technicians working for the National Security Agency. For over a year Beijing's plans to buy influence with large contributions to the Democratic Party and to the Clinton-Gore 1996 re-election campaign were known only to a small group in the FBI.

What shocked the political and national security establishments, however, and again cast suspicions about China onto the national stage, was when the story was revealed by Bob Woodward and Brian Duffy in a March 1997 *Washington Post* article. They said "that electronic eavesdropping had picked up information showing that the Chinese embassy . . . was used for planning foreign contributions to the Democratic National Committee."[33] This time, it seemed, China had made the "wrong mistake"; attempts by foreign powers to manipulate US elections have never gone down well. China's plan to influence the Administration and the Congress had become a public spectacle. It was immediately seen in the context of Administration decisions to loosen controls on the export of militarily sensitive technology and US exporters who had benefited and made contributions of their own to the Democratic National Committee. Either issue would have been sufficient to underscore doubts about China's intentions; taken together, they had the impact of a near-perfect storm. Not unlike the McCarthy period, China was on America's mind both for what was occurring internationally and for what was occurring in Washington. Either way, China's motives, tactics, and character were thought distasteful—or worse—by Americans following the story.

Meanwhile, among China analysts another theme was emerging that took concerns about China from the tactical to the strategic level.

Michael Pillsbury, a defense analyst under President Reagan—and a China specialist—working from original source material, relayed the Chinese view that world socialism is inevitable. "This harmonious world requires a transition away from capitalism in the major powers toward some type of 'socialist market economy.' Just as China has modified the doctrines of Marx, Engels, Lenin and Stalin to produce what Den Xiaoping called 'Socialism with Chinese characteristics,' so will the United States, Germany, Japan and Russia ultimately develop their own socialist characteristics."[34]

Pillsbury adds important connective tissue to the China debate by casting China's embrace of market authoritarianism in dynamic terms. He took the assumption that had been held by many—that China's unique structure for economic growth harnessed the market while avoiding democracy, and was peculiar to China—a step further. He said that China's market-authoritarian format was not static but dynamic, and that the Party leadership believed that this format, or a local variant, applied to "developing and developed countries alike."[35] This begs the question of whether China will actually export its market-authoritarian model, thus harnessing Chinese socialist values to define its role in global affairs.[36]

In effect, the events of the 1990s reinforced earlier perceptions of China as a threat and an opportunity, and established the context for to-day's relations between Washington and Beijing. Chinese political and military leaders, Internet browsers, businesspeople, academics, and visitors returning to China understood all too well the ambivalence Americans felt toward China arising from China's rapidly modernizing economy, and differences on issues such as Taiwan, nuclear proliferation, the environment, and trade practices. Thus, it is not surprising that growing anti-Chinese sentiment was met by more frequent expressions of nationalism in China, particularly charges of US hegemonism.

In the broader sense the hegemonism charge is rooted in the question of who, the United States or China, will predominate in East Asia. China intends that nations not act in the region without first considering China's interests. The United States—cognizant of East Asian twentieth-century rivalries and renewed tensions on the Korean peninsula, and among Taiwan, Japan, and China—is intent on preventing any power in the region from becoming predominant. Thus, the stage is set. Washington and Beijing each believe their security is better served by different circumstances.[37] The narrower charge, frequently seen in the Chinese media and in the speeches and writings of Party officials and military officers, is that the United States seeks to "contain" China—specifically, to limit its territorial claims in the South China Sea, where ongoing disputes over the Paracel and Spratly Islands and Mischief Rock have seen the PRC clash with several other claimants.

China has tried to offset US power by framing US policy as hegemonistic in global councils and by urging that states reject both overt and covert involvement in the internal affairs of others—an obvious reference to Taiwan and Tibet, but also to the Muslim areas in Xingxiang province. But having made little progress in containing US power, and believing that Washington has at times acted irrationally, Beijing's leaders have begun to think they may have to revise their approach. This places US-China relations today in a delicate position.

Differing perspectives in four areas could bring confrontation, even military hostilities: global role, competition over resources, trade practices, and security. In both the United States and China the preconditions of misunderstanding are present. Both are suspicious, both believe the other is predatory in one way or another, the leaders have different values, and, perhaps most importantly, each believes the other represents, more than any other nation, a serious security threat. In these circumstances, where misunderstandings are a continuing concern, policy must be interest driven and rational. Because of the special place each country has come to occupy in the domestic political pantheon of the other, Big Ideas can be especially dangerous. In past decades they have dominated policy to the detriment of both nations, a mistake we cannot afford going forward.

We begin with Taiwan, which, in the context of the US relationship, is Beijing's prime concern. Here Beijing marries hegemonism and militarism to meddling in internal affairs—all themes that are enduring parts of China's domestic political discourse.

TAIWAN

Taiwan's status is a heavy finger on the trigger of Chinese nationalism. It is the issue leaders know will rally the country in times of stress, it is the geopolitical issue most likely to spark a Chinese challenge to America's regional power, and it is an issue with divergent and contradictory US and Chinese histories. Combined, these make Taiwan the most likely point of conflict between the United States and China. Probing the link between China's historical sensitivities and today, James Lilley, the former US Ambassador to China and Korea and US Representative in Taiwan, wrote in *China Hands*:

Threats to China historically had come either from tribal forces sweeping down from the north, such as the Mongols in the twelfth century and the Manchus in the seventeenth century, or from the sea in the form of the British in the nineteenth century and Japanese in the twentieth century. The land invaders had, in large part, been absorbed by China because of its superior civilization, enduring culture and huge size. The later invasions by sea, however, were more devastating. The British and Japanese had shown little respect for Chinese culture and had destroyed the Qing dynasty and damaged China's first attempt at a republic . . . To avoid a repeat of these invasions by the sea, I reasoned, China sought control of an island chain stretching roughly from the Senkaku Islands off Okinawa down to the Paracel Islands in the South China Sea . . . Control of the islands would form a buffer zone around China's most vulnerable areas on the coast . . .

For the Chinese in the 1980s the inheritor of the threat from the sea was the United States with its powerful 7th Fleet and military bases in Japan and the Philippines. A key location for China to control was Taiwan, situated between Japan and the Philippines.[38]

Taiwan's status and the relationship Washington and Beijing maintain with the island have been the subject of an adroit and thus far successful diplomacy. To minimize the prospect of confrontation, relations among the three entities have been more or less regularized by the Taiwan Relations Act of 1979, which formalized an agreement between the United States and China. The pertinent section of the Act states that the establishment of diplomatic relations by the United States with China rests upon the expectation that differences between Beijing and Taipei will be settled by peaceful means; that the United States will continue to supply Taiwan with the arms it needs to defend itself; that the United States will retain the military capacity in the region to defend Taiwan if necessary, and that both the United States and China agree that there is one China.[39]

The PRC asserts, of course, that Taiwan is part of China and demands that the government in Taipei accept that "there is only one China" as the precondition for negotiations over its future. Citing the precedent of Hong Kong, the PRC has advanced the "one country, two systems" formula. It has used its extensive trade and diplomatic relationships to limit international recognition of Taiwan as a sovereign, independent state to only twenty-four nations. Importantly, Beijing maintains that a declaration of independence by Taiwan would invite a military response.

For its part Taiwan rejects China's formulation. It demands that China conduct relations on a "state to state" basis while accepting the possibility of unification when China's market and social and political freedoms have further evolved. Meanwhile, it has expanded routine contacts such as travel, communications, mail delivery, and investment. In some ways the vibrancy of Taiwan's democracy has made unification more difficult. With the independence issue at the center of the island's political life, politicians, the media, and strong interest groups have generated rhetoric and imagery that has often heightened tensions with the mainland—and with Washington.

In recent years the problem has become more nuanced. Not only has China's emerging consumer culture mitigated some of the sharp differences between Beijing and Taipei, but some one million Taiwanese now live and work on the mainland and, continuing a trend seen since the early nineties, Taiwanese companies invested $2.88 billion on the mainland between January and May 2006, which represents a 46 percent increase over the previous year.[40] Given this easing of relations, many in Britain and Europe—as well as China—find it hard to understand why the United States remains so passionate on the question of Taiwan. The answer to this question reveals why Taiwan is uniquely positioned to trigger events that could rapidly lead to confrontation.

While Taiwan's recognition as a sovereign nation by two dozen countries; its membership in numerous international bodies; and its extensive trade, cultural, and political relations with the United States (it is the United States's tenth-largest trading partner) confirm for Americans that Taiwan is a sovereign nation-state, the passion in the US-Taiwan relationship is found elsewhere. Most Americans who follow the issue believe that Taiwan is a democracy of 23 million people who have embraced the principles enshrined in the US Constitution. Taipei's popular consumer culture reflects the choices and values found in many American cities. And, from Washington's perspective, at a time when the spread of democracy lies at the center of US Grand Strategy, the subjugation of Taiwan by a one-party authoritarian state would be unacceptable. No political leader in the United States could accept such a rebuke to the American spirit, the devaluation of America's commitments, or its resulting reduced role in the eyes of the world community. It is because Americans believe that these less tangible elements, centering on the credibility of American security guarantees and the values associated with American Exceptionalism, are essential parts of the US international presence that Washington would have no choice but to meet a Chinese assault on Taiwan militarily.

Such a development would not occur in a vacuum. For the United States to engage China in the Taiwan Strait by deploying the 7th Fleet and requisite air and ground forces, it would require a compelling and forceful "storyline." The war narrative would begin as Chinese assault forces accumulated along its eastern coast. Underscoring ongoing suspicions about China, it would identify the PRC as the aggressor now in process of violating the Taiwan Relations Act, which had managed a delicate situation for three decades. It would further explain why China had made the fateful decision to upend the region's stability. The narrative would underscore a rise in Chinese nationalism and describe how the leaders engaged the nation in conflict to mask domestic policy failures and suppress dissidents in a wave of jingoism. Referring to predatory and unfair Chinese trade practices, arms sales, and domestic repression, the narrative would reach for connections with the various elements comprising the Blue team base—human rights groups, export control groups, the intelligence community, and so on. With the United States cast as the defender of freedom, again threatened by China as it had been in the 1950s and 1960s, the Big Idea would assume a political life of its own, generating a passionate nationalism in the United States, marginalizing experts, and suppressing dissenters.

Any number of pressures could combine to bring Beijing a new calculus of where it believes its interests lie. It could assault Taiwan in response to a Taiwanese declaration of independence—something over which neither Washington nor Beijing has full control. This was underscored in December 2004 when the Standing Committee of the Chinese NPC announced its intention to include a new "anti-secession law" in its legislative agenda for the March session. A few days later China issued a new defense white paper warning that China's military would "'crush' Taiwan if the latter created a 'major incident' regarding independence." While Washington urged that the two sides not escalate tensions, these documents and various statements by PRC officials raise questions about how long the status quo will remain acceptable to Beijing.[41]

In this context, China might choose to act against Taiwan to offset other pressures by wrapping the country in an "anti-splittist" campaign timed to quell domestic chaos arising, perhaps, from disputes over the ownership of rural farmland or deepening coastal-interior differences. These developments would be made worse by the new and distinct identities evident in China, including new consumers in the coastal areas, energized farmers demanding compensation for their land, the "angry-young online," and the Falun Gong. New limits to the government's role and new boundaries for public and private behavior—together with the Party's inability to provide the social adhesive needed to dampen differences—have all set a new and unsettled domestic tone.

A slowdown in China's export sector caused by weakening consumer demand in the United States, the imposition of tariffs in the United States, or higher-priced export products due to rising wages in China would bring chaos as a slowing private sector was no longer able to absorb the huge number of transitioning workers from closing state enterprises. And, of course, pressures would arise should China experience resource shortages, including energy, grain, or fresh water. Problems in any of these areas could heighten tension, reduce the number of new jobs, and slow China's growth, bringing China closer to the chaos the leadership fears. These maladies, should any of them become severe, could alter the calculus and mandate a national crusade—namely "liberating" Taiwan.

Although a Chinese assault on Taiwan would be designed to address domestic pressures threatening Beijing's stability, all understand that success is not a given. With this ambiguity in mind there is yet another dimension that bears mentioning. United States strategic planners must realize that the Taiwan equation holds the real prospect of a reversal for the United States. The timing, conditions, and nature of an assault on the island are all decisions for Beijing to make; Washington can only react. Logistically, defending Taiwan poses the challenge of lengthy supply lines, considerable cost, and the critical factor of time. Can the United States get there soon enough? Equally important is the question of whether the Taiwanese remain dedicated to a military defense of the island, with its attendant loss of life and property. While this issue has arisen in only the past five years, it is of increasing concern to US intelligence analysts.

When these variables are taken together they illustrate that Washington controls neither the conditions surrounding a confrontation nor its outcome. Taiwan, in fact, represents a strategic liability. Should China choose to force a confrontation, Washington would have to successfully defend the island to avoid a loss of credibility—specifically, the credibility associated with a US security guarantee. Even more, a Chinese occupation of Taiwan would threaten Japan, "the linchpin of US forward deployed military in Asia that acted as a stabilizing force in a historically volatile region."[42] Thus, at a time when the US is militarily occupied in the Middle East and elsewhere, China holds most, if not all, of the cards on Taiwan.

Two dimensions offer a source of some optimism, however. First, this exceedingly difficult diplomatic issue has been managed for three decades with a creative mix of power and ambiguity against the backdrop of China's newly powerful presence in global affairs. The issue juxtapositions China's claims of sovereignty with America's regional presence and credibility and Taiwan's embrace of market-democratic freedoms. Trends, timing, rhetoric, and—most importantly—ambiguity have all played a role and can continue to do so. Second, these trends are well understood among analysts in Washington, Taipei, and Beijing, where expanded commercial relations and increasing coordination between Taiwan and the mainland are quietly supported. Neither Beijing, if tempted by the lure of nationalism, nor Washington, if tempted by resurgent American Exceptionalism, would wish a deteriorating Taiwan situation to be defined by Big Ideas.

Taiwan is not the only issue in which there are tensions in the US-China relationship. Beijing and Washington are guided by different principles in addressing the problem of nuclear proliferation. While this is not an issue that seems likely to provoke a direct confrontation, it is a factor contributing to a rise in frustration in Washington, where policy makers conclude that China's mercantile policies are short-sighted, dangerous, and confirm Beijing's unwillingness to enforce the nonproliferation regime when hard currency can be earned by not doing so. As in the case of Taiwan, avoiding "the wrong mistake" means ascribing the right motive to Beijing's actions. It is here that experts, not Big Ideas, provide the perspective needed to determine and pursue American interests.

NUCLEAR PROLIFERATION

North Korea

Not unlike a martial arts expert who uses an opponent's strength to advantage, China has effectively mispositioned Washington in the high-stakes debate surrounding the North Korean and Iranian nuclear programs. While Beijing has achieved little or no progress in resolving these disagreements, President Hu Jintao's pragmatism stands in stark contrast with the Bush Administration's threats of force. Throughout East Asia (except in Japan), the contrast between Beijing's realism and US idealism, and the resulting anti-American sentiment, have accelerated China's growing influence and prestige, effectively replacing Washington as the voice of reason.

Beijing has dominated the story of the North Korean nuclear dispute, emerging as a pragmatic mediator between Washington and Pyongyang despite an uneasy relationship with the Democratic People's Republic of Korea. China's interest in forestalling North Korean nuclear ambitions and its commitment to stability on the peninsula is clear; Texans would say Beijing "has a dog in this fight." An American strike on North Korea's nuclear facilities would spark a peninsular war, with South Korea's dynamic economy sustaining severe damage—though Seoul would ultimately prevail. The collapse of the Stalinist North Korean regime would mean at least one million refugees would stream over the Chinese border in need of food and shelter, imposing a burden and considerable cost on China. United States and South Korean troops would proceed north but stop at the Yalu River.

In warning of the dangers of such an action, Jiang Zemin, then President of the PRC, told one of the authors in 1996, "remember, North Korea is our wife, but South Korea is our favorite concubine."[43] For China, war on the peninsula is a triple loss: the loss of a "wife" (and "comrade"), the loss of a "favorite concubine" (and vibrant market), and the loss of credibility from having been the steward of a failed policy. Meanwhile, were such an event to occur, Beijing's senior management would be obligated to spend time and money to assist refugees and restore stability.

That the road to Pyongyang now leads through Beijing begs the question of how the North Korean issue is affected by the pressures of China's transition. Certainly, many of the familiar elements are there. China has supported—with a notable interruption in early 2003—the North Korean regime and people over time with grain and oil supplies.[44] Many, certainly within the Party, feel a fraternal responsibility for the impoverished socialist state.

The Party leadership wishes relations between Beijing and Pyongyang to remain as close as "lips and teeth," in part, to dilute what they see as a "containment policy" directed against China by Washington. The Party also believes that the degree of pressure applied to Pyongyang to return to the Six-Party Talks can be calibrated and used as leverage on Washington to reign in the pro-independence activities of Taiwan President Chen Shui-bian. And further, both China and North Korea reflect a mix of skepticism and anger in their dealings with Japan.

Thus, a balance of factors, internal and external, generally mitigate toward the status quo, underscoring the calibrated and pragmatic approach China has taken toward the peninsula and North Korea's nuclear weapons program. The net loser is Washington, having been cast by Beijing in the eyes of the region (except Japan) as driven by ideology and as part of the problem, not the solution. At its root, the United States is ideologically wed to a dysfunctional nonproliferation policy formulated in an earlier technological era. It is an ineffective template for managing nations intent on developing nuclear weapons, and it will continue to misposition the United States in world councils until Washington approaches the issue differently, perhaps giving greater credence to the notion of deterrence.

Iran

In the 2006 dispute over Iran's nuclear program, despite heavy lobbying by the US State Department, China rejected the April proposal by the United States, France, Germany, and Britain to refer Iran to the UN Security Council for possible sanctions. While neither the United States nor China wants Iran to acquire nuclear weapons, China has successfully positioned itself as being pragmatic and moderate in this matter, as it has in the North Korean issue, leaving Washington to play the heavy.

In Iran's case, while the United States and China share broadly similar strategic objectives, they differ on priorities, tactics, and urgency. China has tangential geopolitical interests in the Middle East but also vital trade links with Iran: China exports arms and inexpensive consumer goods, and Iran—beyond the orbit of US influence—is China's second-largest source of imported oil.

Seen from Beijing's vantage point, Iran is vital to China's domestic stability, especially since oil analysts say its proven reserves could be depleted in fourteen years. Were China unable to import the oil needed to sustain its economic expansion, Chinese workers transitioning from moribund state-owned industries and seeking employment in the private sector would quickly fill the streets if new jobs weren't available.

It's a hand-in-glove relationship that has cost the United States dearly. Writing in the *Washington Post*, Robin Wright put it this way:

A major new alliance is emerging between Iran and China that threatens to undermine U.S. ability to pressure Tehran on its nuclear program, support for extremist groups and refusal to back Arab-Israeli peace efforts.

The relationship has grown out of China's soaring energy needs—crude oil imports surged nearly 40 percent in the first eight months of this year, according to state media—and Iran's growing appetite for consumer goods for a population that has doubled since the 1979 revolution, Iranian officials and analysts say.[45]

For Washington, China's pledge to block any attempt to refer Iran's nuclear program to the UN Security Council confirms two points: First, energy supply is directly related to domestic stability and is more important to China than cooperation on global security initiatives; and second, China does not presently share Washington's geopolitical preferences in the Gulf and in fact may see its interests served by strengthening Iran.

What should Washington's policy elite conclude from this? Simply that China's position on nonproliferation is a direct function and nothing more or less than a pragmatic calculation of the security challenges it faces. In addition, all policies have costs. United States support for the War on Terror and Freedom on the March, which often seems directed against Teheran, provides the adhesive that binds China-Iran relations.

TRADE:
HARD CURRENCY AS A STRATEGIC ASSET

Beijing uses its hard currency for a range of investments that secure strategic objectives. These range from the purchase of significant amounts of US Treasury debt, which provides Beijing with leverage in the US relationship, to the purchase of advanced weaponry from the former Soviet states and Russia, to investments designed to secure access to commodities, energy resources, and raw materials in Latin America, Africa, and Southeast Asia.

Internationalists and realists like Brent Scowcroft and former US Ambassador James Lilley, though concerned about the amount of US debt held by China, see these expenditures as the steps powerful nations take to deploy their resources to maximum advantage.[46] They believe that China's behavior confirms and reinforces the normal functioning of the international system and that this is preferable to a resentful China "outside the tent looking in." Others, like Richard McCormack, who served the Reagan Administration as Under Secretary of State for Economic Affairs,[47] and Ted Galen Carpenter of the Cato Institute, view these developments with concern, arguing that China's investments are motivated both by self-interested political and security considerations and, to the degree they succeed, may disadvantage the United States.[48]

China's expanded trade in East Asia is a case in point. Japan already imports more from China than from the United States, and is South Korea's largest trading partner. Current trends indicate that China's trade with all of southeast Asia is likely to exceed that of the United States within a few years.[49] Former US Ambassador to South Korea Jason Shapen points to the strategic implications:

> Aware that China is important to their [Japan's and South Korea's] well-being, they are no longer as willing as they once were to position themselves opposite Beijing, even if this means going against Washington. Put another way, while the Bush Administration still thinks the United States is the sole superpower in a unipolar world, Tokyo and Seoul do not share this view. To them the United States and China are both powers to be reckoned with in a bipolar Asia.[50]

The PRC's use of economic power to support its political objectives is apparent throughout the region and took a big step forward in 2004 when Beijing concluded an agreement with the ten-member Association of Southeast Asian Nations with the objective of creating the world's largest free trade zone, encompassing some two billion people.[51] Not only did the pact secure access to vital raw materials, including oil, iron, and nickel, it also helped to secure the sea lanes. Carpenter points out that Beijing's response to the tsunami in Indonesia illustrates a careful and focused use of its resources. While China provided only $63 million in relief assistance compared to the $335 million given by the United States and the $500 million provided by Japan, its high profile at the center of relief operations in Banda Aceh generated more attention than the efforts of other countries.[52]

Of course Beijing pivots much of its policy on its objective of isolating Taiwan. And, while Washington has taken steps to strengthen its alliances with Japan and South Korea in the event of hostilities in the Taiwan Strait, the effort has met with mixed results. Revisions of the 1997 Defense Guidelines of the US-Japan alliance, and a subsequent 2005 statement issued by the US-Japan Security Consultative Committee, reinterpret Article 9 of Japan's constitution to permit Japan to assist with breaches of the peace "in areas surrounding Japan" and commit the two countries to "common strategic objectives" including the "peaceful resolution of disputes in the Taiwan strait through dialogue." Progress with South Korea, on the other hand, has been limited. To date, South Korea remains opposed to broadening its alliance with Washington to cover a Taiwan crisis.[53]

East Asia, of course, has not been the only recipient of Beijing's calculating embrace. In November 2004 Chinese President Hu Jintao visited Havana, where he made loans totaling $2 billion to support joint nickel-iron mining ventures. When alloyed with steel, nickel creates the highly durable metal that is used in turbines, casings, and armor. Innocent as this may be, strained relations between Havana and Washington cast the transaction in a less than positive light. President Hu's announcement was greeted with alarm on Fox Television and in various right-leaning print media where experts were marginalized and pundits embraced. Elsewhere, it was a nonissue. In the *Washington Post* and the *New York Times*, it received dispassionate "sign-of-the-times" analysis.

What is indisputable is that Hu's trip illustrated China's appetite for raw materials and determination to use its hard currency reserves, and offer of broader relations, to acquire the assets necessary for its domestic economic expansion. Hu's initiative was the sharp end of a strategic planning process underway in Beijing since 2000 that should have stimulated Washington to refocus its attention on Beijing's capacity and intentions. But these steps were not taken.

Beijing's interests, of course, extend far beyond Latin America. In 2006, the New China News Agency reported that trade volume with Africa expanded by 400 percent over the previous five years, to about $37 billion. The advantage for China comes not only from the overt benefits of these arrangements but in requiring business partners not to recognize Taiwan and to sever relations where they exist.

In its quest for energy and raw materials, China has turned an unseeing eye toward rogue governments. While the West has generally refused to do business with Zimbabwe, for instance, because of the Mugabe regime's human rights abuses and destructive and impoverishing "land reform" program, China has been attracted by the resources, and willing to exploit Mugabe's isolation. The PRC now accounts for over 25 percent of Zimbabwe's foreign trade, even receiving Mugabe in Beijing for a week-long state visit in July 2005. Sudan, where the China National Overseas Oil Company won exploration rights in 1995, is another example. When the United States cut its ties two years later in protest over the "genocide" perpetrated by the regime in Darfur, China filled the void by agreeing to develop oil fields and build pipelines and refineries. And, as with Iran, Beijing went further, blocking the issue from being considered by the UN Security Council.

In pursuing its mercantile foreign economic policy, China clearly observes fewer constraints than the Western industrial democracies. Its focus on maintaining domestic stability has generated a policy whose values of convenience—including mutual territorial respect, non-aggression, and non-interference in domestic affairs—challenge the conventions observed by its Western counterparts. China has set a new standard in holding the human and commercial realms separate. It is a policy that turns aside the aspirations of millions for basic civil liberties, even though these values are enshrined in the covenants of nearly every multilateral institution of which China is a member. Of course these policies are driven by China's energy needs, which readily translate to domestic security—and this is the message Washington should take away. China's global reach for resources and commodities is a function of perceived domestic need. Its mercantilism and seeming amorality on humanitarian questions are compelled both by tactical considerations and strategic ones.

RESOURCE USE: A TWENTY-FIRST-CENTURY FLASHPOINT

Lester Brown, the President of the Earth Policy Institute, in a remarkable book called *Plan B 2.0*, makes the point that there are simply insufficient resources on the planet to sustain two fossil fuel–based economies the size of the United States and China. At current rates of consumption in critical areas and without an altered course, Brown's argument, which is emblematic of a well-established genre, is that a confrontation centered on "food and fuel," both of which are being consumed faster than they can regenerate, can not be avoided unless certain fundamental changes in resource use and energy production are made by both countries. "Forests are shrinking, grasslands are deteriorating, water tables are falling, fisheries are collapsing and soils are eroding."[54] The question is, will China reduce the rate at which it is depleting its freshwater aquifers, which are critical to grain production, or will it conclude it would cost less to purchase grain on the international market, which would drive up the price of food worldwide?

While the United States, with 5 percent of the world's population, has for some time consumed nearly a third of its resources, China now leads in the consumption of grain, meat, coal, and steel. The United States uses three times as much oil as China, but China has eclipsed Japan as number two, and while US oil consumption grew by 15 percent between 1995 and 2004, China's doubled.[55] If China's oil consumption per person in 2031 reaches US 2005 per person consumption levels, China will use 99 million barrels of oil a day; the world currently produces 84 million a day and may never produce more.[56] Moreover, China's 1.3 billion people are joined by an additional 3 billion living in developing countries, many of whom are dreaming "the American dream," which requires ever increasing amounts of oil; the effect is to "create a politics of scarcity," already a consideration in US national security planning.[57]

Sustaining the supply of grain at current levels poses an equally serious challenge. In the past half-century, population and income growth have tripled world grain demand, pushing it from 640 million tons in 1950 to 1,855 million tons in 2000. Demand for water has also tripled as agricultural, industrial, and residential uses climbed, outstripping the sustainable supply in many regions. As a result, water tables are falling and wells are going dry.[58]

Brown asserts that grain is the commodity most vulnerable to the declining supply of fresh water, adding, "in the troubled relationship between the global economy and the earth's ecosystem, China . . . is on the leading edge . . . over-ploughing its land, overgrazing its grasslands, and over-pumping its aquifers in its effort to become self-sufficient."[59] Water tables under the North China plain, for instance, an area that accounts for a fourth of China's grain harvest, are falling at an accelerating rate. Speaking to this issue in Beijing in January 2006, Chinese premier Wen Jiabao said, "production this year could suffer from unstable grain prices, unpredictable climate and shrinking arable land."[60] Premier Wen's comment would not have come as news to many Chinese: between 1998 and 2005 China's grain harvest fell by 9 percent or 34 million tons—enough to feed 120 million people.[61] In 2002 the world grain harvest, even with new genetic technologies, fell short of consumption by 5 percent, marking the third consecutive year of grain deficits.[62]

A poor grain harvest in the Soviet Union in 1972 illustrates how shortfalls can impact the market. In that year the USSR turned suddenly to the world grain markets to replace some 10 percent of its supply. The impact on world prices was dramatic; wheat rose from $1.90 to $4.89 a bushel, and the price of bread soon followed. Were China to deplete its grain reserves and turn to world markets to cover its shortfall, now 40 million tons a year (but rising significantly if current trends continue), it would quickly destabilize world grain markets—and, of course, that means the US commodity markets. Such a development would present the United States with a rather delicate geopolitical problem: 1.3 billion Chinese consumers, with an approximately $200 billion plus trade surplus with the United States in 2005, would be competing with US consumers for US grain and driving up the price of food at the American breakfast table. Brown says:

> Within the next few years, the United States may be loading one or two ships a day with grain for China. This long line of ships stretching across the Pacific, like an umbilical cord providing nourishment, will ultimately link the two economies. Managing this flow of grain so as to continuously satisfy the food needs of consumers in both countries, at a time when ethanol fuel distilleries are taking a growing share of the US grain harvest, may become one of the leading foreign policy challenges of this new century.[63]

While sales of this magnitude would bolster farm and food industry profits and also help the US balance of payments, the politics of such a situation would be unsustainable. Blue-team sentiment about the rising "China threat" would be joined by a powerful populism. At the policy level Washington's investment in China's stability would, more tangibly, become hostage to China's continuing purchase of US treasuries.

The competition for resources is a serious problem that will in the decade ahead convulse the US-China relationship. The availability of oil and food to Americans at affordable prices is a nonnegotiable part of the American social contract and so requires effective policy. Moreover, an imbalance in this area would be devastating for the worlds' poor—for the millions living in cities on $1 a day or less and spending 70 percent of that on food, rising grain prices would be life-threatening. According to Brown, "a doubling of grain prices today could impoverish more people in a shorter time than any event in history."[64] The social and political pressures resulting from this are hard to overestimate and, of course, people would hold their governments responsible for the resulting instability.

Meanwhile, there is debate within China on whether it is cost effective for the nation to be able to feed itself. Alternatively, China could, like many other countries, purchase the grain needed to make up the shortfall on the international market. Thus, China's continuing commitment to address this problem with large infrastructure projects and attendant expenditures is uncertain.[65]

This said, were Beijing to ignore the effects of its growing dependence on global markets for grain it would be greeted as a hostile act by many in the West and especially among members of the Blue team. It would confirm a mercenary pattern in which China, when confronted with choices that juxtapose values and profit, sacrifices the interests of the global community until it becomes counterproductive to do so. For Beijing to proceed this way would reinforce those who see China as a threat that can be met only by force.

The more productive course would be to adopt water conservation measures that conserve the freshwater aquifers and minimize the overuse of agricultural lands. Success with new rules and standards here would avoid risky dependence on international markets. Moreover, the US-China competition for oil resources should be regularized. The scope for miscalculation and confrontation over both oil and grain is real and growing, and it provides fodder for Big Ideas rather than rational exchange.

CHINA AND THE UNITED STATES:
A STRATEGIC BALANCE

Deepening financial and trade ties anchor the US-China relationship. Together, American consumers and Chinese producers accounted for about half of global growth in 2005. On the positive side, Beijing's purchase of US debt both on a national and local level has kept US interest rates low, reducing the costs to US consumers in the form of mortgages, credit-card payments, and other lines of credit. China's investment in US government debt has more than tripled in the past five years, from $71 billion in 2000 to $242 billion in 2005, making it the United States' second largest lender after Japan, which holds $700 billion. Its dollar purchases have prevented the dollar from falling and stopped bond prices from rising more rapidly. China thus has a large stake in the value of the dollar and, more broadly, in the vitality of the US economy.

Less positive has been China's 10 percent year-over-year, decade-long expansion. Both commodity and energy prices are higher, and the US is laboring under a huge and growing current account deficit. Moreover, even though average wage rates in China are rising now, historically, low wages sent cheap imports to America that depressed prices and profits for US manufacturers, who responded by "outsourcing."

Interest groups have emerged around each of these issues, raising questions and sharpening the political debate over the equities in the US-China relationship. Beijing was strongly criticized during the 2004 presidential election by Blue-team critics on security and strategic issues and by labor and manufacturing interests during both the 2004 elections and the 2006 mid-term elections for causing the loss of American jobs.

There is palpable worry in Washington that the US is tangled in a Faustian bargain that may not end well. William Kristol, editor of the *Weekly Standard*, and Tom Donnelly, a Fellow at the American Enterprise Institute, both neoconservatives, have underscored this, advocating a harder policy toward China since the 2004 elections. Should China manage its reforms effectively, its growth could exceed that of the US even in its most dynamic periods. If present trends continue, within a decade China will be the world's largest exporter—and around 2040 it will become the world's largest economy. So with a new actor on stage in a major role, it is not surprising there is concern from Jakarta to Berlin to New York about whether it will follow the script.

Moreover, China's holdings give it leverage, making many in the US uncomfortable. Under normal circumstances exercising this leverage would be in neither party's interest. But were there to be tensions in the Taiwan Strait—over oil, or over the price of grain, for example—a slowdown in purchasing US debt, or worse, a cessation, by the PRC would send a shock wave through the United States. China's position as a major creditor provides nothing less than a megaphone at policy tables around Washington and New York, leaving no doubt that decisions made in Beijing can reframe the choices for the US government, consumers, and the quality of life in America.

The rapid increase in the US trade deficit, now totaling about $725 billion, became a political issue in July 2003 when a bipartisan group of sixteen congressmen led by New York Senator Charles Schumer, a Democrat, charged that Beijing "has been playing games . . . to get a competitive edge." The group urged President Bush to "pressure Beijing to let currency markets set the value of China's currency," called the renminbi. They charged the weak renminbi keeps China's labor and production costs artificially low . . . The renminbi is 15 percent to 40 percent below its true value, giving Chinese goods what amounts to an export subsidy . . . It's "a nearly insurmountable advantage."[66]

Between 2004 and 2005 the US trade deficit climbed 17.5 percent.[67] In May 2005 the US Treasury Department said China had undervalued its currency, which cheapened its exports, and that this policy amounted to an export subsidy illegal under WTO regulations. The Department said China "must swiftly overhaul its currency system or face the likelihood of being accused of manipulation to gain an unfair trade advantage—with economic sanctions possibly following."[68]

The Treasury was joined by the Federal Reserve, which expressed fears that if the deficit continued to grow, placing downward pressure on the value of the dollar, higher interest rates would be needed to attract foreign investors. Trends had already revealed the growing difficulty in attracting the $2 billion a day needed to sustain current accounts.

Beijing's calibrated response two months later was to raise the value of its currency by 2.1 percent—which left a bitter taste in Washington. It demonstrated that China had little incentive to redress the trade imbalance, that Beijing rejected arguments about the adverse pressure these policies imposed on the broader relationship, and that Beijing and Washington had very different notions of fair trade and, in any case, chose to evaluate and respond to domestic pressures in different ways.

In the US, with the exception of "cooperation" on antiterrorism issues, China was increasingly seen as a menace. Trade, arms sales, tensions with Japan and Taiwan, currency manipulation, the sheer size of China and its economy—taken together these offered the Blue team a platform. But it was the flood of stories about cheap imports forcing American blue-collar workers from well-paying manufacturing jobs into lower-paying jobs as firms failed or moved offshore that gained traction in the hurley-burley of congressional politics. Like a blind man feeling a topographical map, the politicians could feel the heat on this issue and wasted no time exploiting it.

None of this passed unnoticed at senior levels in Washington. Ambassador Richard McCormack, Under Secretary of State in the Reagan Administration, made the point that "America has an absolute requirement, over time, to buy less from abroad, sell more overseas, or some combination of the two. More and more of the fruits of our work and productivity will otherwise go to our foreign creditors in interest payments and other financial transfers. This ultimately could impact living standards here, depending on the size of our accumulating external debts."[69]

Of course the Ambassador is right as far as he goes. But our point is that the present US-China balance is composed of a number of parts, some of which are very much to our advantage while others form disturbing liabilities. Beijing holds significant US debt and could attack Taiwan almost at a time of its choosing, much to Washington's disadvantage. It is worrisome that Beijing could put in play the credibility of an American security commitment and thus our inestimable role in world affairs. Equally worrying is that the quality of American life is, in certain respects, hostage to decisions made in Beijing; a decision to slow the purchase of US debt would push up interest rates. The US, alternatively, with its vast markets and consumer-driven growth, holds the key to China's continuing growth, but more importantly, to China's stability. We have, in effect, a marriage of liabilities.

The watchword in the relationship is *balance*. With liabilities on both sides, a look at the situation from Beijing's perspective reveals that the leadership places the highest priority on stability and economic growth. Acutely aware of the potential for chaos, China's leaders have invested heavily in rural infrastructure and services to slow the migration to the cities. The 87,000 violent demonstrations in 2005 have left little doubt that relations between the Party, the municipalities, and the farmers must be improved and that the question that scarred the NPC, who owns the land, must be resolved. The new coastal identity being forged by rapid modernization and consumer choices is susceptible to nationalist themes—but these tend to be reactive, not proactive. And while Party activists and security circles are more strident in their anti-Americanism, theirs is one of several voices and not likely to predominate unless pushed to center stage by events.

Taiwan, of course, tops the list of such potential events, but current trends suggest a different outcome. Significant investment by the Taiwanese in mainland enterprises, including farms and vineyards, and over a million Taiwanese working in the Shanghai area alone—often attracted by what is called "the Shanghai heat"—and China's expanding social, travel, service, and financial links with Taiwan suggest that both see greater benefits in the status quo than in a course change.

Equally important, both the United States and China are bound by three agreements on Taiwan in an artful diplomacy over three decades that uses ambiguity to sustain what has been a productive arrangement for all three parties. Violating these treaties by any of the parties would end this careful balance, but it would also end an era characterized by relative stability.

The rational center has an important role to play today. Those with expertise in the various parts of this challenge—trade, finance, military, and strategic—should make the point that the "wrong mistake" with China will bring results quite different from the wrong mistake with Iraq. We are, today, in need of an interest-driven diplomacy; there is no room for Big Ideas. Passion and perceived crisis have mispositioned the United States before in dealing with China. We dare not make that mistake again because the consequences could be more adverse than ever.

A CONCLUDING THOUGHT

Where China is concerned, there are any number of issues that seem capable of spinning public emotion to confirm American misconceptions, reinforce the wrong assumptions, and accelerate misguided policy. More than other countries, China has stirred the passionate chords of American Exceptionalism. Avoiding such a development will be a major challenge for US policy makers—now so heavily influenced by talk media and newly minted experts with all-embracing ideas. A repeat of the process in which neoconservative "thinkers" sculpted the nation's perception of the challenge presented by Saddam Hussein would be catastrophic. In a confrontation with China—or in preventing the inevitable tensions from turning into serious conflict—only carefully focused, rational decision-making will ensure that America sustains its quality of life and the future we all expect to live.

US policy toward China must be based on well-informed calculation of its strengths and weaknesses as well as our own. Problems that demand decisive solutions must be accurately distinguished from those that require management. Most important, it is crucial that, as crises unfold, the nation's mainstream institutions dominate the definition of the problem and push back against those who would cast the confrontation in Manichean terms.

Because China's economy is inextricably bound to that of the United States, the United States will share the complexities of China's transition. We should be under no illusion that China's rise can be managed from Washington or that continued market reforms can be taken as a given. Historical grievances toward the West, a crisis of ideology and identity, an occasionally xenophobic history, demand for greater freedoms, the power of the media, and China's entry to the global multilateral system all impose burdens on China's policy makers.

Among the most striking features of China's government today is its ability to integrate tactical goals with strategic objectives—an ability evident in the long-term development of China's military, its mercantile commercial policies, and its deliberate and cautious diplomacy. The essential rationality of China's senior leaders presents both an opportunity and a challenge to Washington. It is an opportunity because such people can be relied upon to act in their country's interest; thus one can negotiate with them. It is a challenge because there is no room for miscalculation or hyperbole. This is not to overlook the chaos China brought upon itself with the Cultural Revolution in the 1960s or the powerful role Maoist factions continue to play in the nation's politics. Nor do we mean to underestimate the dysfunction of important sectors of the Chinese economy. But the leadership has not permitted these pressures to impede the rational conduct of bilateral relationships or participation in global multilateral institutions.

This leaves us with the problem of determining how China's trade policies and modernizing defense establishment might affect the United States. As China continues to expand economically it will come into conflict with the United States, first on the issue of trade and then over raw materials, energy, and commodities, including grain. We can also expect that there will be different approaches to Iran and North Korea in the

UN and that China will take maximum advantage of rising global condemnation of US policies in Iraq and elsewhere to build its own credibility. The Chinese media will advance the notion that the US military, while unparalleled in its ability to win wars, cannot accomplish its stated policy objective of effecting democratic transformation in areas like the Middle East. Beijing will also say that the world has become a multipolar place in the most important sense—economically—and here it can win the peace. Washington's efforts and likely frustration provide China with opportunities for new bilateral relationships with those governments rejecting US initiatives, and to present itself as powerful yet content to offer the example of market authoritarianism as a development model.

Among all of the elements of China's global presentation, the market-authoritarian model may be its most significant export. Having experimented with this since the late seventies, when the "Commission for Restructuring the Economy"[70] began allowing privately owned seven-person businesses to operate, Beijing, drawing on the experience of Singapore and South Korea and others in East Asia, has developed and refined a model with several important attributes. It allows the leadership to navigate treacherous ideological currents, it satisfies consumer expectations, and it preserves power for an unelected elite. Importantly for our discussion, it is uniquely suited to compete with the challenge posed by Washington.

At a time when the Bush Administration is imbued with the Big Ideas of Freedom on the March and the Middle East Project and Democratizing Russia, the market-authoritarian model presents leaders around the world, who are struggling with the complexities of democracy and its many social and political guarantees, with an alternative. Leaders in Russia, Egypt, and Venezuela, to name a few, might opt for the economic growth and political stability—and the continued longevity of the leadership—brought by market authoritarianism. Very simply, it is a way to generate economic growth, accommodate a middle class, insert one's own national value set—socialism with Chinese characteristics in China's case—and retain power. In the sense that it offers an alternative to the democracy proposed by the Bush Administration, it is competitive.

This has several implications for the United States. First, the democratic product proposed by the Administration must be refined. Since both market democracy and market authoritarianism offer growth and the former is more challenging for the leaders who attempt to implement it, Washington must emphasize the benefits of democratic values. This may be harder than it seems. Nations with no democratic tradition or without roots in the Enlightenment, like China, seem to give priority to personal well being, material wealth, and stability over democratic political freedoms.

This suggests that we must contemplate a long-term contest with China; we conclude this chapter with a modest proposal.

Currently, responsibility for China policy is distributed among several agencies and departments, each with separate perspectives on the matters at hand and each with different responsibilities. The US Trade Representative is concerned with the trade balance and open markets, the Pentagon worries about Chinese military activity, the CIA considers political and economic developments within China and analyzes Beijing's impact on others. The State Department considers bilateral relations, political-military questions, and other functional issues that affect relations. If one visits the White House National Security Council, one obtains a certain view based on that staff's perception of the China challenge; a visit to the Vice President's office yields quite a different assessment.

This means that until a major policy proposal reaches the Oval Office, there is no one place where the whole spectrum of issues relating to China can be considered together in the context of US policy priorities. Unlike the Chinese, we are not able to link our tactical goals with our strategic objectives. The varying perspectives and priorities among different departments invite confrontation within the government so that our "policy" is a series of compromise solutions.

To match China's potential to plan strategically, we believe the Administration should convene a China Working Group that includes political, military, economic, fiscal, trade, diplomatic, human rights, and home-land security experts. Collectively, this group would tell us what the chessboard looks like, distill the options, and identify how the United States can best deploy its resources to protect its interests. How do we hedge against Chinese leverage exercised by holding or selling US debt? How do we manage the outflow of jobs from the United States while re-maining open to free trade? What should our trade balance with China be in three years, or five? Should we challenge China's efforts to gain po-litical leverage through energy and commodities joint ventures? Should we deploy our hard currency assets to offset China's strategic impact? Should our information programs exploit divisions in Chinese society—urban/rural, Han/Tibetan, Han/Uighur, old left/consumer culture—or is that not in our interest? Are we comfortable with China's stewardship of the Korean nuclear talks? Exactly what steps can we take to make the market-democratic model more attractive to nations struggling with de-mocracy and tempted by China's market-authoritarian model? There are many issues such a group could profitably address.

The Chinese Communist Party, while disconnected from the people in many ways, is capable of long-term planning in a way that the United States is not. The time has passed when contingencies can be met by showing the colors, rolling the fleet up to the troublemaker's door, and marching parades down the main streets of midwestern towns. Today, serious challenges can emerge silently, invisible to the patriotic heart, and suddenly be met with an adrenalin-fuelled response. That is what we do not want.

TEN

A Return to Rationality

When Air Force One landed in St. Petersburg on July 14, 2006, for that year's G-8 discussions, President George Bush carried a burden as daunting as any US President since the Cold War's end. Among the active issues absorbing top management's attention in Washington were the recent North Korean missile tests, stalled talks at the UN regarding both the Korean and Iranian nuclear programs, incipient civil war in Iraq, and an expanding war among Israel, Hezbollah, and Hamas. United States–Russian relations, once hopeful, had turned cool over the issue of President Putin's antidemocratic initiatives, particularly the steps the Kremlin had taken to extend its control in the nation's energy and media sectors. Moreover, Russia made clear in advance it would not regard the G-8 as a success unless it was asked to join the World Trade Organization; it was not.

There is no shortage of Administration critics, and these reversals will only give added impetus to armchair diplomats and generals who would have done things differently. Our concern, however, is a different one. In this book we have looked at how the public and private components of our foreign policy came together. How influential was neoconservatism as an expression of American Exceptionalism? How important were the Administration's Big Ideas, the War on Terror and Freedom on the March, and its notion of transforming the Middle East? What roles did Congress, the media, the think tanks and the academy play—and when? Was the rational center, the voice of expertise and experience, integral to the policy discussion? Did it contribute all it could have in the first months of 2003, when the Administration announced that removing Saddam Hussein would lead to a regional transformation in which democracies would replace authoritarian regimes? Is it doing so today when so many other crises loom on the horizon?

THE RATIONAL CENTER

Sadly, the rational center was silent on Iraq. Why? Because the lure of celebrity separated eminent academics from opinions critical of the Administration's assumptions; talk-show formats mispositioned the nation's foremost intellects so that they were unable to articulate their arguments; the White House press office created an echo chamber where sympathetic media outlets reflected the Administration's narrative and marginalized critics; think tanks concluded that vital government grants and other funding were dependent on compatible public positions; the political and media cultures celebrated the war as patriots and allowed doubters to be demonized. Others, who can be placed in none of the above categories, were simply unsure and confused about what to believe and said nothing. The effect was to suppress the rational center and the debate that was needed to form effective policy. Put another way, if policy is formed without the benefit of full debate, then one of the nation's most remarkable and indispensable treasures—its free-flowing intellectual energy—has simply been abandoned.

Despite the emotions that attend moments of crisis—fear, anger, patriotic fervor—it is the responsibility of those with area, language, academic, and practical experience to enter the political debate early, as developments are defined. In the months following the Taliban defeat in

Afghanistan in December 2001, when plans were underway to invade Iraq and "transform" the region, the rational center had a responsibility to lend its expertise to the debate. This was the time and the arena for the rational center to engage the "Bush Doctrine," to push back against the policies that would bring so much dysfunction and chaos.

A FATEFUL YEAR

That the Administration faced a distasteful string of reversals in St. Petersburg is readily traced to the foreign policy detailed in the January 2002 State of the Union Address and made operational in the National Security Strategy nine months later. Iraq, Iran, and North Korea were singled out as "an axis of evil, aiming to threaten the peace of the world."[1] To confront them, the Administration stepped beyond the normal diplomatic and economic instruments, and beyond the established doctrine of "preemption," to embrace the notion of "preventive war." "To forestall or prevent . . . hostile acts by our adversaries," the National Security Strategy declared, "the United States will, if necessary, act preemptively."[2] With this statement, the Big Idea Freedom on the March assumed an ominously militant quality.

This was not the first time in American history that megaconcepts framed the foreign policy discussion only to become the common denominator in the domestic political debate. From President Bush came the stentorian reminder that the nation is "at war." The nation was told that these are not ordinary times. Sacrifices would be made—not just the lives of soldiers or the debt to be serviced by this generation's children, but the civil liberties and privacy that would be restricted and the expansion of executive powers Americans would be asked to endure. The President bent the nation to his will in the heady days after 9/11. The War on Terror and Freedom on the March provided the distilled essence of Bush's foreign policy and America's global mission.

Piet Hein, a Danish mathematician who bedeviled the German occupation of his country in the 1940s with his poems, may have captured the odd zeitgeist with his verse:

> *As Pastor [Bush] steps out of bed*
> *he slips a neat disguise on:*
> *that halo 'round his priestly head*
> *is really his horizon.*[3]

FREEDOM ON THE MARCH

Freedom on the March framed the Administration's aspirations following 9/11 without properly matching available resources to objectives. Even more fundamentally, this Big Idea failed to account for the experience and judgment of many regional experts in the United States and abroad who advised that most Muslims, if given the opportunity, might not choose American-style democracy. This Big Idea also spawned deeply misleading notions about the capacity of America's high-tech military to project decisive power. It has taken the bitter experience of the past three years to remind Americans that their military, while technically capable of dominating any specific battle space on the globe, including Iraq, is not trained for police work or institution-building —necessary skills for securing peace after victory. Moreover, Freedom on the March subsumes a host of lesser ideas. In the chapters on intelligence and insurgency we described significant disconnects between our actual capacity in these arenas and the public's perception of our abilities. Intelligence reform will not, for example, guarantee our security at home or the installation of democracy abroad. Nor have democracies had much success in suppressing insurgencies fought on foreign soil. These myths, in service to Freedom on the March, have received far too little public discussion.

REGAINING OUR BALANCE

The Pew Research Center for the People and the Press reported in late 2002 that "negative opinions of the US have increased in most of the nations where trend benchmarks are available."[4] That same year *Newsweek International* editor Fareed Zakaria made the point that "anti-Americanism is emerging as the planet's 'default ideology' which translates into deepening threats against Americans, both as individuals and as a people"—though he added that "the anger may be less anti-American than anti-Bush."[5] America as global conscience and peace-keeper, as honest broker, as voice of reason from East Asia to Caracas to Riyadh, was most clearly seen in the rear-view mirror.

At home there is a parallel reality; the story is told in the metrics. Some 2,800 service men and women have been killed and approximately 18,000 seriously injured. Approximately $350 billion has been spent in Iraq. The Administration has experienced sharp political reversals in the 2006 elections with both the House and Senate now controlled by the Democrats. Some six years after George W. Bush assumed office, the nation is waking up to the bankruptcy of Freedom on the March.

Not only will the Middle East not be transformed by persuasion or force in the foreseeable future, but Bush's remarkable shrinking presidency has delivered a new reality—a shrinking American global presence.

Of course, cultures, especially political cultures, are not static, and reality is a hard teacher. The souring political atmosphere, coupled with policy reversals, compelled the Administration to reinvent itself in a process that can be traced back to early 2005 when, as with McCarthy's Red Scare and then Vietnam, the syndrome proceeded through its cycle and began regaining its equilibrium. As before, as the Big Ideas collided with the realities of public opinion, resource limitations, and a growing realization of ruined and lost lives, lost credibility, and sacrificed values, a resurgent rational center again found its voice. The collapse of one of the Administration's Big Ideas (the other, the War on Terror, is still going strong) brought a changed political atmosphere in which the Administration's discourse was increasingly defensive and explanatory; though still setting the agenda, the ringing hortatory dicta were gone.

The late Gian-Carlo Rota, a controversial mathematician at MIT and the Los Alamos National Laboratories, had his own way of noting the failure of grandiloquent policies and puffery emanating from second-rate leaders: "When pygmies cast such long shadows, it must be very late in the day."[6]

And so it was. In 2005 and 2006, leading neoconservatives left the Administration and were replaced by a generally more pragmatic leadership. The Administration's ideological edge was blunted when Paul Wolfowitz left the Pentagon in January of 2005; John Bolton effectively left his policy job as Under Secretary for Arms Control and International Security to become America's UN Ambassador in March; Douglas Feith resigned in August as Under Secretary of Defense, having been largely inactive for some months; and Lewis "Scooter" Libby resigned in July over the Valerie Plame affair, for which he was subsequently indicted.

Meanwhile, the new Secretary of State, Condoleezza Rice, set a better tone. With the support of the Foreign Service and the intelligence community, she tried to insert pragmatic objectives into several dysfunctional policy areas, including North Korea and Iran, and to stem deteriorating relations with the Russians and the Europeans—a pattern that continued through the 2006 G-8 foreign ministers' meeting in Moscow.

These years saw a newfound willingness to use multilateral settings to advance policy. The Administration began to work with the international grain, not against it—a change that found support in the editorial columns of the *New York Times* and the *Washington Post*, both of which had turned sharply negative toward the President on a host of issues ranging from excessive spending to alleged abuse of executive power to the conduct of the Iraq war. This was reflected in *Time* and *Newsweek* and colored the network and cable news. Vice President Cheney and

Defense Secretary Rumsfeld, both conservative nationalists and also former congressmen, seemed newly sensitive to rising disapproval of US
policy toward Iraq and to America's growing isolation from the international community. The military's lack of confidence in Rumsfeld was
made explicit in April 2006 by a group of six senior flag officers who
specifically objected to his decisions on the military force structure for
Iraq, believing there were insufficient troops to accomplish the mission.
They contended that the Secretary's imperious management style suppressed analysis he did not wish to see and that the United States could
not prevail in Iraq unless he resigned. Though their objections precipi-
tated a torrent of complaints about the conduct of the war, they were
not new. In February 2003 Army General Eric Shinseki had warned that
"several hundred thousand troops" would be needed to stabilize postwar
Iraq, only to be told by Deputy Secretary Paul Wolfowitz that he was
"wildly off the mark."[7] What was new was that the environment had
changed. The rational center academics and think tanks, as well as talk-
show participants, the press, and public opinion, had gone on the offensive and begun the process of recalibrating policy.

Two contemporary crises make this point: North Korea and Iran. One
of the first issues to reflect the Administration's new emphasis on diplomacy was the North Korean nuclear crisis. Recall that President Bush
referred to Kim Jong-il as a "Pygmy" in 2002, adding that he was "im-
prisoning intellectuals" in "a Gulag the size of Houston" and acting like
"a spoiled child at a dinner table."[8] Following their withdrawal from the
Nuclear Nonproliferation Treaty in 2003, the North Koreans requested
Six-Party Talks among themselves, South Korea, Japan, Russia, China,
and the United States. Their demands included a security guarantee and
diplomatic recognition from the United States, relief from restrictive
trade sanctions, and a light water reactor. The ensuing three years have
seen encouraging moments when it appeared that the United States,
China, and Japan had gained North Korea's agreement to abandon its
nuclear program and return to the treaty. At other times, Pyongyang's

rhetoric and actions—six missile tests in July 2006 and the threat to test a nuclear weapon in October, the latter being the most memorable example so far—underscored the regime's dangerous unpredictability.

Between 2002 and 2005, North Korea's missile tests would have brought terse personal condemnations, threats of military action, and a redeployment of the Pacific fleet, but by 2006, with the Administration embattled both domestically and internationally, a new, center-driven consensus had begun to emerge.

On July 7, 2006, President Bush gave a press conference in Chicago at which the majority of foreign policy questions centered on the North Korean missile tests. Bush said on several occasions "we must be patient." He emphasized that it had taken years to for the situation to develop and it would take time to resolve it. At one point he said "diplomacy, diplomacy, diplomacy." Not only were his tone and body posture designed to convey rationality and reassurance, but his policy prescriptions were measured, multilateral, and incremental. It was clear that the President, faced with uncertainty in Iraq, Israel, and Afghanistan, had no intention of inflaming the North Korean situation with "bring it on"–style rhetoric. Morally based, presumptive pronouncements were out; pragmatic diplomacy was in.[9]

The changed policy environment is also apparent in the case of Iran, where the problem is strikingly similar. The rising chorus in Washington—predating Mahmoud Ahmadinejad's election as President of Iran in June 2005—to support dissidents wanting to overthrow the ruling theocracy failed to gain strength even after Ahmadinejad urged that Israel be "wiped off the map."[10] Pragmatism, even in the face of the Iranian President's outrageous comments, carried the day. Putting aside the war drums, Washington allowed the European Union to take the lead, with Britain, France, and Germany negotiating with Tehran to allow International Atomic Energy Agency (IAEA) inspections that would verify the peaceful purposes of Iran's nuclear program. Washington stood apart, threatening military action in a "good cop, bad cop" combination, and there seemed, for a while, some prospect of success. When Teheran refused to supply the information requested by the IAEA and was referred to the UN Security Council for possible sanctions, however, Russia and China withheld full support. And Washington, preoccupied with Afghanistan and Iraq and a sudden war between Israel and Hezbollah, could not credibly threaten military action. The crisis in Israel and Lebanon had the effect of suspending both military and diplomatic options while Iran was left to proceed with its nuclear program outside the IAEA framework and in potential violation of the Nonproliferation Treaty.

As Israel contends with an unstable Lebanon in the north, Hamas in the South, and Iran's burgeoning regional presence, the most striking aspect of the situation is the lack of options available to the United States. Widely blamed for initiating regional chaos with the invasion of Iraq, Washington has limited diplomatic clout. Its overstretched military resources would limit the options for unilateral action even if that were desirable. In less than six years, the pursuit of a Big Idea at a moment of crisis has depleted America's finances, hamstrung its military options, and reduced its global credibility. And the object of this miscalculation was Iraq. Joe Nye, of Harvard University, often says, "it's not whose military wins, it's whose story wins."[11] In Iraq, neither the American military nor the American story is winning. What if it were China in place of Iraq?

A careful look in the summer of 2006 reveals a Washington regaining its balance, as it has done in the past. It is instructive to look at what didn't happen in the first days of the fighting between Israel and Hezbollah. The Bush Administration didn't indulge in paranoid "with us or against us" rhetoric; it did not demonize the Lebanese government; there was no talk of unilateral military action by the United States. Reality is a hard teacher, and whether this newfound restraint reflected a real change of strategy or simply the lack of other options remains to be seen. Nonetheless, the restraint was undeniable.

Yet, in world councils from Delhi to London to New York there is a palpable deflation. The American coin is worth less today than it was just a few years ago. And although we will slowly regain our traction in the world's diplomatic and security debates, we will not return to *status quo ante*. All cultures, including political cultures, change. The Bush Administration has pursued policies that have raised questions about its commitment to the law. The Supreme Court, for example, rebuked the Administration on its claim that detainees in the "war on terror" are not covered by the Geneva Convention, on its use of "signing statements" to impose an interpretation on new laws that modified congressional intent, and on the use of warrantless wiretaps by the National Security Agency against US citizens in circumvention of the Foreign Intelligence Surveillance Act court established to rule on such matters. The doubts raised by the Administration in these areas have allowed America's detractors, particularly in Europe, to label the United States a rogue state rather than an example to be emulated. This criticism, born of America's susceptibility to Big Ideas and the continuing strength of American Exceptionalism, comes at a particularly awkward time. America pictures itself as leading the world to an improved quality of life, fair and predictable justice, and better governance. But for American values to prevail, the American story must prevail, and it cannot if so many of the world's citizens distrust America's response to challenge or crisis.

As the decade proceeds, the United States finds itself locked in violent confrontation with the Islamic world from Iraq to Pakistan. Much is at stake, including the Administration's Middle East Project, the containment of a virulent and growing anti-Americanism, and the credibility of the American security commitment. Samuel Huntington heralds a Clash of Civilizations. The more serious confrontation, however, is elsewhere.

China is the main security challenge for the United States and the West in the century ahead. A misstep here can alter the quality of life across Europe and the United States, and alter the global security landscape. In the twenty-first century the United States will confront China on East Asian security matters including Taiwan, trade matters, access to resources, conflicting models of government, and differing priorities in troubled regions like the Middle East. Rarely in history have such competitions remained free of violence. And as we have pointed out, there are powerful voices, including *Weekly Standard* editor William Kristol, former CIA Director James Woolsey, Bill Gertz of the *Washington Times,* Republican strategist Bill Triplett, and former Acting Assistant Secretary of Defense Frank Gaffney, who believe a military confrontation with China is inevitable. The neoconservative mantra "force as an early option" would make the United States the perfect foil for China's patient multilateralism.

The profound difference between the American and Chinese styles of negotiating international problems is not to America's advantage. The United States, and much of the West, favors coercive diplomacy with force never far behind. This is quite alien to the Chinese tradition, which is based much more on patience and incentives. As China gains increasing weight in international bodies, it will insist that its approach be more broadly accepted, which will be difficult for the United States. To compete successfully in these circumstances, the United States may need to create a centralized mechanism that integrates its security, trade, financial, and diplomatic policies toward China so that they can be proactive, strategic, and effective.

Most importantly—now, and for the foreseeable future—the United States and China share a common interest in a stable and predictable global environment. We share an interest in managing global resources and in sustaining a trade and financial relationship that benefits both.

For all the damage the Iraq war has caused, and for all the disappointment brought by the Bush Administration's policies elsewhere in the world, one could say that America has dodged a bullet. Iraq was a pitifully weak enemy, and all of radical Islam, despite its chokehold on the world's most coveted resource—despite even the sometimes hysterical rhetoric coming from both the Arab countries and our own—is not a threat on the scale of Nazi Germany or Soviet Russia at its height. If we had committed such a blunder against an enemy whose strength was more nearly equal to our own, our future—and the world's—would be in jeopardy. The rational center was silent not exactly at the right time—there is never a right time—but not at the worst time either.

In previous crises our fire power was also directed at weaker foes. During our shooting wars in Korea and Vietnam, our leaders still practiced restraint in dealing with the Soviet Union—a policy that had the virtue of self-preservation. Even at its most foolish, America retains a reservoir of good sense. Let us hope it prevails.

Postscript

Most striking for observers of this vivid morality tale is the process, the recurring cycle, by which the nation is regaining its balance and direction just as it did after the McCarthy era and the Vietnam War. We have noted the changed tone of the Administration's narrative, the departure of key neoconservatives, and the rising criticism evident in the nation's editorial columns and opinion magazines. But rarely does one see the actual instruments of such a course correction as we have this time. The long arm of President George H. W. Bush is seen rescuing his son's presidency. Together with senior members of his former administration, realistic thinkers including former Secretary of State James Baker, former National Security Advisor Brent Scowcroft, and former CIA Director Robert Gates, he has orchestrated the removal of Donald Rumsfeld from the Defense Department and prepared the nation to receive the recommendation of the Iraq Study Group, chaired by Baker and Democratic Congressman Lee Hamilton. The report will urge that dialogue be opened with Iran and Syria who, in turn, will be encouraged to moderate the militias so destructive to Iraq's fledging government. Both Syria and Iran will demand concessions to do this. In Iran's case, agreement for it to proceed with a nuclear weapons program; in Syria's case, agreement to suspend the inquiry into the death of former Lebanese Prime Minister Rafik Harriri. These are high prices to pay, and agreement will not come easily.

But, most importantly, the Study Group appointed by the Administration has emerged as the critical instrument of change. With official status and buoyed by public opinion, it will function to open the policy debate and to underscore what pragmatic steps may be available at this late stage.

For many, the election results, the removal of Secretary Rumsfeld, the removal of the neoconservatives who authored "Freedom on the March," and the prospect of a policy change as described above, and now embraced by former conservative supporters of the Administration such as Henry Kissinger are the last piece of the recurring process in which the nation regains its balance following a bout of "exceptionalism." Unlike the Bourbons who were said to have remembered everything but learned nothing, it seems this lesson must be both remembered and learned by each generation.

Notes

INTRODUCTION

1. Michael Ignatieff, *American Exceptionalism and Human Rights* (Princeton: Princeton University Press, 2005), 1–26.

2. George Lakoff, *Don't Think of an Elephant: Know Your Values and Frame the Debate—The Essential Guide for Progressives* (White River Junction, VT: Chelsea Green), 35ff.

3. "Top Bush Officials Push Case against Saddam," CNN.com, 8 September 2002, http://archives.cnn.com/2002/ALLPOLITICS/09/08/iraq.debate.

4. "The Times and Iraq" (26 May 2004), http://www.nytimes.com/2004/05/26/international/middleeast/26FTE_NOTE.html?ex=1400990400&en=94c17fcffad92ca9&ei=5007&partner=USERLAND.

5. Michael R. Gordon and Bernard E. Trainor, *Cobra II: The Inside Story of the Invasion and Occupation of Iraq* (New York: Pantheon Books, 2006); Paul R. Pillar "Intelligence, Policy and the War in Iraq," *Foreign Affairs* 85, no. 2 (March–April 2006): 15–27.

6. This reference is to the regular "State of Iraq" statistical reports compiled by the Brookings Institution. See for example Nina Kamp, Michael O'Hanlon, and Amy Unikewicz, "The State of Iraq: An Update," *New York Times* (1 October 2006), http://travel2.nytimes.com/2006/10/01/opinion/01ohanlon.html.

7. Gideon Rose, "Get Real," *New York Times*, 18 August 2005, A18.

8. See for example Andrea Mitchell, *Talking Back—To Presidents, Dictators, and Assorted Scoundrels* (New York: Viking, 2005), and Rajiv Chandrasekaran, *Imperial Life in the Emerald City: Inside Iraq's Green Zone* (New York: Knopf, 2006).

9. Alan Wolfe, *Return to Greatness: How America Lost Its Sense of Purpose and What It Needs to Do to Recover It* (Princeton NJ: Princeton University Press, 2005), 160–65.

10. Richard Levin, "Baccalaureate Address: Reviving Public Discourse," Yale University Office of Public Affairs, 10 October 2006, http://www.yale.edu/opa/president/speeches/20050521.html.

11. George W. Bush, "President Thanks Military, Guests at 'Celebration of Freedom' Concert," *The Ellipse*, Washington, DC, 19 January 2005, http://www.whitehouse.gov/news/releases/2005/01/20050119–15.html.

12. "President Delivers State of the Union," Washington, DC, 28 January 2003, http://www.whitehouse.gov/news/releases/2003/01/20030128–19.html.

13. Posting on Poynteronline.com, "A Plea to News Bookers and Producers," 19 September 2005, http://poynter.org/forum/view_post.asp?id=10304.

14. Samuel P. Huntington, "The Clash of Civilizations?" *Foreign Affairs* 72, no. 3 (Summer 1993): 22–49. See Bernard Lewis, "The Roots of Muslim Rage," *Atlantic Monthly* (September 1990): 47–60.

15. Samuel P. Huntington, *The Clash of Civilizations and the Remaking of the World Order* (New York: Simon & Schuster, 1996).

16. Henry A. Kissinger, "The US and Pre-emption," *Washington Post*, 9 April 2006.

17. George Bush and Brent Scowcroft, *The World Transformed* (New York: Knopf, 1998).

18. George H. W. Bush, "A Europe Whole and Free," remarks to the citizens in Mainz, Rheingoldhalle, Federal Republic of Germany, 31 May 1989, http://usa.usembassy.de/etexts/ga6–890531.htm.

19. Steven R. Weisman, "Rice Admits US Underestimated Hamas Strength," *New York Times* (30 January 2006).

20. R. Nicholas Burns, "US Policy toward Iran [Rush Transcript; Federal News Service]," Center on Foreign Relations, 11 October 2006, http://www.cfr.org/publication/11698.

21. See Thomas P. M. Barnett, *The Pentagon's New Map: War and Peace in the Twenty-First Century* (New York: Putnam, 2004).

22. David Halberstam, *The Best and the Brightest* (New York: Modern Library, 2001).

CHAPTER ONE

1. George F. Kennan, *American Diplomacy*, expanded ed. (Chicago: University of Chicago Press, 1984), 62.

2. David Campbell, *United States Foreign Policy and the Politics of Identity* (Minneapolis: University of Minnesota Press, 1998), 130–32.

3. Wilfred McClay, "American History: A Drama of Sweep and Majesty," *American Educator* (Autumn 2002), http://www.aft.org/pubs-reports/american_educator/issues/fall02/index.htm.

4. Ibid.

5. Wilfred McClay, "Mr. Emerson's Tombstone," *First Things* 83 (May 1998): 16–22.

6. McClay, "American History."

7. John Winthrop, "A Model of Christian Charity," sermon given on board the *Arbella* (1630). See http://www.winthropsociety.org/doc_charity.php.

8. Jonathan Edwards, sermon (1742), *The Works of Jonathan Edwards: With a Memoir by Sereno E. Dwight*, vol. 1 (Avon: Bath Press, reprinted 1995), 381.

9. W. W. Rostow, *The Stages of Economic Growth: A Non-Communist Manifesto* (New York: Cambridge University Press, 1967).

10. George Gedda, "Rice Delivers Democratic Message in Alabama," *Washington Post* (22 October 2003), http://abcnews.go.com/Politics/wireStory?id=1239765&CMP=OTC-RSSFeeds0312.

11. Thomas Paine, *Common Sense* (Philadelphia, 10 January 1776). See http://www.ushistory.org/paine/commonsense.

12. Michael H. Hunt, *Ideology and U.S. Foreign Policy* (New Haven: Yale University Press, 1987), 2–5; Walter A. McDougall, *Promised Land, Crusader State: The American Encounter with the World since 1776* (Boston: Houghton Mifflin, 1997), 18–19; Wilfred McClay, "Revisiting Reinhold Niebuhr's *The Irony of American History*," Witherspoon Lecture Series at the Family Research Council, Washington, DC, 5 March 2002; Robert Fossum and John K. Roth, "The American Dream," British Association for American Studies Pamphlet no. 6 (Summer 1981): 1–2; Leland Roth and Marion Dean Ross, "American Architecture: Nationhood and After; 1783–1815," *MSN Encarta*, http://encarta.msn.com/encyclopedia_461575773_2_21/American_Architecture.html#s21, 1993–2006 Microsoft Corporation. All rights reserved.

13. John O'Sullivan, quoted in "The Great Nation of Futurity," *The United States Democratic Review* 6, no. 23 (November 1839): 426–30, http://www.mtholyoke.edu/acad/intrel/osulliva.htm; Paul Rathe, "How Revolutionary Was the American Revolution?" Bradley Lecture, American Enterprise Institute, Washington, DC, 13 January 1997; McClay, "Mr. Emerson's Tombstone."

14. McDougall, *Promised Land, Crusader State*, 24.

15. President John F. Kennedy, inaugural address, 20 January 1961, Washington, DC: http://www.yale.edu/lawweb/avalon/presiden/inaug/kennedy.htm.

16. George Washington, farewell address (1796), in the George Washington Papers at the Library of Congress, 1741–1799: Series 2 Letterbooks, Letterbook 24.

17. McDougall, *Promised Land, Crusader State*, 20.

18. John Quincy Adams, "Fourth of July Address" (1821), quoted in *Respectfully Quoted: A Dictionary of Quotations Requested from the Congressional Research Service*, ed. Suzy Platt (Washington, DC: Library of Congress, 1989), No. 613.

19. Hunt, *Ideology and U.S. Foreign Policy*, 11–13; McDougall, *Promised Land, Crusader State*, 25–26.

20. James Monroe, message to Congress (December 1823), quoted in Platt, *Respectfully Quoted*, No. 40186.

21. McDougall, *Promised Land, Crusader State*, 57, 70–73; Bradford Perkins, *The Cambridge History of American Foreign Relations*, vol. 1: *The Creation of a Republican Empire* (Cambridge: Cambridge University Press, 1993), 167.

22. Ibid.

23. McDougall, *Promised Land, Crusader State*, 57.

24. John O'Sullivan, *New York Morning News*, 27 December 1845 (see John O'Sullivan, "Annexation" in *The United States Magazine and Democratic Review*, vol. 17 (July 1845), quoted in "North America on the Eve of the United States–Mexican War, 1845," The Newberry Online Library, Chicago: http://www.newberry.org/k12maps/module_14/images/o_sullivan.pdf); McDougall, *Promised Land, Crusader State*, 77–78.

25. John Lewis Gaddis, *Surprise, Security, and the American Experience* (Cambridge: Harvard University Press, 2004), 33.

26. William Gilpin, *The Central Gold Region* (Philadelphia: 1950; see Thomas Karnes, *William Gilpin: Western Nationalist* [Austin: University of Texas Press, 1970], 383); congressional testimony of Senator Daniel Dickenson (1847); http://66.102.9.104/search?q=cache:O08UOBpkh8kJ:www.spartacus.schoolnet.co.uk/WWmanifest.htm+%22Our+form+of+government+is+admirably+adapted+to+extended+empire%22&hl=en&gl=uk&ct=clnk&cd=1.

27. Joel Daehnke, *In the Work of Their Hands Is Their Prayer: Cultural Narrative and Redemption on the American Frontiers, 1830–1930.* (Ohio: Ohio University Press, 2003), 229.

28. Ibid, 6.

29. *Boston Times*, 22 October 1847, quoted in Frederick Merk, *Manifest Destiny and Mission in American History: A Reinterpretation* (New York: Alfred Knopf, 1970), 122.

30. Admiral Robert F. Stockton, quoted in McDougall, *Promised Land, Crusader State*, 95.

31. The cause of the *Maine* explosion remains uncertain. A 1976 US Navy reexamination of the facts pointed to a boiler explosion as the likely cause. See Admiral Hyman Rickover, *How the Battleship* Maine *Was Destroyed* (Washington, DC: Department of the Navy, 1976).

32. "I'll Furnish the War," *Time* (27 October 1947), http://www.time.com/time/magazine/article/0,9171,854840,00.html.

33. John Baker, "Effects of the Press on Spanish-American Relations in 1898," 20 Ocober 2005, http://www.humboldt.edu/~jcb10/spanwar.shtml.

34. Baker, "Effects of the Press on Spanish-American Relations in 1898."

35. Matthew T. Herbst, "Methodism and Aggressive Christianity," *Journal of Religion and Society* 7 (2005): 1; Reverand Alexander Blackburn, quoted in McDougall, *Promised Land, Crusader State*, 119.

36. Senator Albert Beveridge, quoted in Richard Vedder, Lowell Gallaway and Stephen Moore, "The Immigration Problem: Then and Now," *The Independent Review* 4, no. 3 (Winter 2000): 351; also quoted in Kenneth Stampp, "The Tragic Legend of Reconstruction," *Commentary Magazine* 39, no. 1 (January 1965).

37. The ad appeared in the *Humboldt Times* on 12 April 1898 and in the *Chicago Dry Goods Reporter* in March 1898. Baker, "Effects of the Press on Spanish-American Relations in 1898"; Rob Schorman, "'Remember the Maine, Boys, and the Price of This Suit'—Clothing and Nationalism in the Spanish-American War of 1898," *Historian* 61 (Fall 1998): 119–34.

38. John B. Judis, "Imperial Amnesia," *Foreign Policy* 8 (July–August 2004): 50–59.

39. Niall Ferguson, *Colossus: The Rise and Fall of the American Empire* (New York: Penguin, 2004), 152–53; see also Gaddis, *Surprise, Security, and the American Experience*, 18–23.

40. Michael Mandelbaum, *The Ideas That Conquered the World: Peace, Democracy, and Free Markets in the Twenty-first Century* (New York: PublicAffairs, 2002), 17.

41. McDougall, *Promised Land, Crusader State*, 126.

42. Comment by Dr. Tarak Barkawi, Centre of International Studies, University of Cambridge, in discussion with Stefan Halper, March 2006.

43. Quoted in Walter Lippmann, *Public Opinion and Foreign Policy in the United States* (London: Allen and Unwin, 1952), 25–26.

44. 55th Inaugural Ceremony for George W. Bush, 20 January 2005: http://www.whitehouse.gov/inaugural.

45. Philip Pan, "In China, Rumsfeld Urges Greater Global Role, Freedom, Military Candor," *Washington Post* (19 October 2005): A18.

CHAPTER TWO

1. Senator Joseph McCarthy, address at the McClure Hotel, Wheeling, WV, 9 February 1950, reprinted in the Congressional Record, 81st Congress, 2nd session, 12 February 1950, 1954–57.

2. Loren Baritz, *Backfire: A History of How American Culture Led Us into Vietnam and Made Us Fight the Way We Did* (New York: Morrow, 1985), 71.

3. Senator Joseph McCarthy, address at the McClure Hotel, Wheeling, WV, 9 February 1950, reprinted in the Congressional Record, 81st Congress, 2nd session, 12 February 1950, 1954–57.

4. John Earl Haynes and Harvey Klehr, *Venona: Decoding Soviet Espionage in America* (New Haven: Yale University Press, 1999).

5. George F. Kennan, "Sources of Soviet Conduct," *Foreign Affairs* 25 (July 1947): 575.

6. George F. Kennan, "Russian-American Relations," lecture given at the University of Virginia, 20 February 1947, quoted in John Lewis Gaddis, "Containment: A Reassessment," *Foreign Affairs* 55, no. 4 (July 1977): 878.

7. Kennan, quoted in Gaddis, "Containment: A Reassessment," 879.

8. George Kennan, *Memoirs: 1950–1963* (New York: Pantheon Books, 1972), 58.

9. Kennan, quoted in Gaddis, "Containment: A Reassessment," 880.

10. William C. Berman, *William Fulbright and the Vietnam War: The Dissent of a Political Realist* (Ohio: Kent State University Press, 1988), 1–2, 197–98.

11. George F. Kennan, *At a Century's Ending: Reflections 1982–1995* (New York: Norton, 1996).

12. Robert S. McNamara, *In Retrospect: The Tragedy and Lessons of Vietnam* (New York: Times Books, 1995), 30.

13. Dana Adams Schmidt, "Saigon's Premier Gaining Strength," *New York Times* (20 January 1955): 3.

14. Clarence Wyatt, *Paper Soldiers: The American Press and the Vietnam War* (New York: Norton, 1993), 64–65.

15. Ibid., 64–68.

16. William M. Hammond, *Reporting Vietnam: Media and Military at War* (Lawrence: University Press of Kansas, 1998), 1–2; Wyatt, *Paper Soldiers*, 67–72.

17. David Levy, *The Debate over Vietnam* (Baltimore: Johns Hopkins University Press, 1995), 21–32; Louis Liebovich, *The Press and the Modern Presidency: Myths and Mindsets from Kennedy to Election 2000* (Westport, CN: Praeger, 2000), 55–59.

18. Michael Getler, "A Parting Thought on Iraq, Again," *Washington Post*, 9 October 2005, B6.

19. C. L. Sulzberger, "Trying to Build Stability in Vietnam," *New York Times* (12 March 1955): 18.

20. Liebovich, *The Press and the Modern Presidency*, 57; C. L. Sulzberger, "Trying to Build Stability in Vietnam," *New York Times* (12 March 1955); and "Crisis in Vietnam," *New York Times* (28 March 1955); Wyatt, *Paper Soldiers*, 60; Hammond, *Reporting Vietnam*, 1–2; Eric Alterman, *Sound and Fury: The Making of a Punditocracy* (Ithaca: Cornell University Press, 1999), 47–53; William C. Berman,

William Fulbright and the Vietnam War: The Dissent of a Political Realist (Kent, OH: Kent State University Press, 1988), 1–2, 197–98.

21. Quoted in Berman, *William Fulbright and the Vietnam War*, 10.

22. Frank Church, quoted in Robert David Johnson, *Ernest Gruening and the American Dissenting Tradition* (Cambridge: Harvard University Press, 1998), 272–73.

23. Melvin Laird, "Iraq: Learning the Lessons of Vietnam," *Foreign Affairs* 84, no. 6 (November–December 2005): 31. See also Michel R. Beschloss, *Taking Charge: The White House Tapes* (New York: Simon & Schuster, 1997), 493–505; Scott Shane, "Vietnam Study, Casting Doubts, Remains Secret," *New York Times* (31 October 2005), http://www.nytimes.com/2005/10/31/politics/31war.html?ex= 1288414800&en=c2f5e349563a32d9&ei=5088&partner=rssnyt&emc=rss.

24. President Lyndon Johnson's message to Congress, Joint Resolution of Congress H. J. 1145, 5 August 1964, quoted in "The Gulf of Tonkin Incident," *The Avalon Project at Yale Law School*, http://www.yale.edu/lawweb/avalon/tonkin-g.htm.

25. Ezra Y. Siff, *Why the Senate Slept: The Gulf of Tonkin Resolution and the Beginning of America's Vietnam War* (Westport, CT: Praeger, 1999), 38.

26. Johnson, *Ernest Gruening and the American Dissenting Tradition*, 254. See also Siff, *Why the Senate Slept*, 100.

27. Quoted in Johnson, *Ernest Gruening and the American Dissenting Tradition*, 233–43.

28. "Ashcroft: Critics of New Terror Measures Undermine Effort," CNN, 7 December 2001, http://archives.cnn.com/2001/US/12/06/inv.ashcroft.hearing.

29. "Cheney Warns Democrats," CBS News, 17 May 2002, http://www .cbsnews.com/stories/2002/05/17/politics/main509395.shtml.

30. Daniel Ellsberg, *Secrets: A Memoir of Vietnam and the Pentagon Papers* (New York: Viking Press, 2002).

31. President John F. Kennedy, inaugural address, 20 January 1961, Washington, DC, quoted in "The Avalon Project at Yale Law School," http://www.yale .edu/lawweb/avalon/presiden/inaug/kennedy.htm.

32. See W. W. Rostow, *Stages of Economic Growth: A Non-Communist Manifesto* (New York: Cambridge University Press, 1967).

33. Thomas L. Friedman, *The World Is Flat: A Brief History of the Twenty-first Century* (New York: Farrar, Strauss and Giroux, 2005).

34. Kimber Charles Pearce, *Rostow, Kennedy, and the Rhetoric of Foreign Aid* (East Lansing: Michigan State University Press, 2001).

35. Michael Wolf, "The Plot to Sell the News," *Vanity Fair* 11 (November 2004), http://urielw.com/refs/0411wolff.htm.

36. Kennedy, inaugural address 1961.

37. Bill Kovach and Tom Rosenstiel, *Warp Speed: America in the Age of Mixed Media* (New York: Century Foundation, 1999); and David Domke, *God Willing? Political Fundamentalism in the White House, the "War on Terror" and the Echoing Press* (London: Pluto Press, 2004), 163–64.

38. Ari Fleischer, quoted in David Dadge, *Casualty of War: The Bush Administration's Assault on a Free Press* (New York: Prometheus Books, 2004), 107.

39. George F. Kennan, *Russia and the West under Lenin and Stalin* (Boston: Little, Brown, 1961), 5–6.

40. Dean Acheson, *Present at the Creation: My Years in the State Department* (London: Hamilton, 1970), 302–3, 374–75.

CHAPTER THREE

1. Quoted in Jacques Steinberg, "The News Is Funny, as a Correspondent Gets His Own Show," *New York Times*, (12 October 2005): B4, http://www.nytimes.com/2005/10/12/arts/television/12colb.html?ex=1286769600&en=262a857c34eb149f&ei=5088&partner=rssnyt&emc=rss.

2. Dan Froomkin, "Caught on Tape," *Washington Post* (14 October 2005).

3. Transcript: "Richard Holbrooke on Kofi Annan," *The O'Reilly Factor*, Fox News, 4 January 2005, http://www.foxnews.com/story/0,2933,143376,00.html.

4. Transcript: Henry Kissinger on *Hannity & Colmes*, Fox News, 29 July 2003.

5. Transcript: "Gen. Clark Reacts to Sen. Durbin on Gitmo," *Hannity & Colmes*, Fox News, 15 June 2003, http://www.foxnews.com/story/0,2933,159907,00.html.

6. Quoted in Eric Alterman, *What Liberal Media? The Truth about Bias and the News* (New York: Basic Books, 2003), 128.

7. Transcript: "Suicide Bomber Blows Up U.S. Military Mess Tent in Mosul; Bush Presents Outlines of Second-Term Domestic Agenda," *The Capital Gang*, CNN, 25 December 2004, http://transcripts.cnn.com/TRANSCRIPTS/0412/25/cg.01.html.

8. Transcript: *The McLaughlin Group*, Public Broadcasting Service, 31 January 2003, http://www.mclaughlin.com/library/transcript.asp?id=342.

9. Transcript: *The Washington Week*, Public Broadcasting Service, 29 July 2005: http://www.pbs.org/weta/washingtonweek/transcripts/transcript050729.html.

CHAPTER FOUR

1. There were notable voices like Brent Scowcroft, Lawrence Eagleburger, James Baker, General Eric Shinseki, and Lawrence Lindsey who did, indeed, speak out, but

they became the exceptions that proved the rule. Yet, there are few, if any, similar examples that lead back to Brookings. A review of the archives reveals considerable Brookings material being produced during the build-up addressing questions of strategy, troop levels, the peril of high-speed warfare, and how best to beat Saddam in the event of war, but little on the actual merits of Administration policy. This would suggest that Brookings analysts directed their analytical efforts to particular elements of the build-up and apparent war-fighting strategy rather than to challenging the Administration's rational for transformational change in the Middle East or war in Iraq.

2. Virginia Campbell, "How RAND Invented the Postwar World," *American Heritage of Invention and Technology* 20 (2004): 50–59.

3. Richard Haas, quoted in "The Role of Think Tanks in US Foreign Policy," *Electronic Journal of the US State Department* 7, no. 3 (November 2002): 2, http://usinfo.state.gov/journals/itps/1102/ijpe/ijpe1102.pdf.

4. Ibid., 20.

5. Heritage Foundation, "Is the European Union in the Interests of the United States?" seminar, Washington, DC, 28 June 2005.

6. New America Foundation, "Why Foreign Policy Matters to the Democratic Party," forum, Washington, DC, 16 June 2005.

7. Charles Krauthammer, "The Unipolar Moment," in "America and the World, 1990/91," special issue, *Foreign Affairs* 70, no. 1 (1990–1991): http://www.foreignaffairs.org/19910201faessay6067/charles-krauthammer/the-unipolar-moment.html.

8. American Enterprise Institute, "Briefing on the London Terrorist Attacks," forum, Wohlstetter Conference Center, Washington, DC, 11 July 2005.

9. Hudson Institute, "America's Mission: Debating Strategies for the Promotion of Democracy and Human Rights" forum, Washington, DC, 20 June 2005.

10. Heritage Foundation, "American Public Diplomacy: A Roadmap to Recovery," forum, Washington, DC, 14 June 2005.

11. See the United States Institute of Peace, Gingrich-Mitchell Task Force on UN Reform: Nations Have International Responsibility to Protect People within Own Borders from Genocide, 15 June 2005, http://www.usip.org/newsmedia/releases/2005/0615_unreport.html.

12. Heritage Foundation, "Finding Inspiration in Black History: Radicals and the Thirst for Literacy," Washington, DC, 15 July 2005.

13. Heritage Foundation, "Job Bank On-line Application," http://www.heritage.org/About/JobBank/JobBankApp.cfm.

14. Vault Career Service, "Internships with Think Tanks,"http://www.vault.com/articles/Internships-with-Think-Tanks–17332861.html.

15. Heritage Foundation, "The Politics of Peace: What's Behind the Anti-War Movement?" forum, Washington, DC, 30 August 2005.

16. Rick Perlstein, "Goodbye to the Vietnam Syndrome," *New York Times* (15 October 2002): A15.

17. Ken Pollack, *The Threatening Storm: The Case for Invading Iraq* (New York: Random House, 2002).

18. Philip H. Gordon and Michael E. O'Hanlon, "Dealing with Iraq," *Financial Times* (30 November 2001), http://www.brookings.edu/views/op-ed/gordon/20011130.htm.

19. Philip H. Gordon, Michael E. O'Hanlon, and Martin S. Indyk, "Getting Serious about Iraq," *Survival* 44, no. 3 (Autumn 2002), http://www.brookings.edu/views/articles/gordon/20020901.htm.

20. Michael E. O'Hanlon, "We're Ready to Fight Iraq: Saddam Is No Match for America's Military," *Wall Street Journal,* (29 May 2002), http://opinionjournal.com/editorial/feature.html?id=110001770.

21. Martin S. Indyk, "U.S. Victory in Iraq Opens Possibility of Palestinian-Israeli Settlement," lecture given at the Ronald W. Burke Forum, UCLA, 9 April 2003.

22. James B. Steinberg and Michael E. O'Hanlon, "Set a Date to Pull Out," *Washington Post,* (18 May 2004): A19, http://www.brookings.edu/views/op-ed/steinberg/20040518.htm.

23. Carnegie Endowment for International Peace, "The Consequences of War in Iraq," forum, Washington, DC, 14 November 2002.

24. Frederick D. Barton and Bathsheba N. Crocker, "A Wiser Peace: An Action Strategy for a Post-Conflict Iraq" (Washington, DC: Center for Strategic & International Studies, January 2003).

25. John McCain, "Containing Saddam Has Failed: Regime Change Only Path to Disarmament," Center for Strategic & International Studies forum, Washington, DC, 13 February 2003.

26. Council of Foreign Relations, http://www.cfr.org.

27. See for example Kenneth M. Pollack, "Next Stop Baghdad?" *Foreign Affairs* 81, no. 2 (March–April 2002): 32–47; and Fouad Ajami, "Iraq and the Arab's Future," *Foreign Affairs* 82, no. 1 (January–February 2003): 2–18.

28. See for example F. Gregory Gause III, "Can Democracy Stop Terrorism?" *Foreign Affairs* 84 (September–October 2005): 62–76; Stephen M. Walt, "Taming American Power," *Foreign Affairs* 84 (September–October 2005): 105–20; and Melvin Laird, "Iraq: Learning the Lessons of Vietnam," *Foreign Affairs* 84 (November–December 2005): 22–43.

29. For example Richard N. Haass, *The Opportunity: America's Moment to Alter History's Course* (New York: PublicAffairs, 2005); and Gideon Rose, "Get Real," *New York Times*, 18 August 2005, http://www.nytimes.com/2005/08/18/opinion/18rose.html?ex=1282017600&en=91e51625204214d1&ei=5090&partner=

rssuserland&emc=rss; Jonathan Tepperman, "Foxes and Hedgehogs," *New York Times* (16 October 2005), http://www.nytimes.com/2005/10/16/books/review/16tepperman.html?ex=1160625600&en=df7bf455017400fb&ei=5070.

CHAPTER FIVE

1. See for example Tony Blankley, *The West's Last Chance: Will We Win the Clash of Civilizations?* (Washington, DC: Regnery, 2005).

2. George W. Bush, "Address to a Joint Session of Congress and the American People," 20 September 2001, http://www.whitehouse.gov/news/releases/2001/09/20010920-8.html.

3. Graham Allison, *Nuclear Terrorism: The Ultimate Preventable Catastrophe* (New York: Holt, 2004). See the table of contents and 121–22.

4. Graham T. Allison et al., *Avoiding Nuclear Anarchy: Containing the Thread of Loose Russian Nuclear Missiles and Fissile Material* (Cambridge: MIT Press, 1996).

5. Matthew Bunn and Anthony Wier, "Securing the Bomb 2005: The New Global Imperatives," commissioned by the Nuclear Threat Initiative, Belfer Center for Science and International Affairs, John F. Kennedy School of Government, Harvard University, May 2005, www.nti.org/cnwn.

6. Allison, *Avoiding Nuclear Anarchy*, 10.

7. Allison, *Nuclear Terrorism*, 5–6.

8. Con Coughlin, "Only a Matter of Time before Terrorists Use Weapons of Mass Destruction," *Daily Telegraph,* 17 January 2006.

9. Michael Ignatieff, *The Lesser Evil: Political Ethics in an Age of Terror* (Princeton, NJ: Princeton University Press, 2004), 113.

10. Samuel Huntington, "The Clash of Civilizations?" *Foreign Affairs* 72, no. 3 (Summer 1993): 22–49.

11. Ibid.; Samuel Huntington, *The Clash of Civilizations and the Remaking of World Order* (New York: Simon & Schuster, 1996).

12. Ervand Abrahamian, "The US Media, Huntington and September 11," *Third World Quarterly* 24, no. 3 (June 2003): 529.

13. Dag Tuastad, "Neo-Orientalism and the New Barbarism Thesis: Aspects of Symbolic Violence in the Middle East Conflict(s)," *Third World Quarterly* 24, no. 4 (August 2003): 591.

14. Andrew Sullivan, "This Is a Religious War," *New York Times* (7 October 2001), http://www.nytimes.com/2001/10/07/magazine/07RELIGION.html?ex=1160452800&en=1bf0956a5b37c096&ei=5070.

15. David Landes and Richard A. Landes, "Girl Power," *New Republic* 225 (8 October 2001): 20.

16. Norman Podhoretz, "Israel Is Not the Issue: Islamic Fanatics Hate American in Its Own Right," *Wall Street Journal* (20 September 2001), http://www .opinionjournal.com/extra/?id=95001175.

17. Richard Lowry, quoted in Abrahamian, "The US Media, Huntington and September 11," 532. See also Richard Lowry, "America's Unspecial Relationship: A Cold Look at the Saudis," *National Review* (25 February 2002), http://www .nationalreview.com/flashback/flashback-lowry080802.asp.

18. Reuel Gerecht, "The Future of bin Ladenism," *New York Times* (23 September 2001): 30.

19. Michael Doran, "Somebody Else's Civil War," *Foreign Affairs* 81, no. 1 (January–February 2002): 22–42.

20. Robert Kaplan, "Looking the World in the Eye," *Atlantic Monthly* 288, no. 5 (December 2001): http://www.theatlantic.com/doc/prem/200112/kaplan.

21. Samuel Huntington, "The Age of Muslim Wars," *Newsweek* 138, no. 25 (3 January 2002): 42–47.

22. "Sixty Prominent U.S. Academics Say War on Terrorism Is Just," Office of International Information Programs, U.S. Department of State, 15 February 2002, http://cryptome.org/60-warheads.htm.

23. Stephen Brown, "Cartoon Clash of Civilizations," *FrontPage* (10 February 2006): http://www.frontpagemag.com/Articles/ReadArticle.asp?ID=21236; "Europe Confronts Clash of Civilizations," *Oxford Analytica* (9 February 2006): http://www.forbes.com/columnists/business/2006/02/08/europe-civilization-clash_cx_0209oxford.html; Daniel McGrory and Dan Sabbagh, "Cartoon Wars and the Clash of Civilizations," *Times* (3 February 2006), http://www.timesonline .co.uk/article/0,,3–2022442,00.html.

24. Michael Slackman, "Bin Laden Says West Is Waging War against Islam," *New York Times* (24 April 2006), http://www.nytimes.com/2006/04/24/world/ middleeast/24binladen.html?ex=1303531200&en=4b9d26a39421dc02&ei=5088 &partner=rssnyt&emc=rss.

25. "Declassified Key Judgments of the National Intelligence Estimate 'Trends in Global Terrorism': Implications for the United States," April 2006, 2: http://dni .gov/press_releases/Declassified_NIE_Key_Judgments.pdf#search=%22 National%20Intelligence%20estimate%202006%22.

26. Associated Press, "London Bomber Outlines Motives in Video," *Washington Post* (7 July 2006), http://www.washingtonpost.com/wp-dyn/content/article/ 2006/07/07/AR2006070700854.html.

27. Pam Bellick, "Towns Lose Tool against Illegal Immigrants," *New York Times* (13 August 2005): A7.

28. Samuel P. Huntington, *Who Are We? The Challenges to America's National Identity* (New York: Simon & Schuster, 2004), xvii.

29. Huntington, 61.

30. Ibid., 362.

31. Frederick Kempe, "Mideast Doctrine's Domestic Hurdle," *Wall Street Journal*, 13 December 2005, A11.

32. Martin Zonis, "Veiled Prejudice," *New York Times* (5 August 1990), http://query.nytimes.com/gst/fullpage.html?res=9C0CEEDD113BF936A3575B C0A966958260.

33. Michael Dobbs, "Inside the Mind of Osama bin Laden," *Washington Post* (20 September 2001): A1.

34. James Klurfeld, "Bush's Go-It-Alone Policy Is to Go Nowhere," *Newsday* (29 August 2002), http://www.anchorweb.org/old%20site/Opinion/090302/bush.html.

35. Bernard Lewis, "The Roots of Muslim Rage," *Atlantic Monthly* 266, no. 3, (September 1990): http://www.theatlantic.com/doc/prem/199009/muslim-rage.

36. Ibid.

37. Bernard Lewis, *The Arabs in History*, 6th ed. (New York: Oxford University Press, 1993). See also Robert Blecher, "Free People Will Set the Course of History: Intellectuals, Democracy and Empire," Middle Eastern Report Online, March 2003: http://www.merip.org/mero/interventions/blecher_interv.html.

38. Quoted in Michael Hirsh, "Bernard Lewis Revisited: What If Islam Isn't an Obstacle to Democracy in the Middle East, but the Secret to It?" *Washington Monthly* (November 2004), http://www.washingtonmonthly.com/features/2004/ 0411.hirsh.html.

39. Lamb interview with Bernard Lewis, "What Went Wrong?" http://www .booknotes.org/Transcript/?ProgramID=1657.

40. Ibid.

41. Bernard Lewis, quoted in Michael Hirsh, "Bernard Lewis Revisited."

42. Ibid.

43. Bernard Lewis, "A Time for Toppling," in *From Babel to Dragomans: Interpreting the Middle East* (London: Weidenfeld & Nicolson, 2004), 378–80.

44. David Horowitz, "America-Haters," *FrontPage.com* (10 September 2002), http://www.frontpagemag.com/Articles/Printable.asp?ID=2930.

45. Condoleezza Rice, remarks at the American University in Cairo, 20 June 2005, http://www.state.gov/secretary/rm/2005/48328.htm.

46. George W. Bush, "President Discusses Freedom and Democracy in Latvia," Small Guild Hall, Riga, Latvia, 7 May 2005, http://www.whitehouse.gov/news/ releases/2005/05/20050507-8.html.

47. Noam Chomsky, *What Uncle Sam Really Wants* (Tucson: Odonian Press, 1993), 7.

48. Ibid., 8.

49. Noam Chomsky, "The Iraq War and Contempt for Democracy," *ZNet Daily Commentaries*, 31 October 2003, http://www.zmag.org/sustainers/content/2003–10/31chomsky.cfm.

50. Chalmers Johnson, *Blowback: The Costs and Consequences of American Empire* (New York: Holt, 2004), xiv.

51. Ibid., 8.

52. Ibid., 12.

53. Ibid., 201.

54. Chalmers Johnson, *The Sorrows of Empire: Militarism, Secrecy, and the End of the Republic* (New York: Metropolitan Books, 2004), 4.

55. Ibid., 11.

56. Ibid., 64.

57. Anatol Lieven, *America Right or Wrong: An Anatomy of American Nationalism* (New York: Oxford University Press, 2004); Michael Scheuer, *Imperial Hubris: Why America Is Losing the War on Terror* (Washington, DC: Brassey's, 2004); Stephen Kinzer, *Overthrow: America's Century of Regime Change from Hawaii to Iraq* (New York: Holt, 2006).

58. Edward M. Graham and Paul R. Krugman, *Foreign Direct Investment in the United States*, 3rd ed. (Washington, DC: Institute for International Economics, 1995), 2.

59. Paul Krugman, *Exchange-Rate Instability* (Cambridge, Mass.: MIT Press, 1989).

60. Paul Krugman, *The Age of Diminished Expectations: US Economic Policy in the 1990s*, 3rd ed. (Cambridge: MIT Press, 1997), ix–x.

61. Daniel Okrent, "13 Things I Meant to Write About but Never Did," *New York Times*, 22 May 2005, D12.

62. Paul Krugman, "The Last Deception," *New York Times* (21 September 2004), http://www.nytimes.com/2004/09/21/opinion/21krugman.html?ex=1253592000&en=5e847f0ef4de23db&ei=5088&partner=rssnyt.

63. Paul Krugman, "Staying What Course?" *New York Times* (16 May 2005), http://www.nytimes.com/2005/05/16/opinion/16krugman.html?ex=1273896000&en=dd8fd52f7c8322d6&ei=5088&partner=rssnyt&emc=rss.

64. Paul Krugman, "The Wastrel Son," *New York Times* (18 May 2004), http://www.nytimes.com/2004/05/18/opinion/18KRUG.html?ex=1400212800&en=d0a34b4187d8a27c&ei=5007&partner=USERLAND.

65. Paul Krugman, "The Uncivil War," *New York Times* (25 November 2003), http://www.nytimes.com/2003/11/25/opinion/25KRUG.html?ex=1385182800&en=856f691e4b7a9076&ei=5007&partner=USERLAND.

66. Paul Krugman, *Pop Internationalism* (Cambridge: MIT Press, 1996).

CHAPTER SIX

1. National Defense Strategy of the United States, Department of Defense, Washington, DC, March 2005. See also Michael Mandelbaum, *The Case for Goliath: How America Acts as the World's Government in the Twenty-first Century* (New York: PublicAffairs 2006); Thomas P. H. Barnett, *Blueprint for Action: A Future Worth Creating* (New York: Putnam 2005); Peter Beinart, *The Good Fight: Why Liberals—and Only Liberals—Can Win the War on Terror and Make America Great Again* (New York: HarperCollins, 2006).

2. See for example General Anthony Zinni, *The Battle for Peace: A Frontline Vision of America's Power and Purpose* (New York: Palgrave MacMillan, 2006); Mandelbaum, *The Case for Goliath*; *Real Security: The Democratic Plan to Protect America and Restore Our Leadership in the World* (Washington, DC: The Democratic Party, 2006).

3. Ari Berman, "The Strategic Class," *The Nation* (29 August 2005), http://www.thenation.com/doc/20050829/berman.

4. Useful information about national defense spending may be found in the respective year books published by the Stockholm International Peace Research Institute, Stockholm, Sweden, and the Institute of Strategic Studies, London.

5. Pew Research Center, "Foreign Policy Attitudes Now Driven by 9/11 and Iraq: Eroding Respect for America Seen as Major Problem," 18 August 2004, http://people-press.org/reports/display.php3?ReportID=222.

6. Madeleine Albright, *Madam Secretary: A Memoir* (New York: Miramax Books, 2003), 182.

7. Hans M. Kristensen, "Global Strike: A Chronology of the Pentagon's New Offensive Strike Plan" The Nuclear Information Project (Washington, DC: Federation of American Scientists, 2005).

8. Theodor W. Galdi, "Revolution in Military Affairs?" Washington, DC, Congressional Research Service, 11 December 1995.

9. Vice Admiral Arthur K. Cebrowski and John J. Garstka, "Network-Centric Warfare: Its Origin and Future," *Proceedings*, U.S. Naval Institute (January 1998), http://www.usni.org/Proceedings/Articles98/PROcebrowski.htm; Arthur K. Cebrowski and Thomas P. H. Barnet, "The American Way of War," *Proceedings*, U.S. Naval Institute (January 1998), http://www.thomaspmbarnett.com/published/awow.htm.

10. David Ignatius, "To Stop an Arc of Violence," *Washington Post* (29 September 2005): A23.

11. Michael Walzer, *Arguing About War* (New Haven: Yale University Press, 2004).

12. Paul Wolfowitz, interview by Sam Tannenhaus, Vanity Fair (9 May 2003). See also http://www.defenselink.mil/transcripts/2003/tr20030509-depsecdef0223.html.

13. Max Boot, *The Savage Wars of Peace: Small Wars and the Rise of American Power* (New York: Basic Books, 2002).

14. Robert Kaplan, "Imperial Grunts," *Atlantic Monthly* 296 (October 2005), and Max Boot, "The New American War," *Foreign Affairs* 82, no 3 (July–August 2003): 41–58. See also Robert Kaplan, *Imperial Grunts* (New York: Norton, 2005).

15. Michael Ignatieff, *Virtual War: Kosovo and Beyond* (New York: Picador, 2001), 246.

16. Alan Wolfe, *Return to Greatness: How America Lost its Sense of Purpose and What It Needs to Do to Recover It* (Princeton: Princeton University Press, 2005), 169–209.

17. Robert Kagan, *Of Paradise and Power: America and Europe in the New World Order* (New York: Knopf, 2003).

18. www.securitypeace.org.

19. Peter Beinart, *The Good Fight: Why Liberals—and Only Liberals—Can Win the War on Terror and Make America Great Again* (New York: HarperCollins, 2006).

20. See Hillary Rodham Clinton, speech at the Woodrow Wilson School for International Studies, Princeton University, 18 January 2006.

21. Contrast David Rieff, *At the Point of a Gun: Democratic Dreams and Armed Intervention* (New York: Simon & Schuster, 2005), and George Packer, *The Assassin's Gate: America in Iraq* (New York: Farrar, Strauss and Giroux, 2006).

22. Michael Scheuer, *Imperial Hubris: Why the West Is Losing the War on Terror* (Dulles, VA: Potomac Books, 2004), 240.

23. John Kerry, remarks at the UNITY 2004 Conference, 5 August 2004, http://www.washingtonpost.com/wp-dyn/articles/A42212–2004Aug5.html.

24. See Michael Ignatieff, ed., *American Exceptionalism and Human Rights* (Princeton: Princeton University Press, 2005); Mient Jan Faber, "Peace, Human Rights, and the Moral Choice of the Churches," in *A Matter of Principle: Humanitarian Arguments for War in Iraq*, ed. Thomas Cushman (Berkeley: University of California Press, 2005).

25. Outcome Document, UN General Assembly World Summit, September 2005, http://www.un.org/summit2005.

26. Andrew Bacevich, *The New American Militarism: How Americans Are Seduced by War* (New York: Oxford University Press, 2005), 32.

27. General Sir Rupert Smith, *The Utility of Force: The Art of War in the Modern World* (London and New York: Allen Lane, 2006), 269–305.

28. Stephen M. Walt, *Taming American Power: The Global Response to U.S. Primacy* (New York: Norton, 2005), 109–79.

29. Russell Weighley, *The American Way of War: A History of U.S. Military Strategy and Policy* (Bloomington: Indiana University Press, 1973).

30. Quoted in Kevin Westerfeld, "U.S. Forces Employ Buffalo to Battle Roadside Bombs," *Morning Edition* (24 May 2005).

31. Fred Kaplan, "Hunkering Down: A Guide to the U.S. Military's Future in Iraq," *Atlantic Monthly* 297 (June 2006).

32. Rupert Cornwell et al., "Iraq: Is the World Safer?" *Independent* (28 January 2005), http://news.independent.co.uk/world/middle_east/article17137.ece.

CHAPTER SEVEN

1. John F. Kennedy, remarks at West Point to the graduating class of the US Military Academy, 6 June 1962, http://www.presidency.ucsb.edu/ws/print.php?pid=8695.

2. Johanna McGeary, "Danger around Every Corner," *Time* (20 October 2003); Dana Milbank, "Rumsfeld's War on 'Insurgents,'" *Washington Post* (30 November 2005).

3. Dick Cheney, interview by Larry King, *Larry King Live*, CNN, 20 June 2005.

4. Michael E. Gordon and Bernard E. Trainor, *Cobra II: The Inside Story of the Invasion and Occupation of Iraq* (New York: Pantheon Books, 2006), 199ff; George Packer, *The Assassin's Gate: America in Iraq* (New York: Farrar, Strauss and Giroux, 2005), 298.

5. Samuel Berger and Brent Scowcroft, "In the Wake of War: Improving U.S. Post-Conflict Capabilities," report of a task force of the Council on Foreign Relations (New York: CFR, 2005).

6. David Ignatius, "A Better Strategy for Iraq," *Washington Post*, 4 November 2005.

7. Steven Metz and Raymond Millen, *Insurgency and Counterinsurgency in the 21st Century: Reconceptualizing Threat and Response* (Carlisle Barracks, PA: Strategic Studies Institute, 2004), iii.

8. Jon Lee Anderson, "The Uprising: Shias and Sunnis Put Aside Their Differences," *New Yorker* (3 May 2005); Peter Maass, "The Way of the Commandos," *New York Times Magazine* (May 2005).

9. Jonathan Haslam, *The Nixon Administration and the Death of Allende's Chile: A Case of Assisted Suicide* (London: Verso, 2005).

10. General John R. Galvin, "Uncomfortable Wars: Toward a New Paradigm," in *Uncomfortable Wars: Toward a New Paradigm of Low Intensity Conflict*, ed. Max G. Manwaring (London: Brassey's, 1991): 9–13.

11. Dick Cheney, remarks at the 73rd National Convention of the Military Order of the Purple Heart, 18 August 2005, http://www.whitehouse.gov/news/releases/2005/08/20050818–4.html.

12. Nigel Aylwin-Foster, "Changing the Army for Counterinsurgency Operations," *Military Review* (November–December 2005).

13. Condoleezza Rice, remarks at the American University in Cairo, 20 June 2005, http://www.state.gov/secretary/rm/2005/48328.htm.

14. Michael Ledeen, "Time to Take Down the Terror Masters in Tehran," *National Review* (1 August 2005), http://www.nationalreview.com/ledeen/ledeen 200508010809.asp.

15. Donald Rumsfeld, interview on *Fox News Sunday*, 26 June 2005, http://www.foxnews.com/story/0,2933,160716,00.html.

16. Martin van Creveld, *On Future War* (London: Brassey's, 1991), 195.

17. Andrew F. Krepinevich, "How to Win in Iraq," *Foreign Affairs* 84, no. 5 (September–October 2005): 87–104.

18. Ignatius, "A Better Strategy for Iraq," A23.

19. The authors acknowledge the help of Lezlee Brown, a PhD candidate at Cambridge University, with this section.

20. Gil Morom, *How Democracies Lose Small Wars* (New York: Cambridge University Press, 2003), 15.

21. Fred Kaplan, "Fighting Insurgents, by the Book," *Washington Post*, 9 July 2006, B2, http://www.washingtonpost.com/wp-dyn/content/article/2006/07/07/AR2006070701151.html. See also Liutenant General David H. Petraeus and Lieutenant Colonel Conrad C. Crane, "Counterinsurgency," Department of the Army, 16 June 2006.

22. Ibid.

23. Thomas X. Hammes, *The Sling and the Stone: On War in the 21st Century* (St. Paul, MN: Zenith Press, 2004), 255.

CHAPTER EIGHT

1. Christopher Andrew and Vassily Mitrokhin, *The World Was Going Our Way* (New York: Basic Books, 2005).

2. Peter Bergen, *The Osama bin Laden I Know: An Oral History of al-Qaeda's Leader* (New York: Free Press, 2006).

3. Comment made to Stefan Halper.

4. Conversations between Stefan Halper and senior SIS and CIA officers (who are not named at their request) in London and Washington between February and August 2006.

5. Ibid.

6. Ibid.

7. Ibid.

8. Nick Walsh, "The Cold War Is Over, but Rock in a Park suggests the Spying Game Still Thrives," *The Guardian* (24 January 2006).

9. Laurence H. Silberman and Charles S. Robb et al., "Report to the President" Commission on the Intelligence Capabilities of the United States Regarding Weapons of Mass Destruction, 31 March 2005, http://www.wmd.gov/report/index.html.

10. "Cats' Eyes in the Dark," *Economist* (17 March 2005).

11. Gary Milhollin, "Mr. Blix Goes to Baghdad," *Wall Street Journal* (26 November 2002).

12. Silberman and Robb, "Report to the President."

13. "Mapping the Global Future: Report of the National Intelligence Council's 2020 Project" (National Intelligence Council, Washington, DC: December 2004).

14. John Lewis Gaddis, "Grand Strategy in the Second Term," *Foreign Affairs* 84 (January–February 2005): 2–15.

15. Viktor Cherkashin with Gregory Feifer, *Spy Handler: Memoir of a KGB Officer* (New York: Basic Books, 2005).

16. Richard Posner, *Preventing Surprise Attacks: Intelligence Reform in the Wake of 9/11* (Stanford: Hoover Institution Press, 2005), 207.

CHAPTER NINE

1. E. J. Kahn, *The China Hands: Ameirca's Foregin Service Officers and What Befell Them* (New York: Penguin Books, 1976), 33–34.

2. Robert Herzstein, *Henry R. Luce, Time, and the American Crusade in Asia* (Cambridge: Cambridge University Press), 133; E. J. Kahn, *The China Hands*, 33–34.

3. The authors express their appreciation to Professor Rodrick MacFarquhar, Director of the John Fairbank Center at Harvard University, for his insights on China's transition, many of which are reflected in this manuscript. Our conversations took place in 2005–2006.

4. Globalis-China, http://globalis.gvu.unu.edu.

5. Quoted in "War of the Words," *The Guardian*, 20 February 2006, http://www.guardian.co.uk/china/story/0,,1713317,00.html.

6. Quoted in "China to Reprint Weekly, Shunts Aside Editors," Reuters, 16 February 2006, http://www.signonsandiego.com/news/world/20060216–0547-media-china-journalists.html.

7. The authors thank Anne Lonsdale, President of New Hall, Cambridge, and a Cambridge Sinologist, for her observations on China's transition concerning

public and private space. Her conversation with Stefan Halper took place in December 2005.

8. "The Long March to Privacy," *The Economist* (16 January 2006), http://www.economist.com/world/asia/displaystory.cfm?story_id=5389362.

9. Ibid.

10. Ibid.

11. "A Sharp Debate Erupts in China over Ideologies," *New York Times* (12 March 2006), http://www.nytimes.com/2006/03/12/international/asia/12china.html?ex=1160539200&en=547fbd6f25b94220&ei=5070.

12. Ibid.

13. Maureen Fan, "Blind Chinese Activist Gets 4 Years," *Washington Post* (25 August 2006): A9.

14. 900 million.

15. Mao Yushi, "Fifty Years of China's Economy with its Background in Politics and Society," in *China's Future: Constructive Partner or Emerging Threat?* ed. Ted Galen Carpenter and James A. Dorn (Washington, DC: Cato Institute, 2000), 19–20.

16. The authors would like to thank Dr. Philip Towle, former Director of the Centre of International Studies, University of Cambridge, for his insights on China's foreign relations and particularly the China-Taiwan relationship. Dr. Towle is University Reader in International Relations. Numerous conversations with Stefan Halper at the University of Cambridge between October 2001 and June 2006.

17. "Annual Report to Congress on the Military Power of the People's Republic of China, 2000," Department of Defense, 1, http://www.defenselink.mil/news/Jun2000/china06222000.htm.

18. Ibid., 10.

19. Professor Joseph Nye of Harvard University uses a related concept called "soft power." This term identifies values, culture, information, travel, and exchange programs as important dimensions of the way nations tell their story bilaterally and to the global community to reach their objectives. China is sensitive to this and uses trade, development projects, and investment narratives to advance bilateral relations under the broader notion that progress in these areas brings improved quality of life to both parties.

20. "Annual Report to Congress on the Military Power of the People's Republic of China, 2000," 4.

21. Tensions over how Japanese textbooks depict the 1936 invasion of China, the prime minister's observances at the Yasukuni Shrine, and Japan's antimissile cooperation with the United States and Taiwan have also resulted in nationalist demonstrations.

22. Defense and Foreign Affairs Strategic Policy November–December 2005; Elias Davidsson, "Simple Math Demonstrates That the Official 9/11 Account Is a Fabrication," www.globalresearch.ca/index.php?context=viewArticle&code=20051229& articleId=1665. This article, quoting NATO sources, claims that the attack was an attempt to decapitate the Belgrade government by killing Milosevic, who was thought to be in the embassy at the time. The US government apologized, claiming the attack was an accident.

23. Quoted in Bill Gertz, *The China Threat: How the People's Republic Targets America* (Washington, DC: Regnery, 2000), 9.

24. For neoconservative analysis see Andrew Scobell and Larry M. Wortzel, eds., *China's Growing Military Power: Perspectives on Security, Ballistic Missiles, and Conventional Warfare* (Carlisle, PA: Strategic Studies Institute, 2002). This book is based on a September 2001 conference held at the Carlisle Barracks and sponsored by the American Enterprise Institute, the Heritage Foundation, and the U.S. Army War College. For scholarly concern see Peter Hays Gries, *China's New Nationalism: Pride, Politics, and Diplomacy* (Berkeley: University of California Press, 2004).

25. Shirley A. Kan, "China: Suspected Acquisition of US Nuclear Weapon Secrets," Congressional Research Service Report for Congress, the Library of Congress, updated December 2000, http://www.carnegieendowment.org/pdf/npp/ chinanukesecrets.pdf#search=%22Cox%20Committee%20Hearings%2C%20US %20congress%20PRC%20nuclear%201994%22.

26. Gertz, *The China Threat*, 19.

27. Robert G. Kaiser and Steven Mufson, "Blue Team Draws a Hard Line On Beijing, Action on Hill Reflects Informal Group's Clout," *Washington Post* (22 February 2000): A01.

28. Bill Clinton, quoted in "Clinton's Legacy Watch," Center for Security Policy, 6 December 1999, http://www.security-policy.org/papers/1999/99-D140.html.

29. Phyllis Schlafly, "Red China: Gatekeeper of the Panama Canal," *Eagle Forum Newsletter* 33 (November 1999), http://www.eagleforum.org/psr/1999/nov99/ psrnov99.html.

30. Retired Admiral Thomas Moorer former Chairman of the Joint Chiefs of Staff, testimony on the Panama Canal and United States Interests, Senate Hearings, Committee on Foreign Relations, 16 June 1998, quoted in Ed Oliver and Joseph Farah, "The Panama Canal Debate Rages: Admiral, Ambassador Sqaure off in Senate Testimony," *WorldNetDaily.com*, 9 November 1998, http://www.worldnetdaily .com/news/article.asp?ARTICLE_ID=16790.

31. Associated Press, "Excerpts from Republican debate in Arizona," 7 December 1999, http://graphics.boston.com/news/politics/campaign2000/news/Excerpts _from_Republican_debate_in_Arizona.shtml.

32. Gertz, *The China Threat*, 15.

33. Bob Woodward and Brian Duffy, "Chinese Embassy Role in Contributions Probed," *Washington Post* (13 February 1997): A1. Also quoted in Gertz, *The China Threat*, 20.

34. Michael Pillsbury, quoted in Gertz, *The China Threat*, 10.

35. Ibid., 11.

36. Conversations between Stefan Halper and Michael Pillsbury in Washington, DC, August–September 2006.

37. Dan Blumenthal, "Get Serious about China's Rising Military," *Washington Post* (25 May 2006): A29.

38. James Lilley with Jeffrey Lilley, *China Hands: Nine Decades of Adventure, Espionage, and Diplomacy in Asia* (New York: PublicAffairs, 2004), 230, 231.

39. Taiwan Relations Act, Section 3301(b):

> It is the policy of the United States:
>
> (1) to preserve and promote extensive, close, and friendly commercial, cultural, and other relations between the people of the United States and the people on Taiwan, as well as the people on the China mainland and all other peoples of the Western Pacific area;
>
> (2) to declare that peace and stability in the area are in the political, security, and economic interests of the United States, and are matters of international concern;
>
> (3) to make clear that the United States decision to establish diplomatic relations with the People's Republic of China rests upon the expectation that the future of Taiwan will be determined by peaceful means;
>
> (4) to consider any effort to determine the future of Taiwan by other than peaceful means, including by boycotts or embargoes, a threat to the peace and security of the Western Pacific area and of grave concern to the United States;
>
> (5) to provide Taiwan with arms of a defensive character; and
>
> (6) to maintain the capacity of the United States to resist any resort to force or other forms of coercion that would jeopardize the security, or the social or economic system, of the people on Taiwan.

40. Dan Nystedt, "Taiwan Investment to China up 46% in 2006: Government Program to Curb Investment to the Mainland Having Little Effect," Infrastructure Development Group News Service, 21 June 2006, http://www.infoworld.com/archives/emailPrint.jsp?R=printThis&A=/article/06/06/21/79482_HNtaiwan investchina_1.html.

41. Ted Galen Carpenter, *America's Coming War with China: A Collision Course over Taiwan* (New York: Palgrave Macmillan, 2005), 134.

42. Lilley with Lilley, *China Hands*, 231.

43. President Jiang Jemin, conversation with Stefan Halper, June 1996, Beijing, while Halper was en route to North Korea.

44. In early 2003 China cut off oil supplies to the North for three days. See Vyjayanti Raghavan, "Six Nation Talks in North-East Asia: The China Factor" (London: Sage Publications, 2005): 71.

45. Robin Wright, "Iran's New Alliance with China Could Cost U.S. Leverage," *Washington Post* (17 November 2004): A21.

46. General Scowcroft and Ambassador Lilley expressed these views in separate meetings with Stefan Halper in Washington, DC, during the summer and winter of 2005.

47. Richard McCormack, conversations with Stefan Halper, 2 July 2005 and 9 August 2005, Washington, DC.

48. Dr. Ted Galen Carpenter, Vice President for Defense and Foreign Policy, Cato Institute, conversation with Stefan Halper, 24 July 2006, Washington, DC.

49. Carpenter, *America's Coming War with China*, 139.

50. Ibid.

51. Ibid., 140.

52. Don Lee, *Los Angeles Times* (6 January 2005): A1.

53. Carpenter, *America's Coming War with China*, 142.

54. Lester R. Brown, *Plan B 2.0: Rescuing a Planet under Stress and a Civilization in Trouble* (New York: Norton, 2006), 3.

55. Ibid., 9.

56. Ibid., 10.

57. Ibid., 11.

58. Ibid., 6.

59. Ibid., 11.

60. Elaine Kurtenbach, "Wen Warns China's Rural Situation Unstable," Associated Press, 20 January 2006, http://www.breitbart.com/news/2006/01/20/D8F8KQVO6.html.

61. Brown, *Plan B 2.0*, 14.

62. Ibid., 7.

63. Ibid., 15.

64. Ibid.

65. Sir Christopher Hum, former British Ambassador to Beijing, conversation with Stefan Halper at, Cambridge, England, 8 March 2006. Brown, *Plan B 2.0*, 17.

66. James Cox, "Congressmen: China's Currency Policies Hurts Jobs in the USA," *USA Today* (31 July 2003), http://www.usatoday.com/money/world/2003–07–31-yuan_x.htm.

67. David Armstrong, "US Racks Up Record Trade Deficit in '05; $725.8 Billion Total Is 17.5% Increase over 2004's," *San Francisco Chronicle* (13 March 2006): C1.

68. Ibid. Meanwhile, analysts across the spectrum maintain that China's refusal to increase the value of the yuan by more than 2.1 percent in July 2005 is partly responsible for the size of the deficit and that its revaluation is an essential first step in correcting the $201 billion trade surplus.

69. "Statement of Ambassador Richard McCormack to the United States China Economic and Security Review Commission," 19 May 2005, Council on Foreign Relations, New York City, http://www.uscc.gov/hearings/2005hearings/written _testimonies/05_05_19_20wrts/mccormack_richard_wrts.php.

70. Chairman of the Commission for Restructuring the Economy, conversation with Stefan Halper, November 1978, Beijing. Halper met with the Commission whilel in Beijing for consultations.

CHAPTER TEN

1. George W. Bush, State of the Union Address, Washington, D.C., 29 January, 2002, http://www.whitehouse.gov/news/releases/2002/01/20020129–11.html.

2. "The National Security Strategy of the United States of America," 15 September 2002, http://www.whitehouse.gov/nsc/nss.pdf#search=%22United%20 STates%20will%2C%20if%20necessary%2C%20act%20pre-emptively%22.

3. Piet Hein, "Circumscripture." Hein, 1905–1996, was a Danish scientist, mathematician, inventor, author, and poet. Piet Hein, *Grooks* (Cambridge, Mass.: The MIT Press, 1966).

4. "What the World Thinks in 2002, How Global Publics View: Their Lives, Their Countries, The World, America," Pew Research Center for the People and the Press, 4 December 2002, http://people-press.org/reports/display.php3?Report ID=165.

5. Sam Parry, "The Bush Exit Ramp," Consortium for Independent Journalism, 22 January 2000, http://www.consortiumnews.com/2003/012203a.html.

6. Gian-Carlo Rota, quoted in the newsletter of the New Zealand Mathematical Society, December 2001, http://www.massey.ac.nz/~wwifs/mathnews/NZMS83/ news83.htm.

7. "Scorned General's Tactics Proved Right: Profile of the Army Chief Sidelined by Rumsfeld," *The Guardian* (29 March 2003), http://www.guardian.co.uk/ international/story/0,3604,925140,00.html.

8. "George Bush: 'Kim Chong Il Is a Pygmy," *Newsweek* (28 May 2002), http://www.msnbc.com/news/754330.asp.

9. "Bush: 'Bring on' Attackers of U.S. Troops," *USA Today* (2 August 2003), http://www.usatoday.com/news/world/iraq/2003–07–02-bush-iraq-troops_x.htm.

10. Nazila Fathi, "Wipe Israel 'off the Map' Iranian Says," *New York Times* (27 October 2005), http://www.iht.com/articles/2005/10/26/news/iran.php.

11. Joseph S. Nye Jr., "Today, It's a Question of Whose Story Wins," *Los Angeles Times* (21 July 2004): B15.

Acknowledgments

A book of this kind could not have been conceived without the stimulation, encouragement, and criticism of mentors, friends, and colleagues. The vibrant intellectual culture of the Centre of International Studies at Cambridge provided all of that and more. I thank Professor Christopher Hill, Director of the Centre of International Studies at Cambridge University, and colleagues Professor Jonathan Haslam, Dr. Charles Jones, Dr. Marc Weller, Dr. Duncan Bell, and Dr. George Joffe. Each has offered encouragement, comment, and criticism on various aspects of this book's argument. Thanks are also due to Professor Christopher Andrew, President of Corpus Christi College, an eminent authority on capabilities and limitations of intelligence and how it relates to the foreign policy process. Al Regnery, Publisher of the *American Spectator*, has provided friendship, support, insight, and guidance throughout the project, and a unique perspective on the contemporary relationship between ideology and foreign policy. Dr. Tarak Barkawi, of the Centre of International Studies, Cambridge University, read and critiqued each chapter, as he did with *America Alone*, providing both vital texture and direction to the manuscript. Joel Rogers, a PhD candidate at Cambridge, made substantial contributions to the chapters on think tanks and the media, and also provided invaluable research on the history of Big Ideas.

Anne Lonsdale, the President of New Hall, Cambridge; Dr. Philip Towle, University Reader, colleague, friend, and former Director of the Centre of International Studies; Lord David Wilson, the Master of Peterhouse, Cambridge; Sir Christopher Hum, the Master of Gonville and Caius, Cambridge; Ambassador James Lilley of the American Enterprise Institute; and Dr. Ted Galen Carpenter, Vice President for Defense and Foreign Policy at the Cato Institute each provided critical perspective on China's transition and its foreign relations. Their anecdotes, suggestions, and corrections were instrumental in the development of the China chapter, which addresses the links between China's internal developments and foreign policy in the context of US–China relations.

Herman Pirchner, President of the American Foreign Policy Council; Dmitri Simes, President of the Nixon Center; Jerry Leach, President of the World Affairs Council; Bob Dean, Executive Vice President of Space Applications International Corporation (SAIC); Captain Robert Mercker (retired US Army Ranger); the Honorable William H. Taft IV, former Deputy Secretary of Defense; John Henry of the Committee for the Republic; Chris James, a former British government official; Jim Campbell, a former CIA Officer; Chet Crocker, former Assistant Secretary of State; Boyden Gray, Ambassador to the European Community; the Hon. Adam Holloway, Member of Parliament; and Tom Twetten and Jim Pavitt, both former Deputy Directors of the CIA, each provided insight and encouragement at various points during the book's development.

The Canadian Donner Foundation and the William F. Donner Foundation have provided generous support for many years and were it not for both, this book would not have been possible. Special thanks are due to David Donner, who was particularly helpful to the 2005–6 Donner Atlantic Studies Programme, and to Curtin Winsor III for his long friendship, distilled advice, and enduring support.

A great deal of credit is owed to Bill Frucht of Basic Books for his superb editing and thoughtful suggestions. Without his good judgment and wry humor this book would not have come to fruition. Alex Hoyt, whose deep knowledge of the book-writing world never ceases to amaze, has done a superb job of navigating the currents of New York's publishing world.

The book owes a great deal to an evening in a thatch cottage in Cambridgeshire, where I joined Professor James Mayall for a chat in the kitchen before dinner. America and the Big Idea, the rational center, the power of Exceptionalism, and America's global role were combined in that conversation to provide the book's focus. Without James Mayall's casual brilliance, these ideas would not have come together the way they did.

Magdalene College, Cambridge, has been a home away from home where I have found friendship and the rare excitement of the "High Table." I am especially grateful to the Fellows of the College and to Duncan Robinson, Eamon Duffy, Andrew Thompson, Denny Murphy, and Mark Billinge in particular for their support, humor, and comradeship.

Finally, this book could not have been written without the insight, love, encouragement, and wise counsel that can only come from a life partner, Lezlee Halper. Profound thanks to her.

Stefan Halper
Southdown Farm
Virginia
September 2006

This book covers an uncomfortable period in American foreign policy. In the run-up to the Iraq war, profiles in courage were hard to find. Elected leaders are entitled to follow their own policies, however misguided. But on Capitol Hill, in the federal agencies and the military, in universities and research institutions, in the media, there were legions of those who knew better but who chose to stay silent or became fellow-travelers. This was not what I expected when I moved my family from

Britain to the America I had always regarded as the default agent for good in world affairs.

Thus, special accolades are due to the heroes who acted upfront on their convictions. Chief among these are the many thousands of ordinary Americans who, though unschooled in international affairs, realized well ahead of the foreign policy elite that what was being planned for the Middle East was both unworkable and illegitimate. Had their elected leaders possessed the courage to listen to the sound instincts of these decent citizens rather than capitulate to the leaden-hearted calculus of their pollsters, the course of recent American diplomacy might have been very different. The country would be safer and the public discourse less toxic.

A number of former high officials did take real risks to their reputations and livelihoods to place on public record their opposition to what they saw as a travesty of American values and effectiveness. In this context I would like to pay special tribute to Brent Scowcroft and Zbigniew Brzezinski, both former national security advisers.

Among those who have guided my thoughts for this book, I would like to record my appreciation to Ahmed Al Abdullah, Elias Aburdene, Mark Allen, Frank Baker, Jim Campbell, Ted Carpenter, James Clad, Steve Clemons, Armeane Choksi, Keith Craig, Andrew Cockburn, Bridge Colby, Ann Crittenden, Chet Crocker, Stephen Day, Alun Evans, Jim Fallows, Graham Fuller, Peter Gooderham, Leon Hadar, Geoffrey Hancock, David Handley, Bill Harrop, Chris Haws, Adam Holloway, Judy Hope, Flynt Leverett, David Ignatius, Christopher James, Harold James, Mahmoud Katirai, David Lambert, Anatol Lieven, King Mallory, Bill Maynes, Michael McDowell, Eric Melby, John Newhouse, Manfred von Nordheim, Bill Odom, Tom Omestad, Doug Paal, Tim Phelps, Alix Platt, Alan Posener, Chris Preble, Gideon Rachman, David Suratgar, Shekhar Tiwari, Tom Twetten, Harlan Ullman, Frank Vogl, Sam Wells, Robert Whitcomb, Tim Wirth, and David Young. I have much appreciated our ability to talk to each other in a sane, informative, and moderate way.

A further acknowledgment is due to a singular association in Washington, DC, founded by Boyden Gray, John Henry, Bill Nitze, and Chas Freeman under the name of the Committee for the Republic. For three years, the Empire Salon has offered an elegant home for foreign policy exchange that, uniquely in these fractured times, draws participation from across the political spectrum. I have never failed to learn from the galaxy of speakers who have passed through its doors.

Finally, human happiness ultimately depends on small circles. In this regard I have been exceptionally blessed through my parents, my brother and sisters and their families, and, closest to home, by my wife of thirty-six years, Suzanne, and my children, Crispin, Robin, and Tiffany, soon to be joined by Robin's fiancée, Clare. They have helped me understand that, while the dull and dutiful usually end up in the corner suites, progress only comes from engagement on the barricades.

Jonathan Clarke
Washington, DC
September 2006

Index